From Chains to Change

One Man's Journey
from God-Hater to God-Follower

From Chains to Change

One Man's Journey
from God-Hater to God-Follower

a memoir by
Steven Allen Young

with *New York Times* bestselling author
Eric Wilson

Clovercroft Publishing

Published by Clovercroft Publishing, Franklin, Tennessee

Published in association with Larry Carpenter of Christian Book Services, LLC
www.christianbookservices.com

Scripture taken from the NEW AMERICAN STANDARD BIBLE®, Copyright © 1960, 1962,1963,1968,1971,1972,1973,1975,1977,1995 by The Lockman Foundation. Used by permission.

Scripture is used from the New King James Version, © 1982 by Thomas Nelson, Inc. All rights reserved. Used by permission.

Scripture taken from *The Message*. Copyright © 1993, 1994, 1995, 1996, 2000, 2001, 2002. Used by permission of NavPress Publishing Group

Cover by Adept Content Solutions

Interior layout by Suzanne Lawing

Printed in the United States of America

978-1-954437-12-8

Contents

Intro   Disclaimers, Excuses, And Stuff Like That 15

PART ONE

1   The End Of The Story 19

2   Somebody's Kid 22

3   Nowhere To Hide 24

4   Counting The Days 29

5   My Little Four-Step 35

6   Crossed Lines 39

7   A Slave To Guilt 45

8   The Numbness 49

9   Love And Thorns 53

10   Hooked 59

11   Point Of No Return 62

12   Time Bombs 64

13   Wreckage 69

14   The Kiss Of Death 73

15   Told You I'd Get You 77

16   Hell And A Bit Of Heaven 82

17   Big Brother 88

18   The Shadows 93

19   Tunnel Vision 97

20   A Drowning Man 103

PART TWO

21   Acts Of Grace.....................................111

22   Black Sheep 115

23   Monsters And Maestros......................119

24   Disney Dreams 122

25   Moving The Metal.............................127

26   Choirboy Behavior...........................132

27   Into The Abyss..................................134

28   Bad News 140

29   No Rest For The Wicked 145

30   Memphis Blues 149

31   Dead To Rights 156

PART THREE

32   Grievances 163

33   Hot Wax 167

34   Better Late Than Never......................172

35   Wasted Years 176

36   Jailhouse Rock 180

37   The Keyring 183

38   Cotton, Coffee, And Tobacco 189

39   The Damage Done..............................193

40   Every Step Forward...........................198

PART FOUR

41   Hard Knocks 205

42   North In The Night............................212

43   The Game 217

44   Across The Field 222

45   Golden Arches....................................226

46   All That's Wrong In The World 229

47   Targeted 234

48   In Short Supply 239

49   Over And Done 243

50   My Terms 247

PART FIVE

51   The Beginning Of The Story 253

52   Alternate Routes 258

53   Mike And Eddie 263

54   A Madness To My Method. 268

55   Survival Games 273

56   Means Of Destruction 277

57   Pandora's Box. 280

58   Going To The Well. 285

59   What Is Truth? 290

60   As Passionate As Ever. 295

61   Better Than Waffle House 299

62   Lifting Off. 305

63   The Biggest Night 318

64   More Miracles 315

65   Start Moving. 323

Sign Off   Headphones, Soundtracks, And Radio Dials 329

Extras   Andy's Corner 333

           Mike's Thoughts. 339

           Eric's Final Note. 341

           Thanks. 343

About the Authors 345

Info   Booking And Other Details. 347

Discussion Guide 349

DEDICATED TO

MIKE DOTSON
For believing instead of leaving. I would not be where I am
or who I am without you. I probably would not be at all.

MY WIFE, ANDY
Yes, you have been the final piece to the puzzle
that made my life complete and whole again, but you also brought
a lot of pieces with you. I could not have done this without you.

THE GIRLS
You know who you are. I hope and pray you know how much you
mean to me, to Home Street Home, and to our friends. You have
touched, changed, and saved more lives than you'll ever know.
Thank you for believing in and loving me, and more importantly
for believing in and loving our friends.

ALL OF YOU, MY FRIENDS, WHO CALL THE STREETS HOME
You do matter. You have not been forgotten. I have not left you
behind and I will never forget, because I will forever be homeless.
Be blessed and, as always, much love.

Intro

DISCLAIMERS, EXCUSES, AND STUFF LIKE THAT

In case you're wondering what you are in for, this is the rambling, semi-coherent, fully entertaining, and life-changing story of Steven Allen Young.

That's me.

I'm a middle-aged white male with loose jeans, glasses, a gray beard, and thinning hair beneath my usual ball cap. I've got a slight Southern accent, stand six-foot-three, and at 240 lb I could stand to lose a few. Guess I like chocolate more than it likes me. Here's the deal, though. This is not an autobiography—me telling my whole story in exhaustive detail. And it's not a biography—Eric, my co-writer, giving you all the dirt he can dig up in the most impressive language possible. That might work for some, the old, the rich, and the famous.

I'm not any of those things. Not really. Not yet. Maybe never.

And c'mon, do you really think I care?

I do like paying my bills, doing nice things for the ones I love, even spoiling my dogs, Hondo and Mickey, but what Eric and I really want is for readers like you to dip your toes into these waters, wade out a little deeper, and then plunge completely into the story.

It'll be cold at times and uncomfortable.

For some, even scary.

Just warning you now, this memoir won't always be nice and polite because we both think being raw and real makes more room for true redemption. A book wasn't even my idea originally. Friends kept telling me I should write one because it might help others along their way. What I think they meant was, if God can handle my shit, He can certainly handle yours.

The names of certain people and places have been changed to protect the innocent—and the guilty too—but these accounts are all true, as best as I remember. Eric even verified some of the more scandalous parts through official state documents and old newspapers.

For those who already know me, you might read this book and suspect I skipped a thing or two. Well, maybe so. And for that, some of you should count your blessings. For those who think I owed you a little more space in these pages, don't worry: once I'm old, rich, and famous—not yet, maybe never—I can always write another book and give you your due.

For now, I want to give God His due.

Thanks for joining me on this journey. As we go stirring up the past, the waters will get muddy, but somewhere along the banks on the other side of these pages, there are pools so pure and beautiful you can see all the way to the bottom.

Alrighty then. You ready to put your toes in?

Part One

"I was tired of secrets, tired of seeing
things I was not supposed to see."

—John Grisham, in *A Painted House*

Steven, 4 months
old, on a horse

back, left to right:
Dad, Mom, & Billy Dean
middle: Robert & Byron
front: Steven & John

Steven, age 5,
on mom's lap

Steven's senior
yearbook photo

Steven's birth
certificate

1

THE END OF THE STORY

It was the wrong place to die. Not that I cared. It was the end of the line for me, my final Christmas. I was not being eaten alive by cancer or some terminal condition tucked away in my medical report, but by something maybe just as deadly. What was it? I couldn't diagnose myself, except to tell you I was done. Done with this world and all its secrets and lies.

So there I was, ready to end things on my own terms.

Always on my terms.

In Nashville, Tennessee, on December 24, 2013, I checked into the Hallmark Inn on Trinity Lane–funny names for a motel and a city street, considering what brought me there. This part of my story definitely didn't involve any sugary TV romance and definitely not the God of the Trinity, the one they taught me about in Sunday School.

If you told me you didn't believe in that God, I wouldn't blame you one bit. I'd also say you were letting Him off the hook.

Oh, I believed. Yes, I did.

And I hated Him.

Like I mentioned before, this wasn't at all the right place, but it was a helluva lot better than spending another night on the streets. For the past five years I'd been one of Nashville's homeless population, keeping mostly to myself, wondering how I ended up sleeping in my old car or in a tent in the woods behind a Walmart. At the same time, I realized this was the punishment I deserved. This was all my own doing.

Just ask my ex-wives.

From wedding rings to divorce. From a six-figure job and company car to eight years in prison. From a locked cell to the front seat of my clunker on many hot and humid evenings, which were almost as bad as the bone-chilling winter nights that turned my breath to ice against the windows. No matter where I ended up, I couldn't run from myself, and after carrying around these chains like some ghoulish Ghost of Christmas Past, well, I was ready for it to be over.

Really, the decision was made a year earlier when I promised myself I'd never again spend my holidays on the streets. Both my parents were dead and gone. I was the fourth of five brothers, and my two oldest were also gone. I and my remaining two brothers hadn't talked in ages. As for my four exes—yes, count 'em, four—they'd done their best to move on with their lives, healing from all the damage I caused.

This was it. On Trinity Lane.

The end of a road called I Don't Give a Damn.

I was at peace with that fact as I pulled a few crumpled bills from my pocket and shoved them across the counter to the hotel clerk. One look at me and judgment hardened her eyes, but I was a paying customer and she couldn't deny me a room. I took the key card and shuffled down the hall.

When I opened the door, bugs scattered inside. They wanted the same thing I did, a little privacy, a few crumbs, a place to settle in without being bothered or stepped on. I slipped into the dank space. Pulled the chain and threw the deadbolt on the door. Drew the curtains shut and plopped onto the edge of the creaky bed.

My bones ached as I wrapped my hand around the object in my coat pocket. Cold comfort. The promise of a swift end.

First, a hot shower.

There were spots of mold on the bathroom ceiling, and the mirror was discolored, but since when did a homeless person get to act snooty? Packaged soap and tiny shampoo bottles were luxuries. Years of dirt from the streets had dug deep into my every pore, and I scrubbed and scrubbed before rinsing. Murky water swirled down the drain and I stood there till the hot water ran out. The starched white towels seemed almost too clean to use.

Still damp-haired, I headed across the street to Waffle House. I figured when the cleaning staff found me later in the hotel room, and the police and the ambulance came, and the coroner determined my cause of death, and some funeral home director did whatever they did to prepare a body for burial, at least I'd be fed and somewhat clean—on the outside anyway.

Not that anything could clean up the inner mess. Believe me, I'd tried over the years to cover, erase, even laugh it away. Tried plenty of other things too. And all those futile attempts, they had left me exhausted.

Done.

Done being a burden to society.

Done being a burden to myself and others.

This was my life, my decision, and this Christmas Eve in this room at the Hallmark Inn, my story was about to reach its quick and solitary end.

2

SOMEBODY'S KID

Nobody sets out to be homeless, not at the beginning. Children don't grow up with dreams of rummaging through dumpsters for scraps, and teen runaways don't look forward to cold nights on hard sidewalks. Alcoholics don't plan to wake up in alleyways, reeking of pee and booze. No, it doesn't work that way.

The truth is much scarier because it can happen to any of us. Our decisions and circumstances, some of our own making and others not, point us in a direction. One step at a time, one foot in front of the other, that's how we reach the highest peaks or find ourselves alone in the deepest valleys.

When I got married the first time around, I was still chasing money, awards, and women, and I never imagined I would later spend years in a prison cell. Or become one of those homeless bums on the corner. Those things could never happen to me.

Then it all came crashing down. My life was a Choose Your Own Adventure book in which my bad choices and sad circumstances led to an ending I did not want.

Couldn't I get a do-over? What if I went back and tried again?

Lemme tell you, it's easy, real easy, to judge others when you have your own act together. It's a lot harder to remember that every person you meet is somebody to someone. Every single person is somebody's kid.

Not that I was a kid anymore, not even close.

But I was a boy once, that much is true, and that's when a series of choices and circumstances began angling me far off course.

3

NOWHERE TO HIDE

My boyhood journey began on May 20, 1956, in Vallejo, California, twenty-five miles east of San Francisco. Dad was a career navy man. Years earlier, during World War II, he had met Mom at a local bar while she visited from Minnesota. Sparks flew and they were married by war's end.

I was their fourth child, a stout, blond-haired, blue-eyed baby. One more in a line of boys to feed. I'd like to believe my parents truly loved each other, but at some point their marriage became a we're-in-it-for-the-kids sort of thing.

Though I attended kindergarten in Vallejo, my main memories of that period involve playing in the canyons, sliding down slopes on cardboard, always seconds away from skinning my elbows or splitting my head wide open. If you think this proves what an idiot I was, you're probably right. Courage and stupidity are two sides of the same coin, and for me it was always a coin toss.

Brave guy or idiot?

Go ahead, call it in the air.

Before I could do any bodily harm or permanent brain damage, Dad packed all six of us into his '57 Chevy—Dad, Mom, Billy Dean, Byron, Robert, and me—then drove us cross-country to his home state of Tennessee. Seat belts were barely a thought in those days and I remember curling up in the back window to watch clouds glide across the wide blue skies.

It was the calm before the storm.

We settled down in Nashville in the early 1960s. Music City was still reeling from Patsy Cline's untimely death. Johnny Cash and George Jones were churning out radio hits, and Connie Smith was proving a woman could top the charts as quickly as any man. The closest thing to a skyscraper was the L & C Tower, only blocks from the Cumberland River.

Still serving five years in the naval reserves, Dad landed a job with Pinkerton Security and found us a place on Horseshoe Drive, north of downtown. While Inglewood was a typical middle-class suburb at the time, our home was small, with two bedrooms and nine hundred square feet. All four of us boys shared a room, stacked in bunk beds with not much space in between.

Home.

I use that word loosely.

Let's put it this way: Growing up, there weren't a lot of warm fuzzies passed around in the Young household. Dad was an honest, hardworking man who bore both physical and psychological scars from his time in World War II. He harbored a lot of anger. Mom was a big-boned woman, even taller than Dad. She played the sullen but dutiful housewife, acting as though her sons were a curse for past sins.

Many nights, we boys stared at the walls or shoved our heads into our pillows as our parents shouted profanities at each other, threw things, and landed blows. They seemed to blame each other for their personal frustrations. Dad, who worked most holidays and Christmases, didn't feel Mom gave him any respect—"Dammit, a man ought to be honored in his own home." And Mom was left alone all day with this houseful of rowdy kids, dirty dishes, and ripe laundry—"So much for any dreams of my own."

Truth is, they were both instigators. They both gave as good as they got, and it often lasted for hours. You might ask who won these fights, but as far as I could tell, nobody came out on top.

We kids, we were always the losers.

The Youngs cleaned up real good, though. Yes, we did. Picture a clean-cut churchgoing family. In public, my brothers and I mostly toed the line, knowing if we didn't, our parents would later make us pay. Even on our best behavior, when we kept quiet and tucked in our shirts and stopped roughhousing in the church pews or in the back of the car, we never knew when the next explosion was set to go off.

Mom was thirty-six when baby John came along, born at nearby Seward Air Force Base. Our family of seven moved a few blocks over to McChesney Avenue, all us older boys crammed into the basement and John sleeping in a crib upstairs.

Why'd they have kids? I often wondered. Did they actually love us?

In years to come, I got answers to some of my questions. And to a few I didn't even know to ask.

As I mentioned, things could turn rough in our household. My parents' policy in regards to the children seemed to be: Punish first, ask questions later. And they both knew how to inflict some damage. Dad's preferred tool was a leather razor strop, the type barbers used to hone their single-edged blades. Mom's was anything within reach, usually off the kitchen counter. As they carried out their punishments, they acted like we were the ones responsible for their violence, like we somehow forced their hands.

I remember Dad wailing on me one time and barking, "I'll stop when you quit your crying."

"Well, hell," I wanted to say, "that's the reason I'm crying."

John doesn't remember things being quite so bad, and for that I am thankful. The youngest, he was mostly spared. As for Billy Dean, Byron, Robert, and me, we were kept home from school more than once while our latest bruises healed. Don't go thinking Dad and Mom felt any deep remorse. It wasn't like that. And they didn't keep us home for fear of the authorities stepping in either, certainly not in that era.

Appearances. It was all about appearances.

This was the South, after all, and looking good for God was almost as important as looking good for the neighbors and our Baptist brethren.

To complete the sanitized image, Dad dressed to the nines, wore a hat, and earned a reputation for helping out the elderly in the area. If something needed fixing, Dad was right on it, replacing a light bulb, tightening a leaky faucet, rewiring a plug. All part of being a good neighbor. Did he help because he was a nice guy? No, he did it for pats on the back, and he was happily obliged by the old men and blue-haired widows.

Dad's people were from Watertown, an hour east, and their roots ran deep. When we visited there, our parents were on their best behavior and everyone seemed to know us by name. We could grab goodies from the local store, no questions asked, and we had more cousins than we could count. Decoration Day was a day-long, small-town event, and the extended family gathered to put flowers on graves, eat loads of food, drink sweet tea, and play games. Mom put all kinds of money into those activities, making her popular with those involved. She was Mama Bea, life of the party.

Back at home? She wouldn't spend five minutes playing with her own kids.

Appearances, like I said. Buckle of the Bible Belt, y'all.

We boys learned to play our parts early on, learned from the very best. We knew all about making good impressions, saying our prayers, and keeping up with the Joneses.

In a house as small as ours, there was nowhere to hide so I stayed away as much as possible. I darted off each morning to Jere Baxter Elementary, and the moment the last bell rang, I ran home, changed into a T-shirt and shorts, then shot baskets at the park or pedaled up and down the streets till dinnertime. When there were no playmates around, I sat in the yard and wore out a toy cannon by firing spring-loaded balls at plastic army men. School was my haven, and the neighborhood was my playground.

Weekends were trickier, though. What to do with all that time?

Five boys under one roof pushed Mom to her limits, and anytime Billy Dean got stuck babysitting us, he resented the fact. If you were smart, you found stuff to do outside the house. Back in time for supper, that was the main rule. Don't be late.

I hear people talk wistfully about the good ol' days—meals together, church as a family, please and thank you and a little respect. I like those things too, but lemme tell you, they sure don't guarantee you any godliness or happiness.

Just ask me how I know.

4

COUNTING THE DAYS

All of us are looking for connection, for something or someone greater than ourselves. I discovered this for myself on Gallatin Pike, down at the old Inglewood Theater. On Saturdays, a pocketful of bottle caps got you through the door, and it was my favorite way of whiling away the day. Those matinees gave me access to a world where handsome princes saved Disney maidens from dragons, James Dean slouched against cool cars in his search for meaning, and John Wayne winked fearlessly at danger and death. Seated in my red plush chair, I was enthralled.

Romance. Purpose. Heroism.

Each one appealed to me on a different level and I exited that theater full of wonder. Within seconds, of course, the sun's glare and Nashville's sticky heat snapped me back to reality. I would never be as cool as The Duke or James Dean and there were no such things as magic-carpet rides.

I kept mostly to myself. I learned quickly it was best to tuck my chin, zip my lip, and mind my own business. Didn't say much in school, or on the basketball court, or in the living room where my father watched his shows on a big black-and-white TV. The less you said, the more others talked, and keeping quiet was a handy way of discovering others' secrets.

One day I was curling up in my bed for a nap, when Dad picked up the phone in the living room and placed a call. He didn't realize I was awake down the hall. Or maybe he just didn't care. As he applied for Social Security benefits and answered a list of questions, he nonchalantly mentioned his previous wives.

Wives? Excuse me?

When Mom got home, I asked her about it and she verified every word. Until then, I'd never suspected Dad was married before, and I wondered what else we didn't know about our parents.

Dad completed his time in the naval reserves and accepted a position at a Nashville branch of the Federal Reserve Bank. This allowed him to upgrade our family to a bigger home only a few blocks away on Howard Avenue.

Gleaming with large reflective windows, that place on Howard was a house of mirrors. While it practically begged the neighbors to slow down and take a look, none of them could actually see what went on inside. On sunny days the glare off the glass was blinding, and on rainy days it was nothing but gray. They didn't really know what went on in there, just as most people had no clue what went on in your childhood home.

Behind closed doors, we never knew what might summon Dad's or Mom's monsters from the depths—a bad grade, a spilled drink, rolled eyes—but their violence often turned on us. All my brothers and I wanted was a sense of love and security, but since neither was abundant, we tried to read our parents' rising animosities and predict which one of us would get the next round of beatings.

Let's just say, it was an inexact science. If my room didn't meet Dad's military standards, I wasn't sure whether I'd be facing Dr. Jekyll or Mr. Hyde. Dad might casually remind me to straighten things up, or he might march in with his razor strop and go to town on my backside.

One chilly morning, I woke up with frost on my bedroom window. Nashville winters were typically short and my heart leaped at the chance of snow. The icy beauty drew me out of my bed and I pressed my hand against the smooth, cold pane. The contrast of my body heat with the freezing outdoor temperature instantly shattered the glass and all I could do was stare.

Boy, was I in for it now.

All day I shuddered at the thought of what would happen. Fear sat on my chest like a pallet of bricks. When Dad got home from work that night, what could I do but fess up and face the consequences? Trembling and tears would only make things worse.

"Dad," I said, "there's something I've got to show you."

As I walked him to my room, I stayed dry-eyed and stoic, ready for anything.

He took one look at the damaged window and his gaze narrowed. He stepped past my toys to the shards of broken glass. His back was to me. I watched for the tensing of his shoulders, the slightest movement of his hands. Here it comes, I told myself. Time to get what I deserve. Oh, well. Bury me deep, where the animals can't pick at my bones.

Dad planted his hands on his hips, then turned to face me. "Things happen." He shrugged. "It's fine, Steven, it's okay. It wasn't your fault."

What? That was it?

The never knowing what to expect, the walking on eggshells, were almost as bad as the actual beatings. Our grandma, Mama Maude, knew of the trouble lurking in our home. She visited one weekend, and I remember her sitting us all down, pleading, "Do whatever you can to not make your dad upset." She knew her son all too well.

That old debate about nature vs. nurture was pointless under our roof since both were negative influences. Despite my brothers' and my best efforts, there was no telling how things might go moment by moment at Howard Avenue, and the instant I let my guard down, I was sure to get smacked upside the head.

Just to be clear, I wasn't the only one on the receiving end.

Billy Dean, being the oldest, he was supposed to be the example. If he messed up, it wasn't pretty.

Byron had his troubles, too. He and Dad once got into an argument while working together out at Poplar Hill Cemetery, near Watertown. Dad hit Byron, and Byron got so mad, he refused to ride back in the same car. He walked home alone and didn't arrive in Inglewood till well after dark.

As for Robert, he was wrong if he thought playing football would gain him any points with Dad. "Why should I go spend a couple hours," Dad grumbled, "just to watch you run up and down the field a few times? It's a waste of my time." The reason for Dad's flippancy toward Robert became clearer one afternoon when my brother was in sixth grade. From down in the basement, Robert overheard Dad and Mom yelling at each other and his strong protective nature propelled him up the stairs.

Dad was growling at Mom. "We should've just got divorced like we said."

"That was the plan," Mom fired back, giving as good as she got. "Why d'you think I did what I did?"

"Oh, I know why. I know. But does he?" Dad nodded his head toward Robert as he arrived at the top of the stairs. "You want me to tell that little bastard that he ain't even my son?"

Until then, we had assumed all five of us boys were from the same father. Apparently, during one of Dad's deployments back in California, our parents had discussed getting divorced. During that time, Mom had an affair. And Robert was the result. Dad let the matter slide since he'd had flings of his own, and they decided to stay together. Nevertheless, this late revelation shook Robert to the core.

Here's one thing I firmly believe: It should not hurt to be a child, and an adult shouldn't have to live with pain. Neither situation is God's hope or plan for us. Though I'm sure Dad and Mom had their own struggles we never knew about, their personal issues became ours. As we got older, some of my brothers tried to justify our parents' behavior, but I refused to paint it as anything other than what it was.

Could things have been worse? Absolutely.

It wouldn't have taken much to get them to that worse stage, though. No wonder Billy Dean and Byron both scurried off at eighteen like cats out of a paper bag. I didn't blame them, and I counted the days till my own escape.

My dream was to be a DJ. At night, I would lie in bed, pull the covers over my head, and listen to my AM/FM transistor radio through an earplug. I imagined I was Wolfman Jack or Casey Kasem, giving each song an intro, an outro, and a "word from our sponsors." Cocooned in blankets and sound, I was in a different world. A world where I had a voice.

"A DJ? On the radio?" Mom smirked when I told her. The look on her face said it all. She proceeded to tell me I should accept who and what I was. Nothing special. Not that smart or talented. Her final words dashed any hope I had of support from my parents concerning what my aspirations. "Get your head out of the clouds and start thinking about getting a real job."

None of us boys were good enough. Reaching for personal goals and striving for success, these were not encouraged. You might think all this was our parents' way of toughening us up, pushing us to greater heights, but you'd be wrong. It became evident over time that Dad and Mom didn't want any of us becoming more successful than they were. That would be getting uppity.

Of course, we weren't supposed to be failures either. Aim for the middle, I guess that was the goal. Settle on mediocrity. Keep your head down, and for God's sake, don't rock the boat.

Things got a bit easier for me once my oldest brothers were gone. I finally had a bedroom of my own and could lock myself away. When I wasn't in my room, at school, or outdoors, I had my other sanctuary:

The church.

But you know how things go. You don't need me to tell you that trouble has a way of slithering in, even in the places you least expect.

5

MY LITTLE FOUR-STEP

Anytime those church doors opened, I was there. I faithfully attended Vacation Bible School and looked forward to youth functions and gym nights. There were games and activities and adults who seemed to actually care. Though I wasn't saved and born again, not yet, church was an earthly salvation from my situation at home, and for the few hours it lasted, it was good.

If any Christian goodness tried to rub off on me, it faded once I was back in our family house of mirrors. Step by step, that's how my troubles began. Tired of feeling shoved aside, I was a moody kid who wanted something to make me feel older and alive.

Rebellion, at age ten. Step one.

I started smoking, figuring it made me look like a cowboy in one of those old Westerns or like my very own father. Dad was a chain-smoker.

Thievery. That was step two.

Dad kept his packs of Pall Malls on his dresser, next to his keys and spare change. I stole one cigarette at a time, tucking each cancer stick into a sleeve or coat pocket. I wasn't exactly on the road to ruin—a few puffs in fourth grade weren't going to make a career criminal out of me—but I wanted to feel big and important.

Step three. Deceit became commonplace.

Since getting caught would mean getting my ass kicked, I never lit up close to the house, and my parents didn't discover my habit till I was much older.

Cursing became step four.

If my stealing and lying made me feel smarter than the adults, my smoking and potty-mouth made me feel somewhat in control. As a kid, you have so little control of anything. You go to school, family functions, Sunday services, wherever your parents decide. You eat whatever Mom cooks for dinner and watch whatever Dad watches on TV. At least, that's how things used to be. In the Young household, Dad had on Porter Wagoner or Glen Campbell with all that old-time twangy stuff. I couldn't even touch the rabbit-eared monstrosity unless Dad gave the orders: "Hey, Steven, turn that up," "Turn it down," or "Go, turn it to channel four." We didn't have a remote. I was the remote, someone always pushing my buttons.

Well, now I was taking things into my own hands. I could cuss when I wanted and steal a cigarette if I so desired. This was my life, thank you very much.

Of course, there were consequences as well. To this day, I still light up regularly, in need of my nicotine fix. Hey, just because I'm writing my story doesn't mean I have things all figured out.

Without even realizing it, I was earning a reputation at a young age, and a reputation is like a dog on a leash. Sure, it earns you some respect and gets you places, but it can also turn and snap at you. I found this out when Mom called me into the kitchen one afternoon. She handed me two paper bills, then slapped a small list into my hand and told me to run down to H. G. Hill's for her.

Wow, she actually trusted me?

I shoved the money into my jeans and hurried off on my mission. Instead of stealing even a penny, I just wanted to impress my mother and make her proud. Less than an hour later, I made my triumphant return with both arms loaded.

"Is that it?" Mom took one glance at the groceries on the counter and at the coins I placed in her hand. "Where's the rest of my change, Steven?"

I knew better than to expect a smile or thank you. I just hoped she would trust me with future opportunities. "That's all there was," I replied.

"But I . . . No, I gave you a twenty-dollar bill."

"You gave me fifteen," I said. "A ten and a five."

"Don't you dare lie to me. You know better."

"I swear, Mom. Check the receipt." I turned out my pockets to show there was nothing to hide. "I stuck the bills you gave me right here. See? Where else would I—"

Mom's first blow knocked me sideways. As far as conversations went, this was already longer than our usual mother/son interactions, and my protests only called down more wrath as she proceeded to beat the shit out of me.

Later, I was slipping through the living room, my eyes red and puffy, when she waved the "missing" twenty at me. "Look what I found in my purse," she said, smug in the realization she still had money on hand. "You were right, after all."

"I tried telling you."

"Now, don't you go getting smart with me. Enough with the attitude."

So much for receiving an apology.

"You know, Steven," she added, "I might've believed you up front, if you hadn't been dishonest with me so many times before . . . "

My own reputation had snapped at me, snarling and taking a bite.

I got my first shot at adult-like responsibility in sixth grade. Though I was a good student and received a certificate for yearlong perfect attendance, I had trouble staying focused at my desk. Figuring I need-ed to work out some energy, the school staff assigned me duties as a patrol boy. I proudly pulled that white shoulder belt over my heavy winter coat. Using flag sticks, I stood at Gallatin Pike and brought cars to a stop so other students could safely cross the street.

My career was short-lived. I never even saw the vehicle that hit me. I was darting across the road when its front end caught my thigh and threw me twenty feet. I came down hard next to the sidewalk. Stunned, I sat up and brushed myself off. I was rushed to the hospital and examined. Nothing. Not even a scratch. With puberty kicking in—body odor, zits, and armpit hair—I was just glad the official scrutiny was over.

"It's a miracle," someone said.

It was my first near-death experience, but certainly not my last. I wasn't so sure miracles were real, and if God existed, did He care about me? Maybe I'd just got lucky, my hard head and thick coat saving the day. Maybe.

6

CROSSED LINES

My maybes turned to hallelujahs soon after my twelfth birthday. It was May 1968, and we were learning in church about Jesus' life, death, and resurrection. Something took hold deep in my soul and conviction washed over me. Begging God for forgiveness, I decided to change my ways and get baptized. I didn't need rebellion, thievery, deceit, and cursing. Jesus loved me, this I knew, and I clung to that age-old truth.

Love.

What a powerful thing.

Before I met Jesus personally, love was just a word to me—and barely even that. As a child, I never heard the words "I love you" out of my dad's mouth. He didn't take me hunting or fishing or out to play ball. Provision over play seemed to be his guiding principle. "My job," he explained, "is to feed you, clothe you, and put a roof over your head. You realize how many hours I put in, busting my back for you boys?"

So that's how it was, I thought. We were just a job to him.

Dad was a good provider, though. I'll give him that. His work ethic was beyond belief, truly deserving of respect. He never let debts linger. He had excellent credit. Bills always got paid first and we lived on the rest, no exceptions. If he saw a hundred-dollar bill on the ground, he'd do anything to find who it belonged to. He never kept something that wasn't his and never looked away when others were in need. While finances were often tight in our household, we never went hungry or slept out in the cold.

Mom, on the other hand, she did tell me that she loved me.

Only after I said it to her first.

She muttered the words back like someone talking in her sleep. The way it seemed to me, she was more worried about what others thought of her than about creating a nurturing atmosphere. If she baked goodies for a school event, religiously gave to food drives, or planned activities for our family reunions out at Cedars of Lebanon State Park, she did it in the service of her own public image. She was beloved Mama Bea, but if I asked for a two-dollar toy, I was told we couldn't afford it.

As far as everyone else was concerned, Dad and Mom hung the moon.

My older brothers and I, we mostly felt eclipsed.

Even though I knew Jesus' love for me, things at home remained tense and both my parents seemed on edge. The cultural clashes of old and new were all around, with miniskirts and sexual freedom en vogue, and the Beatles changing the music scene. Dad watched the nightly news, with Walter Cronkite reporting on Civil Rights marches, draft dodgers, and Vietnam War protests. Only two hundred miles away, Martin Luther King, Jr. was assassinated in Memphis, and then Robert F. Kennedy was also shot.

Tensions across the country were high that summer, but I had nothing to fear. I had angels watching over me. I gathered RC Cola caps for matinee movies, went bowling, and got dairy-dip cones. Some mornings, Robert and I cycled to the end of McGavock Pike and fished along the banks of the Cumberland. I wasn't a big fisherman, but it was a chance to hang out with my older brother. After sunup, we rode the old ferry back and forth across the river, wrapped in the humidity's warm embrace.

With church camp only days away, I got antsy. Boy, this would be the highlight of my summer, and then I'd be heading into seventh grade at Isaac Litton Junior High.

Nothing, however, could prepare me for what was to come. Despite still sneaking an occasional smoke, I was mostly innocent in the ways of the world, and sex was only a vague notion in my head. The girlie magazines at Sturdevant's Five & Dime were tucked up out of view, and when I experienced my first erection, I barely knew what to do.

Not so for a particular deacon in our church.

Innocence was exactly what he was after.

He was a deacon, a respected member of the community, and he should not have been at that summer camp.

He should never have been in that swimming pool.

Church camp had been going for three days already, and I didn't want it to end. I was splashing around in the pool, having a good time. I was taller and broader-shouldered than most kids my age. We played warhorse and other water games, dunking each other, spluttering, giggling. Camp was a safe zone. None of my parents' yelling or fighting. None of my walking on eggshells. Loving Jesus and joking around with my buddies was a whole new existence I could get used to.

Middle Tennessee's heat radiated off the pool's surface. My eyes blinked against the splashing droplets and diamond-hard sun. The water was cool, lapping at my chest. Out of nowhere, the deacon appeared right behind me, his hands grabbing me around the waist, his groin pressing against my buttocks. His body felt rigid and I tried to wriggle free, worried I was about to get dunked. We both laughed. All in good fun.

He wasn't letting go, though.

He chuckled again, and I felt his breath by my ear. There was an intensity in his grip, and as I struggled to break loose, his hand reached into the front of my swim trunks and lingered there. His touch sent a jolt through me. I froze, then watched as he swam away. Had that really just happened?

My buddies were still goofing off. No one seemed to notice that a trusted church member had crossed lines which should never be crossed.

I was in shock. My thoughts swirled. My pulse pounded in my ears.

Why did he do that? I asked myself. Why'd he single me out? Maybe it was just my imagination. Should I tell someone what had occurred? No, if I said it out loud, that would mean it wasn't just something in my head. It would mean one of the leaders in our church, a family man known by my parents, had just groped me beneath the water.

I felt confused as I turned away. I let my body's response die down before climbing out of the pool and toweling myself dry.

The deacon was only getting started. He knew exactly what he was doing, testing, grooming, exploiting a possibility. That night, I was in my bunk. Good luck getting a bunch of junior-high boys to stop farting and cracking jokes after "lights off," but eventually snores filled the cabin. It was late. I dozed off, exhausted from a long day.

A gentle shaking of my shoulder opened my eyes.

The deacon again.

With a finger to his lips, he lured me past sleeping bodies to a space hidden behind a partition. He smiled at me like we were friends, like this was normal. If I didn't want this, he told me, I could have reported what happened earlier in the pool. He was quiet and persuasive and didn't rush things.

Dear Jesus, what was going on?

My body reacted as it had before, betraying everything in me that said this was wrong. No grown-up should be doing this to a twelve-year-old. No twelve-year-old should be doing this at all. I was terrified and confused. I wasn't sure why it felt good, or what to do about it, or who to tell, or how to put a stop to it.

This was our little secret, the man assured me. No one else had to know. In those few minutes that felt like hours, a deacon stole away my innocence.

Sexual obsession. Step five.

Step by step, I moved from typical boyhood troubles into shadows and confusion. A door was opened in my mind, thoughts and images never even considered before. This wasn't some encounter between consenting adults. This was a man who represented Jesus exploiting a boy just entering puberty. It was as deadly as handing a toddler a loaded gun—no instructions, no understanding, no context.

No wonder Jesus said it was better for a person who led a little one astray to have a millstone tied around his neck and be dropped into the sea. This was serious stuff.

The deacon's actions awakened me to sexual things in all the wrong ways. My stomach clinched at just the thought of him. There was no avoiding the man, though. He was at every church service and most youth functions, and he took advantage of me every chance he got. I put up some resistance, but it didn't last long in the dark.

Maybe, I thought, it was my own fault. I mean, was it even so bad? If it felt good, was it wrong? And if I said anything, who would believe me anyway?

What should I do?

My church sanctuary became a prison. I tensed each time I saw the deacon's car in the parking lot or his wife and kids walking through the doors. His smile haunted me. I avoided his eyes.

"I don't want to go to church," I said to my parents, knowing as the words exited my mouth that I was wasting my breath.

"Go comb your hair," Mom shot back. "And stop your whining, for God's sake."

So I played the part. For God's sake.

Not that He was fooled.

Alone in my bedroom, I looked at myself in the mirror and figured there must be something wrong with me. Could other people see it?

How could I think Jesus lived in my heart, when my body betrayed my spiritual vows? And speaking of betrayal, where was God in the middle of all this? He'd spared my life months earlier at that crosswalk, then left me all on my own in that pool and in that cabin. If He was all-knowing, He had seen everything that went on, stuff I would never speak out loud in detail.

He knew.

And still He did nothing.

I felt used and dirty and didn't like what I saw in the mirror. This self-hatred would deepen over the years. At twelve years old, though, I turned the brunt of my anger against God. He seemed to have turned His back when I needed Him most, and this much I knew as a fact:

I didn't want anything else to do with Him.

7

A SLAVE TO GUILT

By summer's end, my withdrawal and isolation caught my parents' attention. More annoyed than concerned, they pressed me for details. Was something wrong? Why was I staying in my room all the time? At last I let everything out, fumbling through the story of what was done to me at camp. Though I didn't even know the right words to describe the events, I got the point across and my parents sat in shocked silence. They barely even looked at me.

Was I in trouble? I almost welcomed the idea of punishment, a price to pay and a chance to move on. No matter how much it hurt, at least Dad and Mom would make sure something like this never happened to me again. They would protect me.

Wrong.

Dad's first question caught me off-guard. "If any of this actually happened, Steven, what did you do to make him think that's what you wanted?"

What did I do?

I was stunned. Those words would echo through my head for years to come.

"It makes no sense," Mom said, arms crossed. "He's a deacon. You're you. I don't even believe you, so do you think anyone else will? No, our family doesn't need this type of embarrassment. We will never bring this up again."

Child molestation was barely discussed in those days, and my parents didn't have the Internet or other materials for dealing with such a scenario. As far as I know, they went to their graves never believing or mentioning what had happened to me.

I'm telling you now, no child—hell, no adult—should have to carry such a secret alone. It was a chain looped around my neck, and at that tender age it set me on a course that would affect the rest of my life. Each day was an act of endurance. Each smile was an attempt to hide my pain. For the next forty-five years I dragged this weight through workplaces and relationships, hurting those around me while simply trying to survive.

As I entered seventh grade, it seemed everything went dim. Shame was a fog, blurring my steps and dulling my emotions. That deacon's face leered at me from the shadows, questioning why I never reported his actions at the pool. Dad's words hammered at me, wanting to know why I made the deacon think any of this was what I wanted.

All I wanted was for the nightmare to end.

Our family continued going to the same church, showing up at least two or three times a week. My parents smiled, nodded, and shook hands with the deacon. He treated me like some annoying kid underfoot, barely even looking my way. When he cornered me in private, though, he got what he wanted.

My distrust and rebellion grew as I witnessed firsthand these treacheries that went on among Bible-toting adults. My own salvation and baptism seemed connected to that treachery, and I started acting out more than ever before.

Shoplifting. Step six, in sync with step two.

Even when I had enough cash on hand to buy items outright, I pilfered them from H. G. Hill's, Sturdevant's, and the nearest Kroger.

Then, from right there in our neighborhood, I stole a bicycle. Didn't need a bike. Didn't want a bike. It was there and I took it, no reason at all. Grabbing pears from Mr. Nolen's trees next door became routine behavior, and skimming money from my parents became a cheap thrill. I often crept out late to light up a stolen Pall Mall, roam the streets, and let the nighttime lick my wounds.

I was no longer the good son, so why keep up the charade? I became hell on wheels, saying and doing whatever I damn well pleased. It was all very liberating and I had some fun along the way, some brief jolts of adrenaline. Mainly, it was about outsmarting the hypocritical grown-ups who preferred things swept under carpets, locked up in closets, and tucked into shadows.

Well, I wasn't at their mercy, not anymore.

I was tired of their masks. Their secrets. The lies.

Of course, the irony is, the more I stole, cursed, and lied, the more I became just like the very adults I despised.

By the time December rolled around, I was ready to fake some holiday cheer along with everyone else. It was the one time of year our parents called a temporary truce and pulled out all the stops for the family. There was lots of fanfare and lots of money spent. Good times were bought and paid for. Even though Dad worked most Christmases, he always made sure this season was special. After all, his birthday was December 24th.

Weeks before the big day, Dad and Mom bundled us up and we drove to a nearby lot, picked out our tree, then gathered by a small bonfire and drank hot chocolate. Back at home, stockings were stuffed and wrapped presents were stacked under the tree.

On Christmas Eve, I spotted Dad on the back porch. In a rare good mood, I pushed through the door, treasuring this chance to be alone with my father and congratulate him on his birthday. He stopped me before I could settle next to him.

"Go back inside," he said. "I came out here to get away from you kids."

He didn't even look my way.

If you've ever seen that old stop-motion Christmas special, *Rudolph the Red-Nosed Reindeer*, you might remember the Island of Misfit Toys. Our family had watched that show on our big TV console, all huddled in the ghostly gray glow.

That was me, I realized. Just a toy that didn't belong.

Okay. Enough with my sob story, right? The fact is, even as a seventh-grader, I didn't have to be a slave to guilt. With God's help, I could have set my compass toward love not hate, forgiveness not resentment, confession not deceit. When the deacon cornered me in the darkness, I could have run toward the light, both literally and figuratively.

But I didn't.

Steps twenty and twenty-one, honest self-evaluation and taking responsibility.

It would be decades before I truly faced what had happened. If I'd taken these steps sooner, I might have spared myself a ton of grief. Instead, I ignored the compass, more stubborn than smart, and headed off aimlessly on my own.

8

THE NUMBNESS

"Steven Young, please report to the principal's office."

As my name was called over the loudspeakers, I frowned. Though I acted out at home and on the streets, I mostly kept my head down here at school. Was I in trouble? Baffled, I trudged down the hall. The moment I stepped into the office area, the class bully looked up at me from his chair. Earlier in the day, he'd thrown a basketball at my face, and the bridge of my nose still smarted from the eye-watering impact. He did it for no reason. He just liked inflicting pain.

I averted my gaze and sat down.

Seconds later, my brother Robert sauntered into the waiting area. He gave me a nod and dropped his six-foot frame into a seat.

This time, it was the bully who averted his gaze.

The principal's door swung open. "Boys, come in," he ordered. "We are going to put a stop to this sort of behavior right here and now."

My questions were answered as Robert admitted that, yes, twenty minutes earlier he had marched straight into the bully's classroom and decked him in front of everyone. "You ever mess with my brother again," Robert had threatened, "and you'll get it even worse." He was defiant, even proud.

The principal tilted his head. "Standing up for your family is a good thing," he acknowledged, "but that's not how law and order are conducted on my school grounds. From now on, if you have a problem here at Litton, you bring it to me. Understood?"

My brother said nothing and the bully stared out the window.

"I'm not asking again, Mr. Young."

"Understood," my brother mumbled.

The principal turned my way. "Steven, why didn't you come speak to me about this in the first place? If you had, we might have avoided this entire mess."

Since when had talking to adults done me any good?

"I'm fine," I said. "Anyway, I'm not a snitch."

Whether or not Robert was suspended for his actions, I don't remember. All I know is, the local bullies stopped messing with me. My parents didn't defend me at home or at church, but at least one family member had my back here on school grounds.

⬤⬤⬤⬤⬤⬤

By the time I started tenth grade at Stratford High, numbness was a way of life. My parents' silence and my own shame leeched the energy out of me, and I shuffled quietly from class to class. I had only a handful of acquaintances. Athletics might have been a good physical and emotional outlet for me, but I quit the football team early in the season. Dad wasn't a sports fan and Mom refused to pick me up from practice. It seemed to me like a whole lot of blood, sweat, and tears for nothing.

What I really wanted, what I needed, was to be heard.

Not an option.

Speaking even a word of my molestation to anyone outside our home would've infuriated my father and mother, and they were viewed as responsible adults who kept their kids well-clothed and fed. Who would even give me the time of day? The first thing anyone would want me to do was go talk to my parents.

Already tried that.

Fifteen years old now, I was awkward around the opposite sex but imagined being with a girl would prove there was nothing wrong with me. Along came Melanie, another Stratford student. Oh, she was cute, and my attraction to her brought all sorts of feelings rushing in. As far as I could tell, she thought I was special too.

We weren't much of an item, despite all the hormones. We exchanged glances here and there. Chatted a few times on the phone. In my house, the telephone was in the living room on a short spiral cord, which made private conversation nearly impossible. It was tough enough figuring out what to say to Melanie at school, and even tougher with my family pulling faces and cracking jokes.

Even so, being noticed and desired meant a lot to me.

And this time, by a girl.

In Melanie's presence, I experienced all the usual male urges and no longer felt like my sexuality was in question. I was a regular guy. I was somebody. Maybe, with her help, I could wash off the grime of a deacon's filthy touch.

I'll never forget the day Melanie delivered the bad news. She'd just learned her father was being transferred to Phoenix, Arizona, and her family was moving that weekend. Whatever there was between us was over. I doubt it was real love or first love or any of that, but at the time it was my lifeline of hope—and it was being snatched away.

I was crushed.

That Friday at school, Melanie and I barely spoke a word as we walked out the front doors and down the hard concrete steps. Her mom was at the curb in their car. Emotion stuck in my throat, and already I felt the numbness returning. Melanie and I had never gone on a real date or even gone to a dance together.

"It seems so unfair," I said to her.

"I know." She turned to face me, her eyes round and brimming with tears. Her mom honked. "I'm sorry, Steven, I have to go. I've still gotta pack."

And just like that she was gone.

School was cold and lonely the following Monday, and at home I locked myself in my room with only the radio to keep me company. Pop tunes and soft rock filled the hours, and I was lulled to sleep by the sound of the DJ's voice. Someday that would be me, I thought, a voice others latched onto as their worlds fell apart. No matter what Mom thought about it, I refused to believe it was a worthless job.

I never saw or heard from Melanie again, and I skipped every high-school dance, including senior prom.

If I couldn't feel normal, I decided, it was best to feel nothing at all.

9

LOVE AND THORNS

I realize now, many years later, that true love isn't about smooth sailing, perfection, and glorious highs. And it definitely isn't about competition, control, or conquering. It doesn't live in the past nor flourish in the presence of fear. Love needs air to breath. It thrives on forgiveness and sacrifice. It's unconditional. Radical. Able to leap tall buildings in a single bound and strong enough to bear the other person's burdens—at least until they can get back on their feet for when you need help, as we all do.

Love is all of these things and so much more.

But I didn't know that yet.

The only selfless love I'd experienced was at the foot of the cross the day I got saved at twelve years old. Jesus fully knew me and loved me as I was. As in the parable of the sower, this realization caused a change in me as surely as water causes a seed to sprout, and for a short time I flourished. Then at that church camp a few weeks later, I awoke and realized the dream was really a nightmare. As the pattern of molestation began, thorns grew and blocked the sunlight. The worries of this world choked the seed as it grew, and I became a shriveled plant, unable to healthily develop and mature.

Why do I tell you this?

Because at sixteen years old, I craved love and acceptance more than ever. The atmosphere in our house didn't do much to satisfy, and with Melanie gone, the craving only got worse.

Don't get me wrong. I did have my good days, and my parents made some attempts at showing they cared. Dad drove our family on long trips through Iowa and North Dakota to visit the relatives on Mom's side. He made stops along the way at Mt. Rushmore and the International Peace Garden. He also paid for a family riverboat ride between the soaring rock walls of Wisconsin Dells, a place of breathtaking beauty.

Dad taught us to appreciate people of color. During World War II, he was on the USS *Yorktown* when it went down at the Battle of Midway. Color, he explained, was irrelevant in the heat of battle. You were all soldiers, side by side. While his ship sank, Dad was trapped in flaming, oil-slick seas, and his legs got badly burned. His scarring was so extensive, he rarely wore shorts even in summertime. He swore he would have died in those hellish waters if not for a fellow sailor, a Black man, who dragged him to safety on a floating piece of wreckage. The sailor earned a Medal of Honor for his efforts, demonstrating courage which left a deep impression on our father.

"There's two kinds of Black people," Dad explained, "the good and the bad. Just like there's white people and there's white trash. Nothing's nastier than white trash."

Dad called it the way he saw it. He thought Blacks and whites should both be treated the same, which was far from the norm at that time in the South. Mama Maude was of a similar mind. For years, she paid an African-American farmhand to work on her place in Watertown—named after Wilson Waters, who freed his slaves before the start of the Civil War—and the farmhand always joined us as an equal at the meal table.

This attitude served me well in Nashville, where my schools were fully integrated and my high-school class president was Black. I saw myself as no better and no worse than my classmates of color.

Dad was a practical man, but he did have a sentimental side. I saw this for myself years later when I suggested he sell all but one of his six cordless screwdrivers. Seemed like a good idea to me, a way to make some extra money. Instead, he said, "Those were gifts, Steven. You don't sell gifts."

Well, alrighty. I had to respect that.

Mom taught me quite a few things too—even if only to help ease her own burdens. She showed me from a young age how to cook, iron, and do my own laundry. By the time I hit my teens, Mom was working outside the home as a buyer at trade shows in Atlanta and New York. With both my abusers away at work, things at home were less stressful and I became proficient at household duties. I liked doing laundry and ironing, since looking sharp played into my ego. If a shirt of mine got stained, it went bye-bye, and you could cut a finger on the crease in my blue jeans.

As for cooking, it became a lifelong passion. At an age when so much stuff felt out of my hands, I had complete creativity and control in the kitchen. Of course, like any good cook, I hated cleaning up. Still do to this day.

Proverbs 14:4 says, "Where there are no oxen, the manger is empty, but from the strength of an ox comes abundant harvests." King Solomon was telling us that you can have a nice clean manger, but if you actually want to reap anything, you'll have to deal with the animals and their piles of crap.

In other words, there's no magic without the mess.

Each one of us, in God's hands, seems a prime example of this fact.

Sometimes, of course, the mess is of our own making and our only reward is a hard lesson learned. I found this out during my first official job at Mr. D's.

Mr. D's was a local seafood chain which later became Captain D's. I couldn't stand seafood, not since a bad incident with some boiled shrimp at one of my parents' parties, but the restaurant was only a few blocks from our house. Though it was hard work for piddly wages, I was earning a paycheck and saving up for my own car.

After closing one night, a handful of us employees got into an egg fight. We went through four crates, winging farm-fresh missiles over counters, fryers, and booths. Yolks ran yellow down the windows and walls. It was all harmless and done in the name of fun, but the place was a disaster zone, and there was no hiding it when the district supervisor strolled in for a surprise store-check.

"We're gonna clean it all up," my coworker promised him.

"Oh, I know you are," he said flatly. "Starting right now."

We worked into the early morning, our muscles sore and our eyelids drooping. We had everything scrubbed and sparkling with minutes to spare before the opening crew was to arrive.

"They're not coming," the supervisor said.

"What?"

"I gave them the day off, with pay. You're today's opening crew."

By the time we finished that double shift, we could barely walk or think straight. Even now, I bet nobody on that crew has forgotten how exhausted we felt. There were no more food fights after that and my fast-food career didn't last much longer. Being a Kroger cashier paid better. Plus, it didn't keep me up all night.

Things took another turn for the better when my parents decided to change churches. I was relieved, knowing I wouldn't have to face the man who had molested me every week.

With a job and a driver's license, I was a man in the making, but I felt out of place at the new church youth program. The boys brushed me off and the girls giggled and whispered when I was around.

Did my hair look okay? Would I ever fit in?

Along came Chad and Deena.

Chad and Deena were the young couple who ran the program. Attractive, lighthearted, and energetic, they gave us all of their attention, and you better believe I ate that up. Chad and Deena didn't act stuffy like most of the churchgoers. We met at their duplex for cook-outs and movie nights. Sometimes, we studied the Bible. Other times, we just hung out and laughed.

As the months passed, my guard came down. Bit by bit, I opened up about family struggles and girl troubles. Chad and Deena, they didn't judge or spout verses or try to analyze. They often let me stick around past the regular group time or invited me over on my own just to talk. They looked me in the eyes. They listened.

Even then, I didn't divulge a thing about my encounters with the deacon—it would be decades before I confessed that to another living soul—but they got an earful anyway. Chad and Deena's personal interest in me bred confidence. My shoulders straightened, my chin lifted, and at six-foot-one, my arrival at youth gatherings began drawing respectful nods from the guys and curious glances from the girls. I felt at ease. Church once again seemed safe, at least when we were meeting at Chad and Deena's.

If this was what God was about, if this was the sort of love Jesus showed to His followers, maybe I'd rethink my opinion of Him.

First Corinthians 13:13 says, "And now abide faith, hope, and love . . . but the greatest of these is love." Those words sounded nice to me as a teenager, but to be honest I didn't have much interest left in faith or in hope. Sexual confusion and secrecy had choked both of them out of me.

Love.

That's the one thing I still wanted.

If the verse above is true, if the Bible has it right, then it makes sense to me that love, being the greatest, is also the strategic weakness, the area most vulnerable to attack. If God Himself is love, what could be more damaging than to corrupt that very concept of Him from the inside out? Wouldn't a warped love create a warped view?

Yes, the Savior would look like a destroyer.

The Friend would look like an enemy.

The Truth would look like a lie.

Even though I was vulnerable in plenty of ways, I'm not here to justify or romanticize the things that happened next. It's easy to say, thinking back, that I should have fled the scene, but that's not how events played out. Sadly, not even close.

For the past four years I'd wallowed in shame, allowing the darkness and fog to thicken, and God's plan, laid out for me from birth, got more and more difficult to recognize, a straight and narrow path glimpsed only here and there through the trees. Each compromise I made led me farther away, and I never even thought to stop.

10

HOOKED

Step seven. Adultery.

Dropping by at Chad and Deena's to chat had become a regular thing, and even the times I found Deena on her own, she seemed happy to have my company. We watched TV, played cards, munched on snacks. The best part was just talking with each other. She didn't treat me like part of her job—think Dad. Or like a nuisance—think Mom. The age difference wasn't an issue between us, and as I saw it, she was fast becoming my best friend.

That Friday night, whatever plans I'd made fell through. Well, hey, I told myself, I will just drive over to Chad and Deena's. I called first to make sure they were home.

"Got home a few minutes ago," Deena said. "It's the middle of tax season, so Chad's working late and I could use the company. C'mon over."

I told her my plans for dinner had fallen through.

She was about to start cooking and said I could just eat there.

Out the door I went. My parents thought I had plans anyway, so what did they care? I looked forward to time with people who cared about me. Yes, Deena was my youth pastor, but we had a genuine friendship developing. For me, these feelings were powerful, rooted in the acceptance I so badly wanted. They blinded me to the danger.

Danger? Are you kidding me? From the moment I walked into the duplex, I felt safe.

Sure, the world outside these doors was in chaos after the recent Watergate scandal and President Nixon's resignation, but what did I care? I couldn't even vote yet. Chad and Deena were my world. Nothing else mattered. Deena and I exchanged small talk as she finished making the meal. We ate together, relaxed as could be, and decided a movie on TV might be nice.

As I was taking care of the dishes, she told me she was going to go change out of her work clothes. Even when I heard the shower running, I thought nothing of it. I was that comfortable. I just grabbed the trash and took it out. There was none of the tension I felt under my own roof, no waiting for the other shoe to drop. I reentered the duplex, closed the door, and smiled.

Home.

So this was how it could be.

Love.

So this was how it could feel.

That's when I realized the shower was no longer on. From the bedroom, Deena called out, "Steven, is that you?"

"Just me."

"Well, c'mon back."

Out of habit, I locked the back door, then made my way toward their room. I had no inkling of the trouble I was in. Feeling welcome here, I suspected nothing.

I found her in front of the mirror, running a brush through her long tresses. She wore a silky off-white robe over a matching negligee. As I entered the room, she glanced at me through the reflection, a smile tugging at her lips, then turned to face me.

I gulped once or twice.

Maybe, I thought, I should excuse myself.

Before that thought could become action, Deena turned and stepped up to me. Though she didn't say a word, the look in her eyes spoke volumes and the kiss she gave me was like nothing I'd ever experienced. It was my first sexual encounter with a female, and the blur of the next few hours left me with a dizzying rush of emotions and sensations. She didn't seem to feel bad about it for one second, and I just followed her lead.

I admit, my opinion of relationships was pretty low at that point. Sure, I wanted to believe marriage was something sacred, and I hoped to tie the knot myself one day, loving and being loved till death do us part. Wasn't that how it should be? But my parents' example was far from that. Not that it'd ever put any dent in their reputations—good, solid Baptists, dressed for the part and widely admired.

For Dad, it wasn't about loving his fellow man. It was about deflecting attention from his affairs on the side and from the problems under his own roof.

Mom, on the other hand, did love her fellow man.

Several, in fact.

All of which left me with some messed up views. As far as I was concerned, screwing around was part of life. Love and sex had nothing to do with each other, and romance was just flowers and fluff. Those fairy-tale relationships in the movies were exactly that. Fairy tales. And recent news that the old Inglewood Theater had closed its doors for good was evidence of this sad fact.

As Deena drew me into her bed, I didn't even feel guilty.

Surprised, yes. Guilty, no.

I relished every moment of it, and I knew, at last, that I was a regular, full-blooded, heterosexual male. She wanted me. She desired me. If there's a headier drug known to man, I don't know what it is.

I was completely hooked.

I was hers.

11

POINT OF NO RETURN

For years, I looked back with dizzy excitement on my encounters with Deena and told myself I had no regrets. Maybe it was wrong, but it was sure fun while it lasted.

I'm guessing you've also made your fair share of mistakes. Do you have any detours you wistfully remember—an old flame, a wild party, a night of crime or adrenaline? Perhaps an addiction that still tugs at the sleeve? Let's be honest, we don't call them sinful pleasures for nothing. Sometimes we relish their memories: "Things got so crazy, I don't remember half of it." "Wow, to be young again." "Those were the glory days."

C'mon, though. Who are we fooling? There's no real glory involved, nothing that lasts more than a few minutes or, at best, a few hours.

Decades after my high-school troubles, as prison guards marched me in chains into the Mississippi State Penitentiary, notoriously known as Parchman, I didn't grin and think that all my youthful, stubborn fun was worth it. I knew better. I wasn't in prison because I minded my own business. No, I turned a blind eye to the warning signs and went walking, even running past the point of no return. You don't just stumble one day into being a criminal. You don't just trip and land in the arms of someone else's spouse.

Did I suffer in prison?

Yes, I did. As you'll soon find out.

Even at that point, though, bleeding and terrified, I blamed myself. My own steps had led me there, and deep in my being, I believed it was what I deserved.

12

TIME BOMBS

In the aftermath of that first time together, Deena told me to never just expend myself and roll off onto the bed. A woman needed soft words, intimacy, and care. I took this lesson to heart and did everything I could to be close to her.

Over the next two years, our moments of pleasure happened at regular intervals, whenever we could find space alone. It wasn't difficult, considering Chad's work schedule and the apathy in my own home. For the rest of my education at Stratford High, I carried on an affair with my youth leader and convinced myself I was in love.

Did she feel the same way? She told me she did.

"Once you're eighteen," she said, "I'll leave Chad and we can get married."

"You'd divorce him?" I asked. "I thought you loved him."

"People change, Steven. I love you."

My whole life I had waited to hear those three words—sincere, unprompted, and passionate—and they instantly melted me.

Tax time. Somehow, in the midst of my liaisons with Deena, I managed to file with the IRS, and by my seventeenth birthday a decent refund was on its way. Deena and I were already making plans, discussing where we would live and work after my graduation. I would apply for financial aid and go to college. My refund would help toward that goal. It all sounded so easy and blissful, and no one seemed to suspect a thing.

How did we manage that? Remember, I had learned to bury my secrets deep. Each one was a time bomb ready to go off at any time, but you wouldn't know it by looking at my face. Keep smiling, Steven. Just show them your pearly whites.

It was Mom who unwittingly put the first wrinkle in my plans with Deena. When I got home one evening from my shift at Kroger, I found my mother making a grocery list at the dining-room table.

"Did we get any mail today?" I asked.

She nodded, not even glancing up.

"Anything for me?"

"I took care of it," she replied.

"Wait, Mom. You opened my mail?"

Her eyes lifted, hard and unblinking. "You live under my roof, young man. Whatever shows up in that mailbox is mine as much as it is yours."

"But I've been waiting on my tax refund."

"I already cashed it."

"What? You can't do that!"

She shrugged. "I figured you owed me. You couldn't even open a bank account without my signature, Steven. Who do you think pays for your food and shelter around here? Would you prefer to discuss this with your father?"

"That was my money," I shouted. "I was saving it for . . ."

"For what?"

Slamming a hand against the wall, I walked out the door. "Never mind."

Dad wasn't much help either. As I considered my college options, all I needed from him was a signature for my financial aid request, but he refused to sign. His exact words: "I don't want anyone knowing I can't afford to pay for your college."

Too poor to pay. Too proud to help.

Alrighty then.

Once again, without mincing words, Dad had reminded me I wasn't anything special. My frustrations boiled within and I stormed over to Deena's duplex. As usual, Chad's car was nowhere to be seen. Though Deena was just as irritated by mother's blatant thievery and my father's stubborn pride, she assured me it would all work out.

"We have plenty of time to get things arranged," she said.

We. I liked the sound of that.

"Come here," she gestured, drawing me into her arms. "Just let it go."

The thought never crossed my mind, of course, that both the deacon's and Deena's actions were forms of sexual assault. With him, it had been violating. With her, it was exhilarating. Even now, it's hard for me to put them into the same category, knowing how special she made this needy and inexperienced teen feel. That doesn't change the fact she groomed and exploited me. Her advances warped my views of love, romance, and sex for years to come, not to mention reinforcing my negative perceptions of God, integrity, and church leadership. Her kind words and feel-goods only numbed the inevitable pain.

A pain which arrived much sooner than expected.

The time bomb was already ticking.

May 20, 1974: The day I hit eighteen, I was legally available according to Tennessee state law. Deena and I could make this happen. Sex and marriage, whatever we wished.

Tick, tick, tick . . .

June 1: Graduation day followed on my birthday's heels, and when I turned the tassel on my mortar board along with my classmates,

I celebrated much more than a high school diploma. Soon, Deena would be all mine.

Tick, tick . . .

June 9: After church service that Sunday, I was headed toward my car when Chad's voice caught me from behind. I turned, smile in place, figuring he was still as clueless as he'd been the past two years. He wasn't smiling, though, and my shoulders tensed. "Steven," he said without any visible emotion, "I think it would be best if you no longer come over to my house unless I'm home."

Boom!

The secret exploded, leaving a crater of questions and distrust between two men in a church parking lot. He knew. How'd he find out?

He walked away, his shoulders straight, seemingly unfazed. I, on the other hand, felt like my ribs had been torn open, my heart pulled out of my chest. Would he tell the pastor or my parents? No, he wouldn't put his wife through that, would he?

Worry churned in me. I could barely get through a work shift without getting a price wrong or fumbling an item onto the floor. At home, I cried myself to sleep. Would I ever see Deena again? Though I was desperate to hear her voice, the only way to reach her was by phone, and I couldn't risk having her husband pick up.

Oh, Deena. Was she okay? What did this mean for us?

Us. What a joke.

As delusional as I was, I still believed there was a past, present, and future to our relationship. She loved me deeply, unconditionally. I was no longer underage and the only thing standing in our way was her husband. These were the things I told myself. She would still leave him, wouldn't she? With time, he would get over it, right?

Tick, tick . . .

Another secret was about to go off, one so surprising yet inevitable that I wonder to this day if I had a part in it.

Deena, I discovered, was pregnant.

If Deena ever meant to leave Chad for me, the reality of a newborn must have changed her mind. Just like that, everything made sense, and heartbroken as I was, it didn't surprise me when our youth leaders stopped coming to the church.

We all know people who try to escape by changing locations, running as far as they can from childhoods and families, mistakes and memories. Maybe that's what Chad and Deena did—no word, no warning, just gone—but for me, escape was never a geographical thing. The things I wanted to run from were in my own head. No amount of distance would change that. Drop me in the middle of Death Valley and I would still have my secrets rumbling around.

Was the child mine? I wondered. Was it a boy or girl? What did it look like?

I never did get answers to those questions, and to this day there's a hole in my heart that will not go away.

13

WRECKAGE

Still under my parents' roof, I had my own vehicle and a job, and I stayed away from home as much as possible. Most evenings I came in from work, cleaned up, slapped on some cologne, and darted back out to make my rounds at Nashville hot spots. I became a popular nightclub presence, with people cozying up to me and calling me by name. It was intoxicating stuff for a former high-school nobody and I took advantage. Music, dancing, and lots of beautiful, flirtatious women.

I didn't care about tomorrow or next week or next month. The moment was all that mattered. And each moment was all about me.

Fun at any cost.

Human beings, I learned, could be a means to an end. One-night stands numbed my pain, and I was always on the prowl. If my behavior was manipulative, so be it. My body was free for the taking, but my heart was kept locked tight so it wouldn't get hurt again. Others had taken what they wanted from me—a deacon stealing my innocence, Mom stealing my money, and Deena stealing my heart—and I was done with all that.

Done with my family and done with church.

Step eight. Done with God.

This deep animosity which had started at age twelve exploded by the time I was eighteen. I became completely and totally who I would be for the next four decades, a full-fledged God-hater. In my heart and mind, I turned that first hard corner onto the road called I Don't Give a Damn, a road I would travel to its end at the Hallmark.

Mom pulled me aside after one of our family gatherings. "Steven, no more."

"What?" I stood taller than her now.

She looked up. "Every time the family gets together, come Thanksgiving, Christmas, or Easter, you bring a different date. Billy Dean and Byron, they make the effort to visit with their wives, and here you are, parading these girls around. If you're not going to take one of them seriously, stop wasting our time. It doesn't look good."

I chuckled. "I'm still just a teenager, Mom."

"Be sensible, Steven. Find yourself a spouse and have a family."

The very thought seemed ridiculous. Sex was the one thing which gave me pleasure, if only for a few meaningless minutes, and I didn't need a wife for that.

"Are you even listening to me?" she said.

"Don't you want me to be happy?" I asked. "Or are you telling me to throw away my life before it even gets started?"

"Happiness has nothing to do with it. It's what's expected. It's what you do."

"But isn't that why you're so unhappy?" I shot back. "You got stuck with all these kids and had to give up your dreams? You know, you could've just put us in a shelter and let us find our own food to eat. We might've been better off." It was a harsh statement, and if ever I deserved one of Mom's beatings it was then. But I meant every word.

Mom set her jaw, looked away, and marched from the room.

At that point, since my own mother couldn't get through to me, my Heavenly Father must have figured I needed a few wake-up calls.

I had survived the crosswalk incident years ago, but my second near-death experience happened in Dad's '57 Chevy. That car was his pride and joy. He had purchased it fresh off the showroom floor back in California, drove us across the country in it, and later passed it down to Robert. My brother spruced it up with a paint job and new upholstery. The thing was a family heirloom.

Robert wasn't tightfisted, at least not with me, and one night he let me borrow the vehicle. With my cousin along for a ride, I roared north on I-65 at close to 90 mph. The Old Hickory Boulevard exit appeared quicker than expected, and as I veered off the interstate, I lost control.

Everything went sideways.

Six times—count 'em—that's how many times the car rolled. My cousin and I should have been mangled bodies, dead or close to it, but that tough old Chevy frame held together until the final roll and the top never did cave in. Dazed, we walked away with barely a scratch. Lucky. Yep, that was me.

The next incident occurred on a warm summer evening north of downtown. Behind the wheel of my Chevy Malibu, I felt in control as the power of the V-8 engine rumbled up through the gas pedal into my foot. My friend Ted was in the passenger seat. We were headed west on Broadmoor Road, going to grab some pizza on Dickerson Pike.

Sixty seconds later, two ladies were dead, and ten minutes later, Ted was slipping from shock into a coma. Two hours later, firemen were still cutting through metal to get my friend and me out of the wreckage.

I woke up early the next morning in my bedroom, sore as hell and needing to use the bathroom. I passed out before I could make it to the bathroom. When my eyes opened again, daylight was pouring through the window. Oh, no. Had I slept through my alarm? I fumbled for my clothes and tried pulling them over stiff limbs.

"Steven?" Dad said from the doorway. "What're you doing, son?"

"I'm late for work."

"They gave you the day off," he said. "Figured you might need it."

My mind was a complete blank. "Why? What's wrong?"

While Mom sat on the edge of my bed and filled me in on the details, Dad stared at me as though I'd gone crazy.

Trauma-induced amnesia is actually pretty common. I didn't remember leaving the house, getting T-boned by the ladies as they ran a stop sign at over 50 mph, or careening over a culvert in my own vehicle and being wrapped around a tree. The only blip in my thoughts was an image of me thrusting out an arm to hold up Ted in his seat. I didn't even realize I had been taken to the ER before coming home.

Turns out I was fine, not even one broken bone. My friend, on the other hand, suffered permanent brain damage, and the two women from the other car were buried later that week. A caution light was installed soon after at the intersection of Broadmoor and Lemont, still there to this day, alerting drivers to potential danger.

You would think all this was enough to get my attention, but instead of heeding the warning, mourning the dead, and praising God for the gift of life, I felt angry. I grumbled about lost work hours, lost pay, and lost time at the clubs. There I was, a miraculous survivor of yet another catastrophe, and I had no idea why.

Was there some heavenly plan at work? Impossible.

As far as I was concerned, I had no redeeming qualities, no reason God should want to keep me around.

Once or twice I visited Ted at the hospital, but seeing him in his condition was too much to handle for someone as self-absorbed as myself. When I went to see my car at the junkyard, I didn't fall to my knees wondering why I alone was spared—not even close. Since the lady in the car that hit us had been uninsured, I still owed $600 on this heap of metal. I mean, what a hassle. The accident wasn't even my fault, and now I had to come up with some money to pay this off and find a new set of wheels.

There you go. That's how pathetic I was.

Not. A. Clue.

14

THE KISS OF DEATH

The price of faking success got higher each day. I needed to update my wardrobe, buy my friends more rounds of drinks, and finance my continued escapades.

For a while, things were okay. As a sales manager at a jewelry store, I made decent money. Girlfriends, husbands, lovers, and older women leaned over the illuminated glass displays, and I sniffed out their weaknesses the way a dog sniffs out a wound. They wanted to feel loved, important, desirable, and special, and since these were my own weaknesses, I knew just how to work them. Even so, my sales commissions couldn't support my lifestyle.

This called for drastic measures.

As a kid I'd already taken steps two and three—thievery and deceit—and it wasn't a big leap into embezzling. I needed more money, just a little here and there, I told myself. My boss trusted me, and for over a year I got away with stealing from him. What did I care? I was just working one lie to live another.

One day a pair of detectives walked into the shop and flashed their badges. "We're looking for Steven Young. Is that you?"

"In the flesh," I said. "How can I help you gentlemen?"

"We have a few questions to ask. Any guesses as to why we're here?"

They knew how to sniff out weakness too. They used innuendo, silence, and subtle threats. They claimed they had evidence they could use in court, and if I just came clean, things would go easier for me.

Despite giving them nothing, I was led from the shop in handcuffs. Before the detectives had me in the patrol car, I was already plotting a way out. I posted bail, with the help of a good attorney, and instead of hitting rock bottom, repenting of my sinful ways, and agreeing to restitution, I thought of ways to manipulate the system.

When at last my court date came, I fed the judge a sob story about being a good-guy-gone-bad due to the evils of drug use. The addiction, I said, was turning me into someone I didn't want to be. I needed help, Your Honor. I pointed out that I had no previous record and my sincere hope was to be a productive member of society.

Can you blame him for eating it up?

He gave me a year's probation after I promised to keep my nose clean, go to counseling, and submit to random drug tests. Since my addiction was a complete load of hogwash, I passed each and every test. My probation officer was so impressed by my clean behavior, he petitioned the court and got my restrictions removed after only six months. I was that damn good.

Without consequences, we humans tend to push the limits even further. Though we complain when things go wrong, oftentimes God gives us an opportunity to learn from our mistakes. He does this out of love, starting with quiet warnings. Gentle nudges. Light correction. Hebrews 12:6 says, "For whom the Lord loves He chastens . . ."

If we ignore these measures, things tend to go downhill quickly.

"Why, God?" we cry out. "Why!"

He is simply allowing us to face the consequences of our own free will. We can decide to care for others and work toward a common good. Or we can follow our selfish desires, swat others aside, and ultimately end up harming ourselves.

I chose the latter.

Emboldened by my success at working the justice system—which had very little to do with actual justice—I went right back to partying, sleeping around, and living it up.

My fourth near-death encounter happened in Donelson, another Nashville suburb. As assistant manager at a small market off Lebanon Road, I was getting ready to close one night when a guy walked through the door, stepped to the counter, and shoved a gun in my face. That silver-lipped barrel was only a foot away, as big as a frickin' howitzer, the kiss of death that close.

"All your money," he demanded. "And don't forget the bag under the counter."

The zippered bank bag contained large bills. How did he know it was there? I didn't know he had been dating the previous late-night clerk, learning details about the store. I didn't say a thing. I didn't move. I couldn't move. Fear had me in its grip.

That's when I heard the click of the trigger.

The fool tried to shoot me!

To my amazement, I was still alive and on my feet, pulse throbbing in my neck. The assailant, equally shocked, spun round and bolted out the door. The police found him later that evening with a fully loaded gun which fired exactly as designed.

If this was supposed to be another wake-up call, I paid no attention.

Here's the thing: Even now I don't always know the Lord's will or understand all His ways, and I certainly can't explain why some people suffer or die while others remain unscathed. We live in a fallen world. Disease and death have their way more often than not, and none of us get out of here alive. That's a fact.

So if you survive cancer, a head-on collision, or a tornado, does that mean you're automatically destined for something greater?

Yes. Yes, it does. Because each and every day on this planet is one more God-given opportunity. Every moment is a seed of destiny, and you are either planting something positive and life-affirming or something wasteful and destructive.

Me? I was more of a lesson than a blessing.

Step right up, friends, and learn from my mistakes, because I've made a lot of them—and suffered the consequences too. My Heavenly Father didn't need to rain down punishment. He rarely does. Crashed cars, handcuffs, and pointed guns are all the warnings any sane person should need.

Oh, wait. Did I say I was sane?

My actions suggested otherwise.

15

TOLD YOU I'D GET YOU

As I saw it, my parents were obstacles to my fun. I moved in and out a few times, but by twenty-one, I figured it was time for a more permanent place of my own. I put down a deposit on a house in nearby Hendersonville and shared the rent with a roommate—though that wasn't all he and I shared. Confused by my past, I had two encounters with men before settling once and for all on the company of women.

To fund my party lifestyle, I found jobs here and there. I worked as a tour guide downtown—good money, with tips and all. I also worked as the cook at a red clapboard barbecue joint—good food and cold drinks.

Which brings me to my job at Davidson County Farmers Co-op.

There was a lot to love about my work at the co-op. In spring and fall, I drove a fertilizer truck to county farms, put the engine into low gear and turned on the spreader, then made slow passes up and down the fields. I rolled the windows down, blasted the radio, and basked in the warmth. It was just me and the truck and wide open spaces. In winter, the truck was fitted for rock salt, which I spread on rural roads and driveways. I had a lot of autonomy and smoked whenever I wanted to. What wasn't there to love?

I also loved taking advantage of an opportunity when I saw one.

And I saw one.

On weekends, when the co-op was closed, I went down in my roommate's truck and loaded supplies out of the warehouse. There were no security cameras. No alarms. And I had the keys to the place. I stashed those supplies in our garage—chainsaws, roofing shingles, gallons of paint, bags of mulch—then sold them off through classified ads in the local newspapers. My roomie had no idea what I was up to.

It was brazen. It was profitable. And nobody caught on.

Until the Sunday one of my coworkers, a good ol' boy, drove past on his way home from church and spotted an unfamiliar truck in the alley behind the co-op. He jotted down the license plate, and when a following tally of warehouse supplies came up short, he raised the alarm.

Unaware of this, I was surprised a few days later when I walked into my house in Hendersonville and found all of my roomie's stuff gone. He had up and moved, no discussion beforehand, no warning at all.

"What's going on?" I demanded over the phone. "Did I make you mad?"

"Something like that," he said.

He told me about the Metro Nashville detectives who'd come to our address wanting to know why his truck was down at the Davidson County Farmers Co-op the previous weekend. They suspected stuff had been stolen from the warehouse. Was he involved? He told them he'd loaned his truck to me and I worked there. Otherwise, he swore he knew nothing about it. Now, sensing more trouble was on its way, he wanted out of our living arrangement. He could no longer trust me.

Unfazed, I thanked him for the information. I moved my stash from the garage to a new hiding place, and sure enough, the detectives reappeared the next day with a search warrant. Did they think I was worried?

"Knock yourselves out," I told them.

When they came up empty-handed, they wanted to know why I had been at the co-op over the weekend. I told them I'd gone in and done some measuring to help price out a job for a buddy of mine.

"We'd like your buddy's number," they said. "Just to corroborate your story."

"I don't see how that's necessary," I replied. "You came in here with your warrant, you've gone through my whole place, and you're walking out with nothing. I don't need any more inconvenience. I think this conversation's over."

It was over, that was true, and they never came back. My job at the co-op was also over. Even if the owners couldn't prove my guilt, they knew. Oh, they knew.

For me, it was yet one more brush with the law, one more warning to steer clear of trouble. A wise person would heed such a warning. Proverbs 1:7 says, "The fear of the Lord is the beginning of knowledge, but fools despise wisdom and instruction." I was the fool, puffing out my chest and congratulating myself on outwitting the authorities yet again. They could send their best after me, but I was a hard man to pin down.

A few weeks later, I moved from Hendersonville into an apartment in Madison, sharing it with a new acquaintance and roomie. I took a position at a nearby Shoney's restaurant and worked my way into management.

It wasn't an easy job. After dealing with inventory, food prep, cranky cooks, and irritable customers, I looked forward to closing times so I could head off to the nightclubs. I also looked forward to hanging out with my latest girlfriend, a Shoney's hostess. While dating a coworker wasn't very smart, it was certainly convenient.

What wasn't convenient was the fact her former fiance was Mr. Pickens, our district supervisor. Let's just say, Pickens wasn't my biggest fan. He criticized my scheduling, ordering, and cleaning. If I was behind it, he was against it. And he seethed every time he paid a store visit and found the hostess and me on shift together.

As district supervisor, Pickens was known throughout the community. He was pals with local politicians, firemen, and officers of the vice squad. He even played golf with some of them. Being on his bad side was not a good idea. To me, though, he was all bark and no bite. I was six-foot-three now, with a head of curly blond hair, and didn't consider him much of a threat.

Big mistake.

One evening, as my roomie and I were getting ready to hit the clubs, the phone rang. Without caller ID to screen my calls, I picked up the hard plastic receiver. "Hello?"

"Steven, glad I caught you."

Regretting my choice to pick up, I said, "What can I do you for, Mr. Pickens?"

"You know how we let the janitor in and out at night? Well, he's done cleaning at the restaurant and I can't find my keys to go let him out. I need you to run down there."

"But my roommate and I were just heading into town."

"Swing by on your way. Won't take you more than thirty seconds."

I grumbled to my roomie during the entire drive, hands squeezing the steering wheel of my Ford Grenada. This was just the sort of thing my jealous supervisor did to get under my skin. This was his way of striking back. I pulled in at Shoney's, left the car running, and jogged to the door with store keys jingling. In the semidarkness, I found the janitor shifting from foot to foot.

"Thought you were all done," I said. "You got everything you need?"

"I, uh . . ."

"C'mon now. I've got places to go."

"Sure. Just, uh . . . just another minute or two." He glanced out the window, seeming awful skittish.

"What's wrong?"

"It's fine. I'm fine." He trudged alongside me. "We can head out."

Before I could even turn to lock the doors behind us, spotlights blinded us, and undercover officers rushed from the parking-lot shadows, weapons drawn.

"On the ground! Get on the ground! Hands where we can see 'em."

In the Grenada, my roomie panicked. He slid into the driver's seat, gunned the motor, and peeled out of the parking lot in a cloud of burnt rubber. He rocketed south on Gallatin Pike with police vehicles in pursuit, blue lights flashing, sirens screaming. On the pavement beside the janitor, I felt knees dig into my back as handcuffs clicked into place. Pebbles pressed against my cheekbone.

"Is this him, Pickens?" a policeman said.

"Oh, that's him alright," my district supervisor responded. Why was Mr. Pickens here? What was going on? His onion-ring breath tickled my neck as he leaned close. "Hello there, Steven. Told you I'd get you, you son of a bitch."

As the janitor and I were manhandled into the back of a patrol car, I heard gunshots—pop-pop-pop!—from the direction of Nashville National Cemetery.

16

HELL AND A BIT OF HEAVEN

Metro Nashville Police informed me of three things related to my arrest.

First, they told me, my roommate was dead. He'd crashed my car outside the cemetery after dozens of bullets were fired in his direction.

Second, they were charging me with third-degree burglary. My district supervisor claimed I wasn't even supposed to be in Shoney's that night. I had unlawfully entered a nonresidential structure with intent to commit burglary or theft. My plan, Mr. Pickens claimed, was to empty the store safe, a plot the assistant manager allegedly heard me cooking up with the janitor out by the dumpster a few nights earlier.

Third, they had the janitor as a key witness. Only later did I find out he was testifying against me to gain leniency on outstanding grand-theft-auto charges.

Justice is a dirty business, everyone in it for something.

Thankfully, the first thing the officers told me was just a cruel joke. Though my car was a bullet-riddled heap, my roomie had only scrapes and bruises. The cops ribbed each other about needing to spend more time practicing at the range. While they thought it was funny, their little lie sowed in me a seed of distrust in the system.

The second thing was a complete fabrication. Pickens set me up, pure and simple. He had the motive—revenge. And the means—

friends in high places. I ranted about how he was the one who sent me to the store that night, but nobody cared what I had to say. Pickens was a community leader, and I was a twentysomething with a record.

No cell phones back then. No text messages. No hidden cameras. My word against his.

The third thing was a potential weakness in their case. The janitor knew I was innocent, and how could the assistant manager have overheard us talking when that dumpster was a good thirty feet from the restaurant. With these things in mind, I hired a bulldog of a defense attorney, who assured me he would use every available tactic to drag out proceedings over the next few years.

Out on bond, I turned twenty-three in the spring of 1979. That same year, America used the electric chair for the first time to execute a death-row inmate. Of course, my issues were much smaller here in Nashville, but I faced a hell of my own as I stared down possible prison time.

To this day, I still insist I was innocent. I was framed.

Of course you were, Steven. Isn't that what they all say?

Sure, but what do I have to gain by lying all these years later? I've already spilled some of my secrets in this book and admitted my guilt at the jewelry shop. I'll be sharing even darker secrets in pages to come, including my part in other criminal activities.

But the Shoney's deal?

Utter nonsense.

Realizing my freedom could be temporary, I applied myself with new vigor to the nightlife. And the party was always on. I wasn't into alcohol or drugs, but I loved wearing expensive fashions, flashing money, and being noticed as I strolled through the doors. Like that old TV theme song from Cheers, everybody knew my name.

Did they know the real Steven Young? Definitely not. No one wanted to hear about my secrets and insecurities, and they for damn sure didn't want a killjoy in the crowd. We were all there to feel better about ourselves and I was the life of the party. I wined and dined strangers and acquaintances, bought rounds of drinks, hopped from bed to bed, and survived on three or four hours of sleep a night.

Was it fun? Hell, yeah, it was fun.

Sin would be a dull knife in the devil's toolbox if it was boring.

To maintain my image wasn't cheap and I needed cash. Some employers balked at my criminal history, but this never stopped me. I had no problem lying, cheating, and conning to get into various jobs and relationships. It was all a big game.

"You know," a friend told me, "you could convince the pope he was an atheist."

"I could." I chuckled. "And I would, if there was something in it for me."

When a DJ at a local bar got sick one Friday night, I offered to fill in, and I landed a regular gig. The pay wasn't bad and I was thrilled. It also made me popular with the ladies. By the time last-call came around, I often had my pick. Deep down, though, I knew the truth. I was crippled—emotionally, sexually, spiritually.

This knowledge was a threat. It whispered in my ear, reminding me that anything I touched would eventually derail. Sure, my life might chug along nicely, with me raking in the dollars and luring partners to bed, but it wouldn't last. It never did.

I didn't trust God, that was the real issue. I completely ignored any signs of His presence and protection.

It's the darkness that allows the stars to shine, but I wasn't even looking up to see the stars. As far as I was concerned, happiness was an illusion, whether I was at a summer church camp or home for the holidays. In a heartbeat, a deacon could wake me from my bunk. A parent could whip out the belt. Better to blow things up on my own terms than have them explode in my face.

Many times over the next year, I drove home with grim thoughts spiraling through my head. I hated to even look at myself in the mirror. I later wrote a poem, trying to capture that ache behind my eyes:

THE LIFE OF THE PARTY

The music drifts on broken wings
And the crowd has all gone home
Spotlights fade into smoky haze
The shadows start to roam
Fleeting laughter turns to silence
As applause slips out the door
A world once filled with joyful noise
Embraces quiet's roar
The smiles leave and lonesome starts
There is no strength to fight
And the life of the party remains behind
He'll die some more tonight

Then, like an angel from heaven, a woman stopped me in my tracks in early 1980. She was nineteen, almost twenty, the Saturday night when we met for the first time. I was DJing at The Showboat, a club near the RiverGate Mall. She strolled in, and at five-foot-two she should have disappeared into the crowd. Instead, she carried herself with confidence, even a little sass, and I couldn't keep my eyes off her.

Normally, I had no problem approaching women. I had nothing at stake, no feelings involved, nothing to lose. This was different. I slipped a few 45s onto the disc changer, then stepped out from my booth. My heart thudded against my ribs, louder in my own ears than the music's bass beat. My legs carried me through smoke and spinning lights to the table where she sat.

"Hi there," I ventured. "I'm Steven."

She stared up with pretty hazel eyes, her face framed by strawberry blond hair. "I'm Andrea."

"Well, Andrea, would you, uh . . . would you like to dance?"

She and her friend shared a sly smile. Were they mocking me? I thought of the youth group girls whose giggles once made me self-conscious. Maybe it was a mistake coming over, following my heart instead of my libido.

"I'd love to," she said.

I took her hand and led her onto the dance floor. Her head didn't even reach my shoulders, yet nothing in the world felt more natural than holding her next to me, my hand resting on the curve of her waist.

As I soon learned, Andrea Thompson was born and raised in Nashville. Her parents co-owned a beer tavern off West End, and her brother, ten years older, had married and moved out, meaning she'd had lots of time on her hands as a young teen. She threw herself into competitive roller-skating, practicing speed and dance at the rinks near Charlotte Pike and on Harding Place.

"So that's where you get your spunk from," I noted.

"What's that supposed to mean?"

"The way you carry yourself, you just look steady and sure. You don't seem like you'd take crap from anyone."

"Especially not from strange guys at the club," she said.

Was she aware of my reputation? I felt a hint of shame.

"Keep dancing with me," Andrea added. "And we won't be strangers for long."

Even as I led her across the floor, a tidal wave of feelings washed over me, and my usual fast-talk that led to pillow-talk seemed pointless. She wasn't the type for a one-night stand. She was the type I would want to spend the rest of my life with.

Whoa now, what was I thinking? Just dance, I told myself. And leave it at that.

We circled the floor. We laughed and talked. Before the evening was over, I walked Andrea out to her car and thanked her for a truly lovely time. There was no way I was ready for a real relationship, especially with my legal troubles looming, but for my own peace of mind I had to know if she had a boyfriend.

She shook her head. "We broke up a year ago, after seeing each other since we were twelve. He was more like a brother, really. Just someone to hang out with."

"Okay." I nodded. "So does that mean I can see you again?"

She lifted her chin, a twinkle in her eye. "Sure, Steven, if you ask nicely."

After a long hug good-bye—could a woman's embrace ever feel more amazing?—I watched her drive off and realized I was more concerned for her than I was for myself. This was not normal for me. In fact, it was a first. You don't have to be an art critic to stand before a Monet painting and realize you are gazing upon something rare and beautiful. Andrea Thompson was that to me.

Don't you dare hurt this girl, I thought. Don't you dare. In fact, you'd be better off if you just forgot about her altogether.

17

BIG BROTHER

Forget about her? Are you kidding? For the next two days, Andrea was all I could think of. I stared at her phone number and fought the urge to call. My trial date was still ten months away and she knew nothing about my class D felony charge. Was it fair to string her along? My attorney said the cards were stacked against me and a guilty verdict was a real possibility. What if I went to prison? I could be facing three to five years.

Phone in hand, I started to dial anyway. I could come clean with the truth about my situation. Andrea was young and innocent, but she wasn't some goody-two-shoes. Surely, she would understand.

I put down the phone.

Who was I fooling? This girl was out of my league.

On the third day, my resistance wore thin and I called her anyway. The moment her voice came through the receiver, I thought of her soft hair and the strength in her eyes and the tilt of her chin and the way she knocked me off balance while also making me feel tall and focused and alive.

Who was this woman?

A gift from above. There was no other explanation.

We talked for two hours straight, learning more about each other. She had faith without being pushy or fake about it. While she was strong in her own opinions, she was more than willing to consider mine. Every minute felt easy and comfortable with her and the mess of my life seemed to fade away. Talking to her, I was just Steven.

I was the boy who loved riding bikes and watching movies.

I was the boy who loved sweet tea and cooking, before a church leader pulled him aside at camp, before Deena called to him in her silky robe.

For two hours I was just me, and through Andrea's eyes I caught a glimpse of the man God had created me to be.

Even so, forgetting the past and basking in the present, I couldn't bring myself to mention the future. Just couldn't do it. The reality of prison was too hard to face, and I had to cling to this promise of romantic possibility. I wanted to stop hurting and start living again, and while Andrea and I conversed, I envisioned a life full of hope.

Before the call ended, she asked, "When can we see each other again?"

My mouth went dry. Legal hurdles. Third-degree burglary. Did I dare string her along any further? She was an angel who still knew nothing about my demons.

"Steven?" She sounded concerned. "Are you there?"

I cleared my throat and heard myself respond, "How about this Friday? Does that work for you?"

"That'd be great."

"I'll pick you up at seven."

Giving me her number was her first act of trust, and giving me her address was the second. She was letting me in and I could not screw this up. If I did anything to cause her pain, I knew I would not be able to live with myself.

We started dating in April 1980. With Andrea around, I was happy and content. Even as screwed up as my childhood was, she saw something worthwhile in me. After dinner, dancing, and hours of talking, I took her home. I never wanted this night to end, and we sealed it with a kiss.

Oh boy!

If our hug outside the club was unforgettable, this kiss was in a whole other realm. It left me wanting more and forged an indelible memory.

She eased away, her eyes finding mine. "Thank you for a great time tonight."

"My pleasure, Andy. Thank you."

"Andy? Nobody calls me that."

"Now I do, so I guess that makes me special."

She chuckled. "Okay, so when are we going to do this again? You know, I'm free next weekend."

"Great," I blurted out. "It's a date."

As she walked into her house, she glanced back over her shoulder. "Call me."

My pulse galloped through my veins. What was happening to me? Andy was a bundle of energy and confidence, leaping over every barrier I tried to put up. For the past few years, my relationships had been disposable.

With Andy, it was different.

And it scared me.

In the past, my casual question had been: What now? Or more accurately: Who now? In this current furnace of chemistry and connection, I had to re-frame my question: Now what?

Now that we were involved with each other, what was I going to do? I still hadn't mentioned my trial date or my previous felony. What if she found out? Would she ditch me? Stop answering my calls? She knew nothing of my sexual molestation by leaders in two different churches. Could any woman love me once she learned of that violation and found out how damaged I was? If not, I wouldn't blame her.

You've really done it this time, Steven.

Now what?

So many times I wanted to tell Andy everything, and each time the fear of losing her stopped me. We were happy together. Fairy-tale relationships were real. I wasn't just living in the moment anymore, but actually thinking about the future.

Within weeks, we even started talking about marriage.

I was in deep shit, and it was about to get deeper.

In Andy's presence, my fears just melted away. I loved the way she fidgeted with her hair and pouted when she didn't get what she wanted. Even when she grew aggravated, her compassion and gentleness won out. Her behavior was unlike anything I'd experienced with Dad or Mom. In just a few weeks with Andy, I began mending inside. My tenderness for her was deeper than any I'd ever felt—or allowed myself to feel. I no longer wanted to settle for the life I'd been living. I wanted to live a life that I chose.

And I chose her.

The night I asked Andrea Thompson to marry me was magical, and when she said yes, the look in her eyes washed away years of lonely anguish and pain. Money couldn't buy the kind of happiness we shared.

Later, we invited her family to a restaurant to make our grand announcement. To say they were less than ecstatic would be putting it mildly. Their questions were reasonable: Why so quickly? What about income? Where would we live?

It would all work itself out, we said. This was for real.

Despite their reservations, we pressed on and set a date in September—only six months after we first met.

Behind the scenes, Andy's big brother went to work. He was a man of persistence and principles, and he was immune to my considerable charm. These traits would serve him well as he went on to become a prosecutor. At the time, though, he we just worried about this stranger who was stealing away his baby sister. He had one of his attorney friends run a background check on me, then, armed with details, he took Andy out to lunch and divulged to her what he had done.

Or more importantly, what I had done.

Embezzlement. Burglary. A rap sheet a mile long.

18

THE SHADOWS

It was over—the romance, the wedding, all of it. I knew it the minute Andy called and said we needed to talk. She sat me down that evening, confronting me with the cold hard facts dug up by her brother. There was no lying or manipulating my way out of this. In some ways, it was a relief.

"So," Andy said, "even with a trial ahead, you asked me to marry you?"

I hung my head. Andy's brother was absolutely right, God bless him. I was bad news. He had done his brotherly duty, sparing his sis the inevitable letdown.

"Why?" she pressed.

"Because I love you."

"Do you?" She leveled her gaze at me. "Really?"

"I do."

She looked away, deep in thought. Finally, she turned back and said, "In that case, Steven, I promise that I'll be there right beside you during your trial."

"What? No, listen, you don't have to feel sorry for me and try to keep in touch. I'll have my parents there, maybe a friend or two. I'll manage." Though not exactly sure of my parents' support, I didn't want her to feel obligated.

"I won't be there as just a friend." Andy took my hand across the table. "I will be there as Mrs. Young."

My heart stopped. Had I heard her correctly?

"I'll be there," she stated, "as your lawfully wedded wife. I'm still wearing my engagement ring, aren't I? I'm head over heels for you. None of that changes, but listen, mister, you better promise to toe the line from here on out. Keep yourself out of trouble, you understand me?"

With moisture welling in my eyes, I swallowed hard and nodded.

"Say it, Steven. Say it out loud."

"I will stay out of trouble, Andy. I'll be the best husband I can possibly be."

As beautiful as the wedding was with the flowers and decorations, my bride was even more so. I could not fathom the grace and love that poured from this woman. She had every right to walk away, and instead she floated up the aisle, a vision in white. If ever I had a chance to redefine my future, this was it, and I beamed from ear to ear.

We left for our honeymoon in Andy's Camaro and started our new life in an apartment on Charlotte Pike. The first four months we lived happily as husband and wife, surviving on my income as a sales rep for Frito-Lay and as a DJ on the side, and on hers as a court reporter, retained by a law firm for divorces, depositions, and whatever else they needed. Andy and I made meals together. Watched TV. Went dancing. Made up and made love. All the normal newlywed stuff. We also adjusted and compromised. Believe it or not, plenty of Nashvillians don't follow country music, but Andy turned me into a fan after convincing me to see *Urban Cowboy* with her, starring John Travolta and Debra Winger. We even bought the soundtrack and wore that thing out.

Life was good.

Then in January 1981, my day of reckoning came. Dad, Mom, and Andy looked on from the wooden courtroom pews, enduring jury selection, opening statements, and hours of witness testimony. The janitor spun his lies, probably fed to him by my district supervisor, and my attorney did his darnedest to oppose every point, wrangling repeatedly with the assistant D.A. It took longer than expected, yet we were optimistic as the jurors left to deliberate. My parents even apologized—something they never did!—for assuming I was guilty, since they now saw clearly these allegations were false.

The jury returned, their decision delivered by the bailiff to the honorable Judge Leathers. Asked to rise, I held my head high and braced for the verdict.

"Guilty," the judge declared, "of third-degree burglary."

The weight of those words rolled over me, the wheels of justice grinding over me the way they do thousands of others every day. There was no stopping what Mr. Pickens had set in motion. It was inevitable. Even so, my knees wobbled beneath the crushing reality and it took everything in me to remain standing.

Sentencing was set for May. The months in between were torturous, full of unknowns and uncertainty. When at last Judge Leathers decided my punishment, he expressed his displeasure with the jury's verdict and stated directly to the cameras that "a personal vendetta was involved." Even the assistant D.A., who knew Andy from her courtroom work, said he was sorry. He had just been doing his job.

The judge gave me the minimum, three years in prison, with ninety days to set my affairs in order. In private, he vowed to keep an eye out for my well-being—a vow he lived up to in the coming months.

Despite the sympathy of the judge and my parents, I felt betrayed by a system which claimed to provide justice for all. Plea bargains, paid informants, and legal loopholes seemed to turn the cogs of this machine as much as any actual evidence, and money was the grease that kept it all churning. Why even try? What was the use?

Andy noticed my mood slipping in the following weeks. "You okay, babe?"

"I'll be fine," I mumbled.

None of it made sense, though. The way I saw it, I had gotten back on track, held a job, paid my bills, found a good woman, and settled down—only to lose it all one fateful evening to a vindictive supervisor who greased a few palms and pulled a few levers.

Feeling sorry for myself, I flipped back into survival mode.

My old four-step—rebellion, thievery, deceit, and cursing—led me toward dark, familiar places. Why even try doing the right thing? Just making it through each day was all that mattered to me. Andy was the only one I cared a hill of beans for, yet each time she reached for me, I retreated further into the shadows. As much as I hated myself for it, I was hiding things from her. What would she do if she knew the full truth? Would she leave me for good? Best to hedge my bets, just in case.

"Something's wrong. How I can help?" she asked me more than once.

I had no answers for her, which just made her—and me—even more upset. There was something broken inside and I didn't know how to fix it.

19

TUNNEL VISION

Andy's twenty-first birthday was only four days away. I would be in prison soon, and with my freedom slipping away, this would be my last chance to celebrate a birthday with her in who knew how long. Like any good husband, I secretly made reservations for a live production at Chaffin's Barn Dinner Theater. With its rustic flair, buffet meals, and quality acting, Chaffin's was both casual and romantic.

Andy would love it.

Except I reserved the seats for me and somebody else.

On June 20, 1981, a warm Saturday morning, my dear wife thought I was leaving on a weekend fishing trip. Loaded with a tackle box and fishing poles, my car served as my accomplice. I waved good-bye to Andy, figuring I'd swing by a Kroger deli on my way home to pick up a good-sized bass or catfish. Look what I caught, honey? Your husband, the mighty fisherman.

As smart as she is, Andy knew something was awfully—pardon the pun—fishy. A month earlier, she had confronted me with an astronomical bill from the phone company. "What's going on, Steven? There are calls to a number in western Kentucky, of all places, and there's another one lasting over an hour to somebody in Gallatin."

"C'mon. You think I'm cheating on you, babe? Don't be ridiculous. You know all the legal calls I've had to make. There's lots going on right now and I need your support, not some wild accusations."

Soon after, Andy had grilled me about a woman's photograph in my wallet. "She's beautiful," she commented, holding up the picture. "Who is she?"

"Oh, I . . . Ha, didn't even know I still had that. Just someone I grew up with."

"Nice monogrammed sweater. What's the S stand for?"

"What is this, Andy? What do you want from me?"

"The truth."

"It's Stephanie, alright? She's like a sister to me. Now stop acting crazy."

For the next few days Andy and I coexisted without another word on the matter. Meanwhile, I resumed my flirting with Stephanie, originally from Kentucky. She thought I was single, and after many phone calls, gifts, and kisses, the two of us hopped into the sack together. Now she was talking about marriage, wanting me to meet her parents.

You're in trouble, I told myself.

Not sure how to get out of this mess, I left on my alleged fishing trip, then quickly reserved a table for four that evening, best seats available at Chaffin's Barn.

The Saturday sun was setting over the nearby hills, its golden rays fanning through oaks and maples, when Stephanie introduced me to her mother and father and they followed me into the theater off Highway 100. We enjoyed a good meal and show, but the best acting that night was done by yours truly. I was suave, polite, and debonair. As always, I was dressed to the nines—just like Dad—and though only weeks away from my own prison cell, I had Stephanie and her parents convinced of my eligibility. It was all a big game. And it made me feel wanted.

It was also pathetic—yes, I know that—and my wife deserved so much better.

Like a dog that returns to its own vomit, I kept going back to my usual ways of coping. By creating a new life, a new persona, I could pretend to be someone else. I didn't have to face the real Steven Young. Looking back now, it makes me sick.

By the time Stephanie and I left Chaffin's Barn, it was dark and humid out, the air electric with the buzz of cicadas. I reached my car and noticed a letter folded beneath the windshield wiper. As I tugged it loose, I recognized my wife's handwriting.

"What is it?" Stephanie asked.

"Nothing. It's just, uh . . . just a friend playing a joke on me." I glanced at my watch. "Wow, it's even later than I thought." I tucked the letter into the pocket of my sports jacket and opened the passenger door for my date. We followed her parents to their place, where they let me sack out on their sofa.

I read Andy's letter twice that night by lamplight. She wrote that she was hurt, angry. She'd received a call confirming reservations at Chaffin's Barn. Suspicious, she had watched with a friend from outside as I led Stephanie and her parents into the theater. Andy had wanted to speak to me in person, but hated confrontation after growing up listening to her parents fight. She was done, Andy said. My unfaithfulness was the last straw.

As rattled as I was, I still believed I could talk her down from the ledge. I'd grovel. Tell her I loved her. Explain it was just an innocent evening with an old friend. Though my wife would be understandably upset, in time she would get over it.

I returned the letter to my pocket and fell fast asleep on the couch.

I awoke early on Sunday, June 21. Father's Day. Before returning to my apartment, I picked up a frozen fish from the deli and tossed it into my ice chest. I pulled on a white T-shirt, blue denim coveralls, and a pair of canvas deck shoes. Oh, you better believe I had a whopper of a fish story all set for my bride when I walked through our door.

Andy stopped me right away.

"Not one word, Steven." Her arms were crossed. "You always come in with some smooth, prepared line and try to make me feel stupid. Not this time."

"What do you mean? It's not what you think. I was fishing."

"You are so full of it. Do you honestly expect me to buy that from you?"

"Listen, babe, I know how you feel, and I—"

"First of all, you have no idea how I feel," she cut in. "I know you got the letter I left on your car. And guess who I heard from this morning? Stephanie's mother. While you were sleeping over there on their couch, she read through the letter and got my number from Information. She told me all about you and Stephanie, how the two of you are engaged, and how none of them had any idea you were already married. Does our marriage mean nothing to you? Did my name just never come up?"

I worked my lips, but my mouth felt full of sand.

"Don't even start," she said.

"Listen, babe, I—"

"No!" Andy pleaded. "Just leave. Please, just go."

All of my scheming crumbled as she moved into the light and I saw her red and swollen eyes, her trembling shoulders. Pain was written across her face in streaks of dried tears. For a brief period at the start of our relationship, I had actually cared for her even more than for myself, and now I'd broken every promise made to her. I was beyond hope. What kind of man went around sabotaging the love that mattered to him most?

Andy was right.

There were no adequate words.

The anguish carved into her features caused something in me to give way. In that moment, my self-hatred sent me storming out to my car, the world narrowing to a black tunnel. All I could see were my hands on the wheel. All I could hear was the pounding in my ears.

Somewhere along the way, I stopped back by Stephanie's parents' house to tell her we were through. Or maybe I lied to her too. All I remember is she slapped me hard across the face.

Back into the vehicle.

Tunnel vision.

Miles flying past and hours creeping by.

West Nashville. Gallatin. Inglewood. Downtown.

Still in a T-shirt and coveralls.

Shadows and soaring metal arches.

I stumbled from my car, leaving the door open, keys in the ignition. I was on Shelby Avenue Bridge, a once-busy thoroughfare which today serves as one of the world's longest pedestrian bridges. Vehicles whizzed by and horns blared. Gasoline and diesel fumes stung my nostrils. Gravel hissed at my ankles, and from far below, the Cumberland River called my name.

When someone does something crazy in the news, there's always that neighbor or coworker who says they never imagined so-and-so could do such-and-such. People shake their heads in disbelief. Friends or spouses might even, in complete honesty, swear they never saw it coming.

Gimme a break.

It was coming, alright. Step by little step.

I'm no therapist—hell, I'd just lost two women in the space of an hour—but I'm pretty sure each of us have our own private trails of shame. Some trails meander off through the grass, others straight into tangled thorns or through haunted woods or off steep cliffs. Each small surrender, each compromise, nudges us toward a larger one. Each step leads us further into darkness.

That same darkness now called my name.

Steven, the voice whispered from the waters below, *no more hiding, no more secrets, no more pain. Wash it all away in the murky depths.* Desperate as I was, I could believe almost anything. At age twenty-five, after years of battling nightmares and shame, I was ready to put it all to rest. Now was as good a time as any. Andy was done with me, and my mother was gone on a visit to California, insulated by distance from whatever choices I might make.

One leg went up.

Then the other.

An updraft tugged at my curly blond hair.

Over the railing of the Shelby Avenue Bridge I crawled, scrabbling for traction on a horizontal length of pipe. Teetering there, I peered down between the toes of my deck shoes. The height was dizzying and I took a deep breath.

20

A DROWNING MAN

Andy got the call early that evening. It was Vanderbilt Hospital's psychiatric ward letting her know I had just been admitted. They provided very few details. When she showed up at my bedside with my oldest brother, Billy Dean, neither of them seemed happy.

"What'd you do, Steven?" she asked.

I offered no reply from my position beneath the sterile sheets.

"You look alright, but you must've done something or you wouldn't be in here."

"My hair hurts," I said. I knew it sounded strange, but my head ached right down to the roots of my thick curly mane.

Andy took a deep breath, clearly exasperated.

"We wanna help," Billy Dean said. "You and I don't talk much, not since we left home and went our separate ways, but we're family. That's gotta mean something."

I wasn't so sure. I had nothing to share, nothing I wasn't deeply ashamed of.

My wife's eyes were hollow, her voice flat. "Aren't you going to tell us what happened, at least the basics? Please, don't you think you owe us that much?"

"I can't talk about it right now."

"You can't? Or you won't?"

I set my jaw and looked away. Billy Dean shifted his weight, his hands shoved deep into his pockets.

"If you won't talk to your own wife, who will you talk to?" Andy implored. "You know how I feel about you, Steven, but this is toxic. As much as I want to help, I can't play this game with you anymore." She waited for a response, then added, "Well, if this is a ploy for sympathy or to get a lighter prison sentence, it's not going to work. I will bring you some clothes and toiletries and leave the rest of your stuff at your mother's house."

Fiddling with the ID tag on my wrist, I nodded.

My brother said, "If you have nothing to tell us, I suppose I'll be going home to the wife and kids. If you have it in you, you might wanna at least give Dad a call. Not sure how he'll respond, but it would be a nice gesture, being as it's Father's Day and all."

As sick as I was, that thought hadn't even crossed my mind. My world had crumbled and all I could think of was myself. My wife and my brother left me there, locked in my own bitterness toward family, the system, and God.

A few weeks later, after my extended stay at Vanderbilt, the Tennessee Department of Corrections sent me to a rundown classification unit in Cockrill Bend, just off I-40 on the western edge of town. This is where authorities would determine my security level and eventual destination based on the nature of my crimes and on my interaction with other inmates.

Two weeks in, my parents came to visit.

Dad didn't say much. What was going through his mind? Was I a failure in his eyes, a disappointment? Did he see in me a reflection of his own mistakes?

Mom, never much of one for maternal gestures, did one of the most motherly things I ever saw her do by placing a call to Judge Leathers. These were no conditions for her son, she told the judge, and by that afternoon I was moved to the much newer and nicer medical ward down the road. I was grateful.

Eventually, I was designated as medium-security and transferred by a TDOC bus to a facility over a hundred miles away. It seemed like the middle of nowhere, and the reality of my situation struck me hard as the bus chugged around the final bend. Down there between limestone ridges and green hollows, the Turney Center prison complex bristled with chain-link fences and razor wire.

Only years later did I get the full story of what happened after Andy left me that night at the psych ward. Though my shrink resisted my wife's quest for answers, Andy kept pressing until he relented. After exhaustive evaluation, he had diagnosed me as a "sociopathic, pathological liar, borderline genius and insane." The way he saw it, my self-fabricated world had caved in the moment Andy confronted me with the evidence of my lies and adultery.

The smells and sounds of the psych ward were still fresh in her thoughts as she got back to our apartment that Sunday night. Her heart was broken. She had ignored her brother's warnings, putting everything on the line for me, and I'd torn it all to pieces. She felt angry and overwhelmed.

And the phone would not stop ringing. Initially, she answered the calls from the fast-talking reporters, confused by their barrage of questions.

"Is this the home of Andrea Thompson Young, wife of Steven Young?"

"Yes."

"Do you have anything to say about what happened earlier tonight? Had the two of you been fighting? Was there another woman involved?"

"Where'd you come up with all this?"

"So it's true, then."

"I don't know what you're talking about."

She stopped picking up after the third or fourth call and disconnected the cord when the jangling became too much.

Early the next morning, her thoughts were interrupted by a thud at the front door. What now? Was it someone knocking or just the paper delivery? Were news vans outside? When she peered through the window, there was nobody in sight.

She cracked open the door. On the front step, rolled and tucked into a plastic bag, sat the early edition of *The Tennessean* newspaper. Dated June 22, 1981, the front page bore a photo of me. She found an article on page nine by Perry Hines, beneath the headline, **Ex-Classmate Diverts Man From Suicide:**

> A young Nashville man threatened briefly yesterday to jump from the Shelby Avenue Bridge . . . Steve Young, 25, of 6319 Charlotte Pike, apparently was despondent because of his marriage, said Sgt. K. I. Wright, who added . . . "I believe he would have jumped if we hadn't arrived when we did."
>
> Young had been standing outside the bridge railing, perched on a pipe that runs the length of the structure, for about 20 minutes, when he was grabbed by police officer Randy Carroll. The officer made the grab while Young was talking to Officer Don Long, who recognized Young as a former classmate at Isaac Litton . . .
>
> Long said that Young struggled when first grabbed by Carroll, but that once he had been pulled back over the railing, he became subdued and burst into tears . . .

Andy's own eyes welled with tears when she saw the staff photo of Metro police yanking me by the arms and hair back to safety on the bridge. No wonder I'd complained of my head being sore.

Would Steven really have jumped? she wondered. Would he really have married another woman while married to me? What the hell was wrong with him?

As much as she was worried about my state of mind, she realized a drowning man would only drag her down with him, and she wasn't about to let that happen. She had to keep her own head above water and do her best to move on. Seeing no other option, she met with her brother's attorney friend and filed for a divorce.

In the following months she came to visit me in prison, but for all intents and purposes our relationship was over. I didn't even try to fight it. I signed the papers, knowing I'd sabotaged the one good thing in my life.

She was an angel. And I'd dragged her through hell.

Maybe I belonged behind bars, after all.

Part Two

"Success had brought him nothing but misery;
he couldn't handle it."

—John Grisham, in *The Testament*

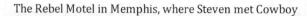

Steven's first Christmas with
his son, Josh Young

Steven's certificate from Nashville
School of Broadcast Technique

The Rebel Motel in Memphis, where Steven met Cowboy

21

ACTS OF GRACE

Some people try to tell you that prison isn't all that bad. They make it sound like an extended visit to a state-run country club, where inmates are spoiled with three square meals, hot showers, and hours of cable TV. No wonder, they figure, so many released convicts get locked back up again. Well, I can tell you, the ones who spout such crap have never been to prison or known a friend or family member who has been. We weren't human beings. We were numbered, warehoused, and treated as damaged goods.

I shared a 12x6 space with my cellmate. One exposed toilet between our beds. A shower twice a week, cold before your five minutes were up. Constant noise. Clanging, yelling, cursing. A total lack of privacy. Every minute regimented, every movement accounted for. I was always on edge, always alert. The only time I breathed easy was when they locked our door at night and turned out the lights.

Thanks to my shrink at Vanderbilt, I could see now that my fabricated reality was a pipe dream, a life tacked together on a shaky base of deceit.

No more wife. No girlfriend. No job.

My life was now a dumpster fire, and if I hoped to survive prison, I needed to set goals and take practical steps toward achieving my dreams. Think about it, Steven? What have you wanted to do since childhood? The one thing I'd always imagined was being on the radio, larger than life. A personality beyond the reach of my abusers.

A somebody.

My first step toward accomplishing this was to keep my nose clean. I did my best to stay invisible at Turney Center by showing respect to the guards and avoiding conflict with other prisoners. I kept my head down, ate in silence. My good behavior was soon noted, and it wasn't long before I was slated to face a review board for possible reclassification. If downgraded to minimum-security, I could apply for work release.

Everything seemed on track until two days before my review, when a fellow inmate tried to pick a fight with me. Words were exchanged, a scuffle ensued, and I got shoved into a metal railing before falling hard. Bruised ribs landed me in the clinic, and I knew any word of this could ruin my chances before the board. My hopes of a new life seemed in jeopardy, all because some angry S.O.B. had targeted me that morning.

And then an act of grace took place.

With nothing to gain from it, the guard on duty wrote me a recommendation letter in which he explained how I had slipped and fallen into the railing, a silly accident and nothing more. The board members read the letter, considered my case, and only two months after my arrival at Turney Center, they sent me back to Cockrill Bend.

Cockrill Bend is nearly three thousand acres of Nashville farmland tucked into a bend of the Cumberland River. In the late 1700s, early settler James Robertson owned the property before deeding it to his son, John Robertson, who for decades ran a slave-based operation there. After passing hands from the Robertsons to the Cockrills to the Morrows, the site became a prison complex in 1898, with the Tennessee State Penitentiary dominating the landscape.

By the 1980s, the thousands of acres at Cockrill Bend contained a maximum-security building known as The Castle, and a minimum-security area known as The Farm. The Castle housed eight hundred inmates and was featured most memorably in the movie *The Green Mile*. A mile or so away, the Farm included fields, a work release center, and other correctional facilities. From the Farm, convicts went out on road crews to gather trash or went to state office buildings for janitor duty.

Though I bunked at the work release center, I found myself spending six days a week off-site. Thanks to a second act of grace, the warden had granted my counselor's request for me to enroll at Nashville School of Broadcast Technique, near Music Row, taking courses from 8 a.m. to 2 p.m. And the state even paid for it. From NSBT, I went to my job as a second-shift cook at Ruby Tuesday. The guards looked forward to my return at curfew since I often brought pies and goodies from the restaurant.

As a broadcasting student, I also interned from midnight till 6 a.m. on Fridays and Saturdays, in the booth at WMAK, a popular Top 40 AM station. If the warden ever wondered where I was, all he had to do was tune in to hear me live on-air.

Busy as I was, Sundays were my only full days in prison. I filed paperwork for a third act of grace, which would spare the prison shuttle drivers from carting me to NSBT to Ruby Tuesday to WMAK and back to The Farm. I was not only granted use of my own vehicle but also furloughs to pursue a social life. I could rub shoulders at a few parties and laugh like I hadn't a care in the world. Nobody there would know any different.

Did I thank God for these opportunities, for His amazing grace?

No, not for a second.

But I wasn't about to squander them. Since drugs and alcohol had never been my issues, I had no trouble making curfew the way some inmates did. The obstacles I faced came in other forms.

One afternoon at Ruby Tuesday, I spotted my ex-wife at the bar. Andy was with a young man—a gay friend of hers, as I later found out—and jealousy took hold of me. I marched out from behind the grill in my work clothes and confronted the two of them. This drew the attention of others and it could've turned ugly. Thankfully, it did not.

Another time, Andy dined in with her older brother and his girl-friend. I figured I would pop over to say hi to my ex. Oh, her brother didn't like that. Next thing I knew, the two of us were tussling in the parking lot. Not exactly my proudest moment.

Despite these momentary setbacks, I stayed the course and retained my work privileges. I was only a year and a half from completing my NSBT certification, and I was setting aside money from my paychecks. Back in June my world had crumbled, but already I was constructing a new life that would be mine once I got out of here.

Part of that new life came much sooner than expected.

Only nine months later, to be exact.

22

BLACK SHEEP

His name was Joshua, born August 4, 1982, and he was beautiful. I first held my son in my arms while in the prison visiting area. My emotions were all over the place—proud of this little boy who looked like me, curious as to whether he was actually mine, and sad that my introduction to him should be as a ward of the state penitentiary system.

In case you're wondering, no, Andy was not his mother.

Back in November, during furlough, I had met with Joshua's mother while out on the town. She was an old flame of mine, and I was a lonely divorcé. Josh was the result. She said he was my flesh and blood. Something told me she was right, and a year later I signed documents legitimizing his birth, bestowing on him my last name, and agreeing to child support. For now, though, all I could do was stare in wonder.

New life.

A little bundle of squirming energy.

An entire future of hopes and dreams, pain and regret.

I wished him all the best on this cold, crowded planet before handing him back to his mother and telling her I had to go. For a man who could barely keep his own life together, the thought of being a father was just too much.

Approved for another 48-hr furlough—ostensibly, to get things in order for my upcoming release—I finished my Ruby Tuesday shift on a Friday evening, cleaned up, and slapped on some cologne. Invited by the hostess of a house party, I slipped into my old ways, mingling, smiling, and dancing. The place was loud, full of revelers.

For me, it was a night of celebration. Adding the time from my stint in Vanderbilt, my stay at Turney Center, and my duties in work release, I'd served nearly a year of my prison sentence, and the warden had hinted at parole by month's end.

A free man again? I couldn't wait.

Of course, if you're thinking this was too good to be true, you would be correct.

The day after the party, when the hostess realized some of her rings and bracelets were missing, she called upon her father for help. He just happened to be a Metro detective. He ran background checks on those who'd been there the previous night and came up with the obvious suspect—one Steven Allen Young, formerly convicted of embezzlement at a jewelry store and of burglary charges at a Shoney's.

I am no angel, I think I've made that clear, but I had nothing to do with this woman's stolen jewels. Regardless, due to her father's pending investigation, my release was suspended and I was sent from The Farm to strict lockup in The Castle, a decrepit old structure, like something out of a horror movie. My privileges were stripped away.

I'm never getting out of here, I thought. I am truly screwed.

A few weeks later, I heard my name called over the loudspeakers. It was a hot, humid morning and I was feeling lazy. I didn't move a muscle till I heard the message again: "Inmate Young, number such-and-such, report to the yard sergeant's office."

I meandered across the yard and stepped into his office.

The sergeant looked up at me. "Go pack your shit."

So this was how it would go, I realized. They would lower the boom by sending me back to the sprawling Turney Center complex.

"What're you waiting on, Young?"

"I'm not packing anything till I know where I'm headed."

"Listen, you really wanna go start packing." The sergeant gave me a blank stare. "You're going home."

Was this a joke? Was home a euphemism for something else? I headed over to the sally port, where guards informed me I was going to The Farm. When I arrived back there at the work release center, the officers seemed unsure of what to do with me. At least my old bunk was still available, they said. Since they couldn't provide me any further details, I dragged myself down the hall and collapsed onto the bed.

That afternoon on my way to chow, I was spotted by my counselor. "What're you doing here?" he said.

Exactly, I thought. They'll never let me out.

He marched me up to the overseer's office. "Hey," he barked, "you know, you've been keeping this man incarcerated when he should have been gone hours ago."

The overseer shrugged. "What can I tell you, Young? You're good to go."

It was true. I was officially discharged. Instead of walking out of here earlier in the day, I had submitted to fear and doubt and climbed back into my bed. That's what the system does to you. It numbs you and grinds you down. You become a pawn in the game, shifted from here to there as others see fit.

Truthfully, this first prison term was nothing compared to what still lie ahead. Before it was all over, I would serve three more terms in three separate states and witness things I still don't like to talk about.

For now, though, I was free. What was I waiting for?

I gathered up my belongings and made a phone call. Andy, God bless her, picked me up and let me sleep on the floor in her new apartment. For tonight only, she insisted. She could no longer be responsible for me. A full foot shorter than me, she had a backbone made of steel, and I knew she wouldn't budge. She had already put me in her rearview mirror, and to this day, she barely remembers coming to get me. All I could do was thank her, since one night was more than I deserved.

Nearly forty years would pass before we saw each other again, which still hurts just to think about. All that time wasted. All because of me.

At twenty-six, I tucked my tail the next morning and moved back into my parents' house. My physical freedom from guards and prison bars didn't free me from the mental chains that weighed me down. Nightmares and vivid memories still haunted my nights and days. The demons of anger, hatred, and loneliness rarely left me alone. There was no escaping from myself.

I tried, though. I really did. Still determined to carve out a new existence, I made a mental list of positive things to focus on.

I was out of prison, with only a parole officer to answer to.

I had a son.

I had my old car and a temporary place to lay my head.

I even had a good portion of my broadcasting certification completed. Since I was out of prison, I had to pay the remaining tuition, but that was manageable with my income and tips from Ruby Tuesday.

As committed as I was to making it all work, Dad and Mom showed zero interest in helping. Resentments, old and new, rumbled through my bones, and I let them fester there for the next three decades.

As far as I was concerned, there was no one to turn to. My ex wanted nothing to do with me, my brothers had their own lives to figure out, and my parents were embarrassed by their fourth son, the convicted felon. I'd been marked as the black sheep ever since Mom sent me on that errand to H. G. Hill's only to accuse me of stealing her money. The way my family saw it, my bad was worse than all of theirs.

As for the churchgoers, personal experience told me they were just as hellbent as the rest of us. And the system, the powers-that-be, they were as crooked as the day was long. They took bribes, called it justice, and rolled over anyone who got in the way.

Well, so be it. From here on out, I would live life by my own rules.

As for everyone else?

They could . . . Kiss. My. Ass.

23

MONSTERS AND MAESTROS

Pride is a monster. Whether it chases you up a cliff and makes your head spin with arrogance, or stalks you into a cave and chills your blood with self-doubt, it focuses all your attention on you. You can revel in accomplishments or wallow in failure, but either way you become the center of your own universe. Others become mere afterthoughts.

In May 1983, on my twenty-seventh birthday, I received my broadcasting certificate from Nashville School of Broadcast Technique. I'd already interned at WMAK, and now I was getting paid to work there. It wasn't much, but it got my voice out on the airwaves, and with that voice I could be anybody I wanted to be. Like many radio personalities, I refrained from using my legal name, and listeners knew me simply as Steven Michaels.

I was becoming a known entity. I felt important.

The monster, always huffing.

Not that my parents were the least bit impressed. It was frivolous as far as they were concerned and they refused to listen to me on-air.

"I don't like the music," Mom stated. "What about getting a real job?"

"I'm at the station at least thirty hours a week. It is a job."

On a deeper level, all I wanted was to earn my parents' approval. Not everyone was able to go live and on the air, and I believed I had a talent for it, an actual gift. They never saw it that way. To them it was a joke, and their words cut deeper than they knew.

Despite what they thought of it, my career as a DJ soon allowed me to move out of their house. Since I didn't have to fill out job applications, my prison record never came up. The Steak and Ale, a club by RiverGate Mall on the north end of Nashville, wanted to increase their business by bringing in a DJ, disco, and dancing. They built a booth that I designed, and they paid me well to liven up the weekend crowds.

My DJ services expanded beyond that small lounge to others—the 11th Frame, the Blue Max, the Brass A—and my growing popularity was even noted in a local newspaper article. I hired other DJs to meet the demand, with up to six at a time working for me. I got a cut from each of these gigs, and I also mobile DJed, which was exhausting. One particular wedding party kept me busy long past my allotted time, requesting song after song as the party nudged toward midnight. Some family members and I almost came to blows over the pittance they wanted to pay me.

The thing I couldn't explain to my parents was the intoxicating effect of being behind the microphone at the clubs and on the airwaves. Until the night's final song played, it kept the shadows at bay and lightened my chains of shame.

By the time I got home each morning, shoved some food in my mouth, wound down from adrenaline, and lumbered to bed, I was lucky to get four or five hours of sleep before starting the cycle all over again.

High. Low. High. Low.

Cocky. Insecure.

The monster ever near, breathing down my neck.

Only in the silence did reality kick in. These people didn't want me for who I was, only for what I did for them. If Steven Michaels wasn't spinning discs and setting a mood, someone else was sure to take his place. Maybe that's why I lived on the edge of exhaustion, the monster running me ragged to keep me from facing the ugly truth.

High. Low. High. Low.

As busy as I was, I certainly wasn't looking for a serious relationship. I'd been down that road before. Crashed. Burned. Barely survived. Now I just used people and had myself some fun. I was a maestro, playing a symphony of promises and lies. I didn't even care if I broke a few hearts along the way.

Until I was the one who got played.

24

DISNEY DREAMS

She was seated at a table with her sister, one of my regulars at the 11th Frame. Right away, she had my attention. I strolled over from my booth, suave and relaxed. Most women loved to be singled out from the crowd, and I was sure she'd be impressed.

"Hi there," I said. "I'm Steven. I hope you're having a good time tonight."

"This is Kate," her sister told me.

"Kate," I said, "you sure are pretty. You'd be even prettier if you just smiled."

"I'll smile if you go back to that rock you just crawled out from under."

Well, that was the end of that, I assumed, and went back to my booth.

I later found out Kate had gone through a bitter divorce, her wounds still fresh. I also heard that Kate told her sister that same evening that she'd just met the man she was going to marry. Not if you're gonna treat him like crap, her sister responded.

Kate knew what she was doing, though. She played my pride against me and I couldn't get her out of my head. As the attraction between us grew, my aloof demeanor vaporized in the heat. I did my best to resist Kate's charms, but her way of bruising and then stroking my ego kept me coming back for more. A common yet unhealthy pattern. It was nothing nefarious on her part. She was just a master of the game, good at reading others. When she wanted something, she went and got it.

My defenses gave way a few weeks later when Kate opened the door to my DJ booth. The Frame was closing in twenty minutes, with only a handful of customers at the bar. She stepped inside in a pair of tight jeans and looked up into my eyes.

"Are you ready to get serious about us?" she asked.

I didn't know what to say. Andy still had a place in my heart, an undying love wrapped in pain and regret, and I feared getting close to anyone else.

"Okay, here's the deal," Kate said, "I'm going to leave you something." She pulled two bar napkins from her pocket, sketched a map across them, and handed them to me with a coy grin. "If you're interested, Steven, those are the directions to my house. Follow them, if you can, and I'll cook you breakfast in the morning."

Heart pounding, I watched her turn and walk out of the bar. Boy, had someone just turned up the temperature in my booth? With one glance at the napkins, I knew I'd never find her place from these rudimentary scribbles. I put the booth on autopilot, convinced the manager to shut down the equipment for me, then dashed outside.

Was I too late? Was she already gone?

Beneath the dim parking-lot lights, I found Kate leaned against my car with arms folded and hair glistening. Oh, she was good at this game. She knew my every move. Instead of being aggravated, I just felt wanted and alive. I shook my head and laughed. She had wondered if I was serious about the two of us and now she had her answer. Real serious wasn't far behind.

One thing led to another, and before I knew it I was popping that question I never thought I'd ask anyone again.

Kate and I got married in 1983. I did my best to conceal my secrets and chains, afraid of being rejected if all were exposed. Kate also had issues to deal with. Years earlier, her first husband had left her with no explanation, and she compensated in our relationship by playing the doting wife, trying to anticipate my every want and need. These behaviors were set early between us and for years they diverted us down paths we were never meant to follow—as you'll soon see.

As much as I loved Kate, I realized I wasn't in love with her. Despite all her good qualities, she was trying to occupy a space in my heart that was filled by someone else. Kate was a good wife and I tried to love her, I did. But she deserved better.

Though my son Josh lived with his mother at the time, I suddenly had two girls under my roof, stepdaughters from Kate's previous marriage. The oldest was twelve, headstrong and smart, resentful of my intrusion. The youngest was five, taking her cues from her mother and calling me Dad from the day Kate and I exchanged rings.

As a wedding gift, Kate gave me a Mickey Mouse watch with white-gloved hands indicating hours and minutes. I wore it religiously. I was nostalgic for those matinees at the Inglewood Theater and the *Wonderful World of Disney* on TV. With nothing else special to hold onto, I trusted Mickey to point me to a time before the abuse and depression, a time of relative innocence. Though I'd never been to Disneyland or Disney World, Mickey represented a dream of the way life could be.

Sadly, even Mickey wouldn't be able to save my marriage to Kate.

We lived in White House, a half hour north of Nashville. To friends and neighbors, Kate's and my relationship was the epitome of normalcy. Kate was an adoring wife and great mother, keeping track of all the details. I was a successful radio personality and business operator, always good for a joke or for some barbecued ribs on the home grill.

We were recognized members of our community. Kate's oldest daughter became a cheerleader, and when the youngest joined the softball team, I joined in the fun by becoming commissioner of the local Dixie Youth league. I had no idea of its racist history, and by the 1980s our teams tried to be inclusive.

At games and team picnics, Kate and I were a popular couple. Though we weren't church people by any stretch of the imagination, we tried to treat others the way we wanted to be treated. We attended school functions, invited friends over for cookouts, and took the kids on trips. We wore the smiley masks of white, middle-class Americans, and in many ways we lived a good life. Now that I had the appearance of being a respectable member of society, even my own family treated me better.

You know, maybe that's what irritated Kate's oldest daughter so much. Like many teens and preteens, she wasn't yet conditioned to fake it till you make it. Her mom and I were actors in a masquerade, and she probably saw right through it.

My own mom had once told me of a discovery she made while doing trade-show sales. During a factory visit, she'd seen firsthand how the brand-name products sold for top dollar in department stores were often the same exact items stuffed into generic packaging and sold elsewhere for a third the cost. Behind all the fancy names and labels, they were essentially the same thing.

It was all about perception. Not everything was as good as it seemed—or as bad.

For the next decade or so, Kate and I worked hard at presenting a stable marriage for the world to see. Most days we even fooled ourselves. While helping Kate with her issues, I imagined myself as her savior. The problem was, I had no idea what a healthy relationship even looked like. Instead of healing from my own past, I tamped stuff down and pressed on. In the flurry of activity, I did fine, but when I was all alone, everything closed in. I would never be happy this way. And I knew it.

Something shifted in me in 1984, during my ten-year high school reunion. Hired as the DJ, I hit a level of popularity I never dreamed of back at Stratford High. I was now the picture of success, married to a beautiful woman and making a living at something I loved. My classmates didn't know what to think. Was this the same Steven who avoided dances all through school, dropped out of football, and kept mostly to himself? Our class vice-president pointed me out from the stage and said he wished he had my job.

The monster of pride did a real number on me. I went from feeling cocky at the reunion to feeling empty afterward. My well-wishers were the same kids who wouldn't give me the time of day back in high school. It all seemed wrong. I was Mickey Mouse in Fantasia, beaming beneath the wizard's hat until his magic broom got out of control.

It wasn't long before I gave up my nightclub business and ditched my life as a radio personality. I went back to being Steven Young. If there was one thing my father had modeled for me it was being a solid provider, and I now had daughters to look after. For extended periods, Josh also came to live with us. He was a quiet kid, who needed more from me than I knew how to give. I wasn't able to meet his emotional needs.

What would I do for my next job? I wondered. Who would hire an ex-con?

Did I even deserve to make a decent living?

The scars of incarceration go far beyond realizing you are unable to apply for a gun permit or to vote in many states. As a convict, it was hard for me not to feel marked, carrying a blemish in my own head as much as on my record.

25

MOVING THE METAL

Within a couple of years, against all odds, I was winning awards and earning real money. I had always been good at reading people, knowing when to push and when to back off, a prerequisite for any profitable salesperson. One that also benefits pastors, politicians, and con artists. For good or for evil, I suppose it's how you use your skills that matters.

In addition to any God-given skills, my crude mouth, smoking, and cutting humor helped me fit right in at the latest Chevy dealership in Middle Tennessee. Tom Bannen Chevrolet was a car lot near the Nashville National Cemetery, just north of Briley Parkway. Eventually it relocated to RiverGate Mall, but it wasn't yet that big. Festooned with flags, balloons, and bright signage, the dealership was just getting started.

Tom Bannen was a hoot. He was an athletic man, a good golfer, with warm eyes that danced behind his glasses. He was more than just a name and figurehead. He drove up everyday in the latest floor-model Corvette and threw himself into the daily business of showroom displays and sales-lot etiquette.

"I've been in sales before," I told him early on, "but never cars."

"You'll do just fine, Steven. No two salespeople are alike, just as no two customers are alike. The key is figuring out how to sell cars the way you sell cars."

He taught me so much in the years that followed, pushing me to do better while keeping things loose and fun. He treated his people right, with fairness and respect. He was more than just a boss. He was a friend and confidante. Being an avid health nut, he ribbed me constantly about my smoking habit.

"Those things'll kill you one day," he warned.

"If working for you doesn't do it first," I fired back.

One drizzly afternoon, I sat in my sales office and griped to myself about the chances of making even one wooden nickel in these conditions. I barely flinched when Tom zipped into his parking space and popped out of the car. He was shaking off moisture by the time he got inside.

"Why aren't you out there moving the metal?" he said to me. That was his term for selling cars, and he liked nothing more than to see sold vehicles drive off the lot.

I raised an eyebrow. "You looked in the mirror? It's pouring cats and dogs."

"It's just water, same thing that comes outta your shower head."

"I like my showers hot."

"I like my customers being helped."

"That's the problem," I said. "Who wants to shop cars in this weather?"

"What about that fella there? Anyone talked to him yet?"

I followed Tom's gaze to a gray-haired man easing his old pickup between the rows of cars. Pulling on a jacket and ball cap, I headed out to say hi. The man and I shook hands through his window, he told me what he was looking for, and I sloshed off through the rain, shivering and cursing under my breath, to point out some options. I imagined the rest of the sales team sipping coffee and hot chocolate inside, maybe even sharing Jim Beam from a flask, grinning and elbowing each other as they watched me wander from one end of the lot to the other to humor this old fart.

Eventually, my customer narrowed things down to three vehicles. He told me he wanted to pay cash. How much was it gonna cost him? As I tromped inside to run the numbers with our finance manager, my customer remained in his pickup with the window cracked, smoking a cigar like he had nowhere else to be.

This guy was wasting my time, I thought. Look at the old clunker he was in.

I walked back out with some figures, in no mood to negotiate while wiping drops from my fogged-up glasses. Who thought I'd be wearing prescriptions by age thirty?

"How much're we talkin'?" the old fellow asked around his stogie.

I gave him the sticker-price numbers and mentioned a few payment options.

"Son," he said, "you're not listening. I want all three, and I'm paying you cash."

Let's just say my day brightened considerably when he pulled a brown paper bag from behind the seat and showed me he was serious, to the tune of over twenty grand in hundred-dollar bills. As he signed papers and I handed over keys, he told me his story. As a kid, he had learned how to run a bulldozer, and now he had his own company renting out equipment. Every couple of years he bought new cars for his wife, daughter, and son, and he always shopped on rainy days because he couldn't effectively operate his machinery in wet weather.

Thanks to Tom Bannen, I learned to never write off a day before it was over and to never judge a person by age or appearance. Over the years, I sold that older gentleman at least a dozen vehicles.

"There ya go," Tom applauded me. "Guess I wasn't all wet, after all."

On another occasion—because I'm a slow learner—I had my feet up on my desk as I sipped coffee and scanned *The Tennessean*. My team, the University of Tennessee, wasn't playing to expectations.

Business was slow and things at home were strained. Kate and I were on the hamster wheel, running all the time and getting nowhere.

Tom's Corvette announced his arrival with a throaty purr.

"What're ya doing sitting around?" he demanded of me.

"It's a beautiful day and I'd really rather not be here," I admitted.

"I hear ya, I do, but it's near month's end. Here's the deal, Steven. I'll give you a $500 bonus for every car you can sell and deliver before the end of the day."

"In cash?" I ventured.

"You betcha. If that's what it takes to get you off your lazy butt."

Well, that's what it took alright. By closing, I had delivered my fourth automobile and I walked out to my car—a demo provided at no charge by my boss—with two grand stuffed into the folds of my wallet. My Mickey Mouse watch told me it was time to head home and surprise Kate and the kids with a late dinner out.

If being a car salesman wasn't exactly a prestigious job, at least it ranked higher in my parents' minds than being a DJ. I was even treated a little better when we attended family Christmases, big productions as always in the Young household. My brothers and their families were there as well. Dad's birthdays on Christmas Eves were followed by gift-giving, food, and games, which continued on through the next day and late into Christmas evening.

One year we chipped in and got Dad and Mom a top-of-the-line color TV to replace their old black-and-white monstrosity. Another year I got them cordless phones. In his seventies now, Dad soon bought himself another rotary phone.

"What happened to the cordless?" I asked. Not that I really cared.

"Oh, you know your mother. She leaves those damn things in the back, and I can't ever find them when they start ringing."

Nowadays, I'm the one complaining about kids on their iPhones.

Seems the generation gap never closes.

One Thanksgiving, Dad and Mom fished around, wanting to know what gifts my brothers and I had always wanted as kids and never received. This was a rare glimpse of my parents' good side. The truth was, I'd often made lists for Santa that went ignored, but I wasn't about to dig up the past and seem ungrateful.

A remote-control car, I told them. That's what I'd always wanted.

Okay, so Dad and Mom may not have encouraged me in the pursuit of my dreams, but that year I found a remote-control car beneath the family tree. In their own unique way, my parents helped me move the metal.

26

CHOIRBOY BEHAVIOR

My brothers and I all had our own issues to deal with, from marital strife to addiction to clinical depression. Billy Dean and Byron are no longer with us, and Robert and John have their own stories to tell. Those are up to them to divulge. However, Robert's life and mine did overlap a few years after Kate and I got together.

Robert was always a good older brother, taking me bike-riding and fishing, standing up to bullies for me, and these days the two of us are closer than ever.

In the mid-1980s, though, Robert was struggling. He liked to drink, which I'm sure was one of his ways of numbing the childhood wounds inflicted by Dad and Mom. Robert had uniquely personal scars, of course, including the realization that he was our half brother. He set out for California to track down rumors about his birth father. He burned some bridges on his way out of Nashville, and when he returned after sharing little more than a beer with his father, Robert was in worse shape than before he left.

I was in White House a few weeks before Christmas, grilling outside with friends on a clear day, when an unfamiliar car pulled up. I couldn't see who was inside. When my older brother stepped out, I hardly recognized him. He seemed like a shell of his usual self.

"Robert? What the hell are you doing here? How'd you even find me?"

He had already stopped by each of my brothers' places and been turned away. One of them, he said, gave him directions to my house and suggested he look me up.

"You had anything to eat?" I asked. "Well, c'mon and grab you something."

Kate and I let him stay the night in our guestroom, then offered to let him stay longer if he would work a job and not drink in the house. If he was drunk somewhere, he could give me a call and I'd come get him so he could sleep it off, but I didn't want that stuff around the girls. He was compliant, and I found him a good-paying job. Our parents had no idea he was back from California, and we surprised them by sneaking Robert into a group of carolers at a family outing. They were very happy to see him.

But things with Robert took a turn soon after.

And you know what?

That's okay.

He and I both made our mistakes, and who am I to go around pointing fingers? We've long since made amends and I love my brother. He's never further than a phone call away. Plus, as you'll soon see, I made some choices which made his indiscretions seem like choirboy behavior in comparison.

27

INTO THE ABYSS

This is my book of secrets, so hold onto your seats, guys and gals.

You have your secrets too, I'm sure, and most people have no clue what went on in your childhood or your teenage years or even in your adult life last week. Secrets are long-nailed fingers, clawing at your thoughts. They're under-the-breath whispers, telling you to give in. They don't care about you. They'll soothe and seduce, or form fists and beat the hell out of you. Often, they do both.

Kate didn't know most of my secrets and I didn't know hers, so I'm sure we went into our relationship dragging those things behind us. As we ran the hamster wheel, they weighed us down and tripped us up.

Why, we wondered, were things turning sour between us?

Was there something wrong with her?

Was the problem with me?

It reached the point of desperation. With a bit of nervous excitement, I decided it was time to add a little spice to our marriage and I put some pressure on Kate to follow along. Listen, I'll just put it bluntly: We got involved with a swingers club.

I'm not proud of it, and it certainly offered no long-term solutions, but our secrets led us by the nose from our wedding altar to wandering thoughts to other people's beds. We skipped right along as though this would heat up our cooling relationship and, I've got to be honest, for a while it did just that.

We felt liberated. We were footloose and fancy-free. We flirted with others by candlelight and chose to do as we damn well pleased.

We were those spoiled brats you see flailing in the store. You know the ones. If you give kids anything and everything they want, it does not make them content, well-adjusted, and satisfied. The fun only lasts for a season and then they just want more.

And if they don't get it, there will be hell to pay!

Kate and I spent the late '80s as part of the "fun bunch," a growing circle of mostly well-to-do and well-regarded men and women who lowered their inhibitions and went wherever the mood directed. It was all hush-hush, all part of the fun. None of our friends or family knew. We kept this to ourselves, even if we spotted another of the bunch at a church picnic or town hall meeting. Our ringmaster was a lean, nondescript guy who coordinated events and locations and charged nominal entry fees.

Our spicy new lifestyle gave Kate's and my marriage a temporary jolt that made us feel alive—before leaving us dead—while also presenting me with a lucrative business opportunity. By this time, I was pals with our ringmaster and told him he could be earning ten times the amount he was making off his clientele in Greater Nashville and beyond. He possessed the clean-cut look and slippery demeanor to pull the whole thing off without too many legal hassles. He just needed a partner to help him think bigger.

Our clubs spread. Our contact lists grew. Soon, over a million dollars were pouring in each year. We tapped into an even larger scene and flew out to Las Vegas for a swingers convention at which I was a keynote speaker.

My topic: How to meet others and converse with mutual respect.

All very dignified. This was serious business.

I'll say this much, all masks were set aside at these gatherings, all desires laid bare. There was something appealing in that, knowing we were done with the polite gestures and moral hypocrisy of society at large. We could let our hair down and be ourselves. Aren't most of us looking for something real? Isn't that what church should be? I'm not justifying a thing, but somewhere in here is a lesson to be learned.

Adding to my troubles, I started gambling while in Sin City, USA. This was a new drug for me, a heady sort of escape. The lights never dimmed. The rush could last for hours. Money kept the games flowing, and I now had lots of it from my side gig. The casinos knew just how to play to a person's vanity, making me feel special as they escorted me into top-floor hotel suites or into private rooms for high-stakes games.

They pampered me. They catered to my every whim.

I believed I was a VIP.

Once again, I fell prey to the pride monster, and over the next few years it teased me, toyed with me, then threw me onto the garbage heap.

The best way to disguise my hedonistic lifestyle was to keep my day job and carry on with the usual routines. I was still a car salesman, bouncing from Tom Bannen Chevrolet to Trickett Oldsmobile and back, but a good part of my income flowed in from my other activities. I'd never seen so much money, and I got to pocket a fair portion of it.

Sex. Money. Power.

Some of you, I'm sure, are disgusted by now, and others are privately envious, thinking I had it all, the world at my fingertips.

Lemme put that thought to rest right now. In the end, the sleeping around made me just another item on the menu and all I did was pour dollars down the drain of my fragile ego.

By the early '90s, my relationship with Kate cooled to sub-zero, even though she did everything a good wife could do—and much, much more—to make her man feel happy and alive. Her pandering actually made me feel trapped and suffocated. I'd tried it all and was still left wanting. Our divorce was inevitable.

If I had any sense, I would have gone running to God. I would have walked, stumbled, or crawled to the one who knew my deepest needs.

But I was still stuck back at step eight.

God-hater.

I didn't trust fathers or cops, judges or juries, deacons or the God they served. The only person I trusted was myself, even as I drowned in self-loathing. I was that spoiled brat in the aisle of the store, throwing a tantrum and out of control.

Christmas, 1994. My family bonds were on the verge of snapping. I no longer had my wife or her daughters to bring over during the holidays, and being alone with my parents stirred all sorts of old animosity. My brothers and I didn't have much to say to each other, and I was tired of going through the motions.

I had nothing to show for my thirty-eight years on this godforsaken planet. Everywhere I looked, I saw the evidence of my failures—lost jobs, marriages, relationships. No sooner did something good come into my life, then I sabotaged it with anger and cynicism. I kept waiting for the other shoe to fall. Waiting for a beating, so to speak. Nothing I did would impress my dad anyway. We didn't have much to say to each other. In his mind, he'd already done his job by putting a roof over my head and clothes on my back. What more could he possibly do for me?

Well, an attaboy would've been nice. Or some indication he was proud of me.

Good luck with that.

I was no better as a father. My oldest stepdaughter had been a tough nut to crack, and she had every reason to be. I wasn't worth her time. My youngest, on the other hand, had given her love freely, and all I did was trample it on my way out the door.

As for Josh, well, he was eleven now, almost twelve, a young man with all the usual male struggles. On occasion I flew him over from his mom's in South Carolina—or wherever else she might be at the time—but there were few words exchanged between us. He lived on and off with us, but I was woefully inadequate in my fatherly role.

I later tried to capture these frustrations in a poem:

A DAD

I have been a lover
I've been a husband and a friend
I've shared so much with many
Yet, before this journey ends
One thing still remains
One bond I've never had
Although I've been a father
I've never been a dad
Passing days move swiftly now
Can forgiveness still exist?
So much I walked away from
So much that I have missed
From a little boy to a strong young man
He's done without me there
I can only hope that within his heart
A trace of him still cares
And one day hope can overcome
When joy replaces sad
I'll hear those words I long to hear
"I love you . . . you're my dad"

There was just no way I could share these sentiments with my son. The emotions were too raw, the regrets too deep. If I were to ever hear those words from Josh, they had to come from his heart unprompted. I wanted the real thing or nothing at all.

Deep down, I was still aching for that home life I'd never had.

No wonder, my therapist now tells me, I got involved with yet another divorced woman with two kids. Not Kate this time. No, Ashley was her name, and little did I know, she was hiding a dark side that would drag me deeper into the abyss.

28

BAD NEWS

When God goes from being a concept in your mind to a reality, it is truly life-changing, He becomes so real, so alive. Of course, I didn't believe any of it at the time, not since my salvation and baptism as a twelve-year-old. Any hopes of a real experience with Him were crowded out by my fixation with my own pain. I hated what I saw in the mirror, hated the dreams that plagued me in the dark. I was still that scared little boy who'd been beaten with a razor strop and fondled furtively in a camp cabin.

The way I saw it, I could run my own life better than God. All He'd ever done was sit idly by while I suffered. I'd take it from here, thank you very much.

Pride. The devil's original sin.

Thinking we know better than God.

Thinking our ways are better than His.

Thinking our self-preserving lies are more important than His truth.

If God is the loving Father I now believe He is, there will come a day when this world with all its secrets will be no more. The darkest moments will be washed away in a light so radiant and pure they'll be gone from our thoughts forevermore. Even our most glorious earthly experiences will pale in the gleam of love we find twinkling in God's eyes. When He reaches out for us and smiles, oh, we'll drop every one of our grievances and go running into His arms.

I long for that day.

And I get foretastes of it every now and then on this earth.

But as 1995 rolled around, all I tasted was loneliness, which goes a long way in explaining my attraction to Ashley. I was a twice-divorced man, living on my own in a big house in Hendersonville, selling cars off and on, while managing a local club.

Ashley, the sister of a friend, worked as a waitress at a nearby eatery and she was easy on the eyes. We had undeniable chemistry, and while there was no real love or emotion between us, she was game for anything.

And I mean anything.

She was bad news.

There were times when I heard something primal take over her, with shrieks that sounded ungodly and sent a shiver down my spine. That should've been warning: Steer clear, Steven. You're completely out of your element.

Like Kate, Ashley was divorced, with two adorable daughters. The parallels were too obvious to miss for anyone less thickheaded than me. Was I trying to reconstruct the last marriage I ruined? Trying to get a do-over? If you're wondering why you should read through another one of my doomed relationships, I promise each step down took me closer to hitting bottom—and from there, the only way was up.

Oblivious to any trouble ahead, I asked Ashley and her daughters to move in with me at my three-bedroom house. The girls ushered laughter and joy into that empty space and I was crazy about them. For once, I felt I was doing something positive for someone, accomplishing something good.

Then Ashley's demons began surfacing, and it all quickly went to hell.

There were red flags beforehand, as always, but I refused to accept the truth of her drug habit until I discovered her stash of paraphernalia. Suddenly, it all made sense—the erratic behavior, the glazed looks, the unexplained disappearances for hours at a time. When I confronted her about it, she turned vicious. Even as our arguments grew more heated and frequent, I stuck it out, convinced she and her girls needed me.

I could fix her, I thought.

The broken trying to fix the broken? Yeah, good luck with that.

Then out of the blue, Ashley vanished. I got home from work and found her girls' half-eaten bowls of cereal on the table. A cigarette was still burning, smoke rising and fading away as easily as the women in my life. I called out their names, looked through the house, the backyard.

Nothing.

Where was my girlfriend? Where were her kids?

I freaked out, all sorts of horrible scenarios running through my head. I called her sister, my friend from years back, and found out Ashley's ex-husband had come down from Indiana and was trying to talk her into going back with him.

"Is she there at your place?" I pressed.

"Not for much longer."

"Don't let her leave. Please. I'm on my way over."

"Okay," her sister said. "I'll try to convince her to talk to you first."

With some coaxing on my part, Ashley left the girls at her sister's and agreed to meet with me. Her ex showed up right beside her. I could barely look at the guy, knowing the stuff she'd told me about him. His father was a sheriff in Indiana and he thought the world bowed to him.

"Let's take a walk," I said to Ashley.

"You're not going anywhere without me," her ex interjected.

I squared up to face him. "Listen, hoss, you're not calling the shots here."

Ashley muttered to me, "He has a gun."

"Is that right?" I said. "You have your gun?"

"I do. And I'm not afraid to use it."

"I bet you don't have a Tennessee permit for that thing," I fired back. "If you're going to use it, use it now. Ashley and I, we're going to take a walk."

We walked. We talked.

"Sorry, Steven," she concluded, "but I'm not gonna leave him."

I knew this man would treat her and the girls as poorly as he had the first time around, which would only make her drug habit worse. I watched her climb into his vehicle, then followed them through the streets of Hendersonville. Finally, her ex pulled into a gas station and called the cops on me. I was still sitting there when they arrived.

"We hear you won't leave this couple alone," they told me. "What's going on?"

"They're not a couple, not anymore. She lives with me."

"That's between y'all, but she's in his car now and I don't see her getting out."

"He has a gun," I said. "She's afraid of him."

"You've seen this gun?"

"She's the one who told me about it."

After some discussion between all those concerned, the police searched the ex's vehicle and located a firearm for which he had no permit. They informed him it was in his best interest to head back north without stopping. He could go crying to his daddy if he wanted, but he best never show his face around here again.

Conflicted, Ashley picked up her girls and moved out of my place. Over the next few months, she bounced from spot to spot. She went to rehab—which didn't work. She slept around—with at least four other guys. She returned to Kentucky to be near her dad and stepmom—a family even more dysfunctional than my own. Whereas my parents had covered up sexual abuse, her father perpetrated it.

Toward the end of 1995, I heard Ashley was back with her ex. In hopes of wooing her away from him, I regularly sent her a dozen roses. Just thinking of her with that blowhard made me cringe. Dangerous thoughts filled my head. I worked like a dog so I'd have as little free time on my hands as possible.

All the hard work paid off and my sales numbers shot through the roof, one of my best years ever. With cash to burn, I took trips every now and then to a casino in Mississippi. If money couldn't heal my pain, it could at least buy me a temporary sense of self-worth. Most important, it kept me from wallowing in the past where my demons dwelt, and from looking to the future where they waited for me. At the blackjack tables, I could let myself go numb and lose myself in the thrill of the game.

It was an escape, that's all it was. An escape and nothing more.

Said the addict to the man in the mirror.

29

NO REST FOR THE WICKED

As the hours wound down at Tom Bannen Chevrolet that New Year's Eve, I was tied with one other guy for salesperson of the year. We had the highest gross sales, and I needed to land just one more deal to break the tie and earn a $10,000 bonus.

Late in the afternoon, a customer pulled into the lot with an empty trailer and Alabama plates. He stipulated that he was looking for an '83 Monte Carlo SS. That was the first year the car came out, and for that reason it was still a hot item.

"You're in luck," I told him. "Those aren't easy to come by, but we have two of them, a factory model, as well as a customized convertible on our showroom floor."

I was already imagining that coveted five-figure bonus.

"I've got a set amount I can spend," the guy added. "I won't go a penny over."

As it turned out, his amount was $500 under the car's factory cost. After driving all the way from Huntsville with a trailer just waiting to be loaded up, he insisted he would go home empty if we didn't meet his price. Scrambling for top honors, I spoke to our finance manager in private. I suggested we sell the Monte Carlo below cost, then I could chip in three hundred bucks and he could chip in two hundred to make up the difference. We'd both profit from bonuses and everyone would go home happy.

Except, of course, the salesperson currently tied with me. Sucked to be him.

I wrote up the contract, loaded that trailer, and beamed from ear to ear as my customer headed south on that cold December evening.

My monster of pride showed two faces, cockiness and insecurity, as I called Mom to tell her about my bonus and award. They were proof I was not a complete failure. Even as hopeless as it was to gain my parents' approval, it didn't stop me from trying.

"Well, Steven," Mom said, after hearing my good news, "you best not go around bragging about it. You did your job, that's all."

At least she referred to it as a job. That was progress. Nonetheless, her words left marks much as my father's beatings once left marks on my backside.

Success, for me, was ammunition in a gun. The more bullets I loaded, the more chances of doing damage to myself. My childhood shame and abuse drove me to find meaning in money and accolades. If I had success, I had value. Yet I knew from experience that nothing ever lasted and things eventually went wrong. No matter how many dollars I banked or honors I earned, it was never enough. I always knew the barrel of that gun was swinging round and the trigger was about to be pulled.

No rest for the wicked, as they say.

If my brushes with the law and my failed relationships weren't proof enough of my self-obsession, I got involved with yet another married woman. She was a busty teller at the bank, and every Friday I made eyes at her as I cashed my checks. Rather than waiting for someone else to pull the trigger and do me harm, I did the deed myself, jumping into bed with her. Her husband, one of my customers at Tom Bannen, was often out of town, which made it that much easier to pull off our frequent trysts in her home.

Turned out, her husband wasn't as clueless as we thought.

One morning he pulled onto the sales lot in the S-10 truck I'd sold him and asked to see me. My conscience was seared black and I didn't even flinch. Oh, I knew who he was alright, which just made my infidelity that much more exhilarating.

"Hey, Steven," he said, "hop into the truck with me for a minute."

"Sure, buddy, what's going on?"

"The engine's making this weird noise. I want you to hear it."

Casual as could be, I slid into the passenger seat and he took me for a spin. I didn't hear anything at first, and then he pushed a cassette tape into the player in the dash. He had bugged his own house. Clear as could be, the factory-issue speakers blared his wife's and my voices as we interacted intimately.

My face turned beet-red.

That was his first round of revenge. The second came as he used my fingerprints around his house to implicate me in a home burglary. When my lawyer explained to detectives the real reason for my prints being on the property, the case got thrown out. Not to be outdone, the husband used round three to throw a knockout punch by getting me fired. Despite my drama on and off the lot, Tom Bannen had always been good to me. He cut me a fat final check and let me keep my demo until I could buy a car of my own.

Grace, I've heard said, is receiving something you don't deserve.

Mercy, on the other hand, is not getting what you do deserve.

Time and again, God extended both His grace and His mercy to me, whether it was through levelheaded judges or bighearted bosses. Though His love for me was always there within reach, for so many years I just failed to see it.

And I still had more years to waste, dead ahead.

All starting with a phone call from Ashley. She and her girls were back at her ex's in Indiana. He had turned abusive again, big surprise. Could I please come get her?

She needed a hero and I couldn't resist.

After a few more zigs and zags in our relationship, Ashley decided we must move to Memphis. She had connections there, a brother, a cousin, some old friends. We could leave our pasts in Music City and start fresh. It might be good for us.

I wasn't so sure. I mean, who wanted to live in Memphis?

Ashley said we could eat good barbecue and visit Elvis's estate at Graceland. We could go to the casinos across the Mississippi River. She made it all sound wonderful.

In my travels around the country, from San Francisco to Vegas to Miami, I've never felt more at home than in Nashville and I couldn't imagine spending my life anywhere else. Then again, my parents and I were barely on speaking terms, and everywhere I went in the Metro area I dealt with memories I'd just as soon forget.

Like a fool, I blurted, "Sure, Ashley, if it'll make you happy."

"You won't regret it."

She was wrong. I regretted it almost right away. Memphis was my final step toward serious addiction and prison time. Though it all led to where I am today, God probably had a shorter route planned, if only I'd heeded His voice from the start.

30

MEMPHIS BLUES

Ashley's and my first priorities were finding jobs and a place to live. With my experience in nightclubs and restaurants, I got hired as a day-shift manager at Alfred's on famed Beale Street. The music, lights, and drinks kept the atmosphere electric. Ashley worked as a night-time server, which allowed us to take turns watching her daughters. It also meant we didn't have much free time together, but we had to start somewhere, right?

Our lead cook at Alfred's was a real piece of work. Right off, he and I didn't get along and it only got worse. One day I gave him some instructions, nothing unusual.

He cussed at me and barked in my face, "I don't have to listen to you."

"You're going to apologize, then do as I asked," I said, aware of the kitchen crew gathered around. "Or I'll fire you."

"You can't fire me!"

"I just did."

He threw a cold drink in my face and refused to leave, raising a stink.

When word got round to the owner, he jumped all over the kitchen manager. "Your cook's outta there! We can't allow that sorta behavior in here. And the next time Steven fires someone, you better back him up."

On his way out, the cook informed me in the crudest of terms that he was sleeping with my girlfriend. Other staff members glanced away, nodding their heads. Apparently, I was the only one who didn't know.

The owner pulled me aside. "Steven, I know it puts you in a bind, but you've gotta let Ashley go."

"We just moved here. Just leased an apartment."

"Your personal life, that's your business. All I'm saying is, she can't be working here anymore. This sorta stuff's bad for team morale."

Nice start to Ashley's and my new life together.

With Ashley's looks and energy, she landed another job just across the street and began messing around with a tattoo artist from a parlor a few doors down. She even packed her daughters' stuff and made plans to take off with him. Though I managed to talk her out of it, I had my doubts about the next time around—and there would be a next time. The pattern was pretty clear.

To forget all that, I hit the blackjack tables in Tunica. I wasn't playing to win but to escape. I lost a lot along the way, and one Christmas Eve I was down to almost nothing. I hadn't even bought Ashley and the girls presents yet. I scooped up the last dollars I had and hit the tables once more. I had a specific goal this time. I would be disciplined and walk away once I got ahead. I could do that when I set my mind to it.

Lord knows what would've happened if I'd lost that night. Thankfully, I won a couple hundred dollars and wandered the aisles at Walgreens in search of last-minute Christmas gifts. Ashley and the girls woke up to wrapped presents under the tree.

Our zigs and zags continued, from Memphis to Clarksville and back to Memphis. Ashley hopped into beds everywhere she went as I trailed her like a lost puppy. I had her girls to think of. I'd invested so much already. There was hope for us yet.

Then I caught her with her cousin.

I was done!

Mad as could be, I whipped into a gas station, tripped over the hose while filling the tank, and ended up at the hospital getting a cast for my broken ankle. I hated this city. Hated everything about this place. As soon as I could, I would go back to Middle Tennessee. Ashley could screw up her own life and leave me the hell out of it.

But what was there for me back home?

A few weeks later, I made a quick trip to Nashville for my nephew's wedding. With nothing to wear but a pair of nice blue jeans, I stopped at a Walmart on my way out of Memphis, bought a dress shirt, then cruised east along I-40.

From the moment I entered the church till the moment I left, I felt out of place. Everyone else was dressed up. I had shoes with no socks. It wasn't just the attire, though. It was the indifference from my own family members, the lack of any real connection. I didn't belong there. I didn't fit in. That was the vibe I got.

Feeling lonelier than ever, I shot straight back to Memphis.

It's hard to describe the doubt that consumed me—doubt in anyone and everyone, including myself. Happiness was a forbidden fruit, a sweet thing always just out of reach. Many nights I cried myself to sleep. Doubt turned to anger and hate. Even the sight of others going about their lives with any normalcy inflamed me. I used it to fuel my destructive behavior while holding my pain at bay.

The hatred, at its core, was self-hatred. I hated the man in the mirror. I gave him all the freedom and justification he needed to destroy himself piece by piece. Bad dreams and childhood trauma robbed me of genuine rest until perpetual exhaustion became the norm. With every heartbeat, sanity slipped further from my grasp.

From down the river in Tunica, Mississippi, the glamour and bright lights of the casinos called my name.

Come escape, Steven. Come forget.

Forty and single, I had the job at Alfred's and an apartment all to my lonesome. Working extra hours and having one-night stands didn't do much to mitigate my misery. I had nobody to spend my hard-earned money on, so I started gambling now in earnest. It was back to the game for me, a rush like nothing else. A surefire strategy to stop feeling at all. My life spun in an endless cycle, from all-nighters in Tunica, to quick morning showers, to my day shifts on Beale Street, and back to the casinos again.

I coasted on adrenaline. I could vanish for hours, even days. I won some. I lost a lot. It wasn't unusual to drop thousands of dollars in a single night.

And I loved it!

An addiction? Ha. It was an escape, that's all. Don't you tell me how to live my life.

Casinos became my home, my oasis. The lights, the action, the thrill of it all. I soon knew every doorman, barkeep, and limo driver. I didn't do too shabbily with the ladies, either. The people who ran these establishments treated me like a king. At one place, the manager actually gave me a free room and laundry services. I could gamble, shower, head to work, and race right back. Here, I could hide from the world outside and from the pain within. Here, I was never alone.

You might find this hard to believe, but my work ethic began to suffer.

Yep, I got fired.

I found another job and lost it, another and another. It wasn't long before word spread up and down Beale Street. No one wanted me on their staff. Even as my bank account dwindled, I couldn't shake the casinos' hold. The people in those places loved me. They smiled and waved, calling me by name as I came through the revolving doors.

Some days I got on a roll, and like a coke-head selling drugs to feed his addiction, I managed to finance my gambling with more gambling.

Most days, however, I lost a bundle.

I emptied my apartment, sold off the few things I owned, and bulled ahead as though nothing could stop me. Each night was a shovel with which to dig a deeper hole. The site for my burial was nearly complete.

When you are at your lowest, there's always someone ready to capitalize. It could be a credit lender, pawnshop, or cash-checking place. It could even be someone close to you. Satan is the enemy of our souls and he sniffs out desperation like a dog sniffs out death. In the moment, that pawnshop or enabler or demon can seem like a long-lost friend.

I thought I was done with Ashley until her brother came sniffing around.

"You know, Steven," he said to me, "word on the street is you're in dire straits."

"Dire's a strong word."

"Don't try to con a con, man. You know I just got out of prison, right?"

I nodded. Nothing about this conversation was putting me at ease.

"Listen," he continued, "I got an idea."

"Not interested."

"Why you gotta be that way? Just hear me out."

"I wasted a few years of my life with your sister and, no offense, I'm not exactly a fan of the family."

"You're a straight shooter. I like that, bro. Respect."

"So what's this idea of yours?"

He grinned. "Alright, now we're talking."

When he was finished, I turned him down on the spot. As pitiful as my finances were, I wasn't ready to prey on others to feed my addiction. I tucked my tail and returned to Nashville, slinking into town without telling anyone I was back.

It wasn't long before Ashley's brother contacted me again. What now?

"It's my sis," he said.

Deep in my chest, emotion still stirred at the mention of her name.

"She's in deep this time, Steven, on drugs and working for a pimp named Cowboy. I don't know nobody else gonna get through to her. You gotta help me out."

It was like the bat signal drawing me out of my cave. I rounded up two friends, one of them a sheriff's deputy, and we reached the edges of Memphis three hours later. As I gave directions, my friend nosed his car into a seedy section of town. The asphalt was cracked and sprouting weeds. Stores had bars on the windows. With streetlights flickering or shot out, the darkness was almost palpable.

I must be out of my mind, I thought. What do I hope to get out of this?

"You sure we're in the right place?" the off-duty deputy asked.

"Look, that's it right there," I said. "The Rebel Motel."

"And this pimp, you think he'll be cool? I don't feel good about this."

"Just pull into the courtyard. Someone's supposed to come out and talk to us."

We eased into the space. A guy with tattoos crawling up his arms sauntered out, hand tucked into the front of his pants, and looked in the front and back seats.

"I'm here to see Cowboy," I told him.

"That right?" He reared back, smirking. "Well, follow me. Naw, not your friends. Just you, big guy. Alone."

"Don't do it," the deputy hissed at me.

Too late to turn back now, I exited the car and was ushered around the corner into an empty motel room. I waited there by myself for fifteen minutes, palms sweaty, pulse pounding. I stayed near the bathroom, eyes on the front door.

When at last it opened, I had no doubts about my host's identity. A tall, thin Black man, Cowboy strode in wearing boots, a big belt buckle, and the air of a man who owned the place—which for all intents and purposes, he did. Two brawny guys stood watch outside the door.

"Whaddya want?" he said.

"I'm here to see Ashley."

"That's gonna cost you."

"I'm not a john, okay? She's got two little girls who love and need their mama. I love her too—don't know why—and I just want to take her home."

Cowboy leaned back, his eyes unreadable. He looked me up and down, then gave a slight nod to his goons. They fetched Ashley and propped her close to me on the edge of the bed. Just looking at her broke my heart. Even makeup and lingerie couldn't hide the gauntness in her face and the skin pressed against her ribs.

I tried speaking to her with all the stern affection I could muster, but she clearly had no interest in getting out of this motel or being with me or seeing her daughters. She knew exactly where her next fix was coming from.

To his credit, Cowboy addressed her himself. "Ashley, baby, you need to go. You got someone here who loves you. I'd give anything to have someone walk in here and do the same for me. You hearin' what I'm sayin'? Go get your stuff."

She wandered off, trained to respond to the sound of his voice.

I dipped my head in Cowboy's direction. "Thank you."

"You're a good cat," he told me.

For a moment, the vulnerability in his voice made me forget my fears in this pitiful motel room. I turned and allowed my eyes to meet his.

"Do me a favor," he added. "Next time you talk to the Big Guy up there, please tell Him Cowboy ain't so bad. You tell Him that, alright?"

31

DEAD TO RIGHTS

Against their better judgment, my friends left me to my fate and headed back to Nashville. Though Ashley and I had nothing left to build a relationship on, I couldn't walk her out of the Rebel Motel and just drop her off on someone's doorstep. I had to see this through. Her brother arranged for her and the girls to stay with family, then thanked me for stepping in.

"You're solid," he said. "You need anything, you hit me up."

"Sure," I said.

"And don't forget that other thing I told you about. Easy money, man."

It was clear to me I was a captive to Memphis once more, and from downriver my newest love still called my name. My job options were limited, my income not even worth mentioning, and my moral compass badly broken. I hopped from bed to bed, including Ashley's a time or two. I lived in hotels for a while. The gambling got so bad, I napped in my car between trips to the casinos. I shoplifted to eat and to "cash back up" for my next visits to the blackjack tables.

I was a hostage to the game. It wasn't about winning or losing. It was about getting lost in a sea of forgetfulness. Make no mistake about it, addiction is a sickness—and I was a sick man, damaged in spiritual, mental, and psychological ways. Even so, I knew better. I just didn't give a damn.

At one point, I spent forty-one straight hours at the blackjack table.

In a span of a few days, I cashed $20,000 of bad checks to build my nest egg.

Over eighteen months in Memphis, I burned through an estimated $300,000.

Somewhere in that journey of depression and despair, I finally crumbled and gave Ashley's brother a call. I steeled my voice and made a fateful decision.

"Okay," I spat out.

"Okay, what?" he said. "You telling me you're in?"

"Yes, dammit, I'm in. But I get a say in how we operate."

"Partners," he agreed. "Hell ya!"

We got to business right away. He had a whole list of addresses, ranging from his dad's neck of the woods in Kentucky—"a whole band of Barney Fifes up there"—down through West Tennessee into northern Mississippi. These were middle-class homes, prime targets for burglary. To avoid suspicion, we cased the places in a spendy Lexus. We then returned in a work van and loaded up in broad daylight. Ball caps and coveralls made us indistinguishable. By the time we moseyed out of a neighborhood, we could be carrying thousands of dollars of cash, jewelry, credit cards, and electronic equipment.

We stored and distributed the stuff from a rented stash house on the outskirts of Memphis. Ashley lived just down the street, but her brother's and my names were in no way attached to the property. We never left the van there and we garaged the Lexus off-premises. Both vehicles, I insisted, were for work and nothing else.

My criminal activity funded my gambling addiction, and my addiction often sent me back out on the road. There was money to be made and money to be played.

It wasn't all fun and games, though. A battle raged inside my soul between my screw-everything-and-everyone attitude and my last shreds of decency. Looking back, I realize my spiritual battles would have been best fought with God on my side. You can either worry until it hurts—and boy, did I hurt—or pray until it feels good. Jeremiah 29:12 says, "Then you will call on me and come and pray to me, and I will listen to you."

But did I call on the Big Guy?

No, I did not.

If Cowboy expected me to put in a good word for him, he was sorry out of luck.

My own luck ran out in early 1997. I was stepping out of our stash house when two officers, guns drawn, ordered me down on the ground with hands behind my back. The smell of grass filled my nostrils as they slapped the handcuffs on.

The ride to the station seemed to last forever. Panic blurred my vision and deafened my ears. If the officers said anything, I couldn't decipher it. As the guilt of the past year pressed upon me, threatening to do me in, I went into self-preservation mode.

I racked my brain. What was in the stash house? Not much. They couldn't prove I lived there or had any ties to the place. I was visiting a friend there, for all they knew.

I was fine, I thought. They didn't have shit on me.

I soon found out how wrong I was.

Not only had Ashley spotted me loading stuff into the stash house and called the cops, but earlier in the week a robbed homeowner had spotted and described our Lexus to detectives. Later, against our rules, Ashley's brother took the car for a spin to impress a blackjack dealer he was dating, and an eagle-eyed officer pulled him over. As a result, we were now both in handcuffs at the station, in separate interrogation rooms.

My partner in crime sang like a bird, at least that's what the detectives told me. He gave details about our activities, working a deal for himself. They put the screws to me and I knew there was no squirming my way out this time. They had me dead to rights. With multiple charges of grand larceny and aggravated burglary, I could be facing decades behind bars. I had just turned forty. I could very well die in prison garb.

Of course, it didn't have to be this way. They promised to only charge me with one incident per jurisdiction if I simply confessed to all of the cases.

What other option did I have?

The next week I rode along with the detectives, confessing to jobs I'd done—and even some I hadn't—in various towns and neighborhoods.

When the dust settled and guilty verdicts were handed down, judges in Tennessee, Kentucky, and Mississippi sentenced me to three years, two years, and four years, to be served consecutively. Once again, I belonged to the Department of Corrections, and this time they weren't cutting me any slack.

I had no idea what awaited me.

Part Three

"I didn't dare think of the future;
the past was still happening."

—John Grisham, in *The Street Lawyer*

Turney Center, where Steven's season in hell began

Steven's dad, L. H. Young

Logan County Detention Center, in Kentucky

Last photo of Steven and his dad together

Steven's first view of Parchman Prison, in Mississippi

Steven's last view of Parchman

32

GRIEVANCES

My first hint of how rough things might get came pretrial, in Fayette County, Tennessee. I was locked in an eight-man cell with over two dozen men. We were elbow to elbow, fights breaking out all the time. We got an hour a day to roam about the yard, then it was back inside for another twenty-three hours. Nights were spent on the floor, with sleep coming in fitful increments. Only toward the end of my five weeks did I work my way into one of the coveted bunks.

I sent my parents a few letters during this period. Dad wrote back in beautiful longhand, his attention to detail reflecting his unspoken concern for me.

Mom wasn't such a pushover.

"I want you to quit writing," she told me during a short call. "Right there on the envelopes, there's a stamp saying they're coming from prison. The mailman, he sees that. How do you think that looks, huh? What if a neighbor saw?"

When her friends or coworkers asked where I was, she wasn't about to admit that her black-sheep son was incarcerated.

"He's moved outta state," she'd reply.

Which wasn't a lie, once I was transferred to Kentucky and Mississippi.

I'm told that when Dad was asked about my whereabouts, he took the direct approach. "Steven's in prison," he would say. "He's holding his head up and I'm proud of him. He's made some mistakes, but he's paying for them."

After my day in court, I was bussed to a West Tennessee unit. Here I would go through classification before they sent me to one of the state penitentiaries.

The county jailer, unbeknownst to me, had filed a note in my jacket saying I was depressed. Really? You think? Next thing I knew I was on suicide watch, dressed in a paper gown and locked in a room with three glass walls for 24/7 observation. I had a plastic mat on the floor, no pillow, no blanket. Since I could potentially harm myself with utensils, I had to eat with my hands and brush my teeth with my finger. I was allowed only a Bible as reading material—and I'd read that story before, no thank you.

I was barely hanging on. Was this intended to cure my blues or brighten my mood? You tell me.

Welcome to the correctional system.

During my eight or nine years as their pawn, Tennessee was bad, Kentucky was okay, and Mississippi was no joke. Not once did I witness any real corrections going on. A young guy coming in with a year or two sentence was often paired with a cellie staring at fifteen or twenty years. I met one guy, a twenty-eight-year old, who'd been in and out six times since his teens. You were not prepared in any way for release. The guys who got back out on the streets were usually worse off than when they came in.

Corrections? I don't think so. It was all about punishment, period.

After two weeks, I was visited by a psychiatrist who refilled my antidepressants and got me removed from suicide watch. I was also able to get a medicated cream for severe athlete's foot, one of the gifts picked up while living in that cramped county jail.

Still awaiting classification, I went to a follow-up appointment at the clinic. The nurse, she was a real piece of work. I told her I was fighting allergies and needed sinus medicine. With thick eyebrows above icy eyes, she told me too bad, there was no appointment written down. Well, I wasn't leaving till I spoke with someone. We argued this way for a few minutes as others shifted in their seats in the waiting area.

"I have a right to be here," I insisted. "You can't just turn me away."

"Oh, is that so?" The nurse leaned forward. "I can treat you any which way I please and you can't do a damn thing about it."

I was a forty-year-old man now and didn't take kindly to her attitude. I managed to take a deep breath. "All I want is some medicine and a few minutes with the doctor."

She shrugged. "You're wasting your time. The doctor's not even in today."

A minute later my attending physician walked through the door.

"Thanks for lying to me," I hissed at the nurse.

With the help of an inmate who happened to be a paralegal, I filed a grievance. I listed an inmate, another nurse, and the doctor as witnesses.

A few days later, I was on gym time when a voice over the speakers called me back to my cell. The sergeant stood by my bunk, stern-faced. My stuff had been tossed and he'd discovered handfuls of sinus tablets along with my prescribed antidepressants. Earlier, the nurse had given me a month's worth of sinus medication in what I assumed was a form of apology but now realized was part of a setup.

Shaking his head, the sarge wrote me up for hoarding meds.

I filed a second grievance, naming the nurse and the clinic. This time, I found myself in the warden's office along with the assistant warden, the physician, and the nurse. The nurse, I was told, had noted in my jacket that I was "angry, out of control, abusive, and threatening." This jacket would follow me throughout my time in prison and those comments could make things tough for me going forward.

She watched me smugly, her arms folded, her lip slightly curled.

"Do you have any response?" the warden prompted me.

"I do." Since ranting would only hurt my cause, firm yet calm was the best approach. "I have three witnesses, Warden. Speak to any of them and they'll corroborate my story. This all started because the nurse refused to honor my appointment and then treated me disrespectfully and lied to my face."

She tried to interject something here, but the warden held up a hand. "What're you after, Inmate Young?"

"I want her sanctioned and her comments struck from my jacket."

"Those are high demands."

"Remember, three witnesses. I'll be honest, Warden, if I don't get this resolved, I'll seek outside representation and sue you, her, and this facility."

The warden smiled and patted the papers stacked on a filing cabinet beside his desk. "Feel free. I'll just add it to the pile." He sat back in his padded chair. "None of this is really necessary. If you'll withdraw your complaints, I will personally see to it that you get through classification quickly and sent to where you want to go."

"I want to go to Turney Center."

"You sure about that? Things've changed since you were last there."

His concerns didn't register with me. I knew the place, the routine. It was only a hundred miles from my parents and my brothers. If I went there, this might all seem manageable. "There's one other thing," I said. "I still need those comments removed."

The nurse shot up from her chair. "Warden, you can't—"

"He can," my physician cut in. "I would also like to see them removed."

Between the warden and the doctor, I was good to go, and soon found myself handcuffed on a TDOC bus en route to Middle Tennessee, back to guard towers and glittering razor wire. As much as I hated to be there, at least the place felt familiar.

33

HOT WAX

The warden was right. Things had changed, and not for the better.

Located in Only, Tennessee, the Turney Center Industrial Complex simmered in the humidity between rolling hills and lush vegetation. The shrill drone of cicadas was an assault on the ears. The only reason Only existed was to support this correctional facility, which functioned as a city unto itself.

I was dumped off for processing and issued a button-up shirt and heavy denim pants with a stripe down each leg. I got socks and underwear, which would be replaced every six months as they turned gray in the vast laundry services. Assigned the same inmate number from my first go-around fifteen years ago, I was seen as an "old head."

Being an old head gave others the impression I'd done hard time and knew my way around. They figured at six-three and 240 lb I wasn't someone to mess with.

Even so, my head was on a swivel. Despite our highly structured environment, things could turn ugly in a flash. Rival gangs and paybacks were usually involved, and you could get swept into the violence if you weren't careful.

And it wasn't just inmates you had to be wary of.

There were some guards on the take and most of the drugs entering the facility passed through their hands. They could buy an ounce on the street, then sell it at four or five times the cost behind bars. Since we were potential customers, they treated us with basic respect. They chatted us up, even using our names: "Hey, Steven, how's that book you're reading?" "Jose, you hear from your girl?" "Whatcha think, Big D, who's gonna win the SEC this year?" "Anything y'all need, you talk directly to me. I gotcha covered."

In prison in those days, saggy pants were a sign of being both gay and available. Some guys were flamboyant and others kept it on the down-low. While I had some gay acquaintances who were loners like me, I was never approached or messed with. I'll tell you, these guys were good wing men in a fight. They'd as soon cut you as look at you.

New convicts came into the system as wide-eyed as deer in the headlights. For protection, they tried to integrate and make connections. The ones who already had street experience, they often formed alliances with like-minded inmates.

I didn't do any of that. I sat. I observed. I stayed to myself.

No groups or gangs ever tried to recruit an old head like me.

A typical day started at 6:30 a.m. I made my bunk, washed up, then headed to chow, with pancakes always served on Fridays. We returned to our cells for count. Some mornings were so foggy that we weren't released to our duties until 10 a.m, though generally we split off at 7:30 a.m. to laundry, maintenance, cleaning, and so on, with lunch before noon. After evening chow, we had summer free time in the yard or winter free time in the gym. Chapel services were also an option. Before nightly lockdown, the showers were available—good luck getting more than a couple minutes of hot water—and the day room was open for TV viewing.

The most popular show while I was there? Take a wild guess.

Nine times out of ten, Cops was playing, accompanied by running commentary from the inmates: "You dumb ass, no wonder you got caught." "Whatcha doing hoppin' a fence like you some Olympic athlete?" "Don't look up, fool. Now they got your ugly mug on camera."

"Well, if you're so smart," I would sometimes ask, "how'd you get here?

"Got snitched out."

That was the standard reply. I'd shake my head, thinking, here they are in prison calling someone else who got caught stupid.

By dark, I retreated to my cell to read and use the toilet before my cellie came in. Privacy was a joke. Each solid cell door had gaps at the top and bottom, too small for a person to squeeze through, but large enough for guards to peek in whenever they felt it necessary. My actions and inaction were always under scrutiny. Though I'd never been much of a reader, I became a fan of John Grisham's novels. Story was a form of escape in a world without a moment's peace. It connected me with those outside these walls.

Once count was taken and the cell doors clanged shut for the night, danger was no longer a threat, but the claustrophobia, the trapped feeling, preyed on my fears.

Not all prisons are made of barbed wire and barricades.

Not all chains are made of iron.

Cornered by thoughts and memories, I felt the psychological pressure of those walls bearing down on me. Some nights it took everything within me not to break down in tears or start yelling at the top of my lungs.

"Can I come into your house?"

I glanced up from my bunk. A young guy, a lifer, stood in the doorway. I swiveled into a sitting position, planted both feet on the floor. "Sure," I said.

He stepped in, looked around, made a disapproving sound in his throat.

"What?"

"I'm not dissing you, brother, but you need to put some pictures on the walls, some posters, or something. It's bare bones in here. You gotta fix up your house."

I shook my head. "Forget that."

"Might as well make yourself comfortable, that's all I'm saying."

"I don't want to get comfortable. I want every day in here to be miserable, so I make sure to never come back."

As it was, there was enough misery to go around. The worst of the human condition is on full display in the American experiment called the correctional system. In four decades on this planet, I had never seen anyone killed in cold blood. I would witness my first at Turney Center and several more over the next eight years. I still relive those moments over and over in my dreams. Or should I say nightmares?

The first happened one evening just after lockdown.

What the hell? That was the one time of day I thought we were all safe.

A small crew of inmates was working a night shift, scrubbing and waxing the floors while nobody else was moving about. One of the men stood calmly, lit his can of highly flammable wax, and tossed it like a grenade over the top gap of a door two cells down from me. The man inside was a known snitch, and within seconds an inferno raged. The screams were bloodcurdling. Angling for a glimpse, I saw flames dancing yellow and hot, casting stark shadows against the opposing row of cell doors. The smoke curling from the cell smelled of burnt hair and flesh. By the time guards managed to get inside, it was too late.

You learn real quick in those situations to turn deaf, blind, and dumb. You don't get nosy. You don't ask questions. If you do happen to know anything, you sure as hell keep that information to yourself.

Another time I watched a guy get pinned against the brick wall of the equipment building. A group of inmates stabbed him from head to toe over a hundred times. It happened in seconds. He slid down the wall, gasping for air, blood bubbling out of his wounds. When the emergency response team rushed in, his attackers walked into the middle of the field, dropped their knives, and surrendered without a fuss. They'd acted according to some gang code of honor and accepted the consequences.

Snitches and gang members were the most common targets of violence, but daily fights could erupt anywhere over anything.

I was in the rec hall one evening when a Black guy on the land-line phone ignored another inmate wanting to make a call. The frustrated inmate, a white guy, reached over, hung up the call, and snatched the receiver away. He started dialing his own call. As he did, the first guy walked over to the pool table, picked up a cue stick, and broke it over his knee. He rushed straight at the man who had disrespected him and stabbed him through the neck, the cue stick going in one side and out the other.

The wisest thing to do in those moments was freeze. Any sudden movement made you a target. By remaining unattached, I avoided attacks and repercussions.

Hear no evil, see no evil, speak no evil.

34

BETTER LATE THAN NEVER

There are two things inmates respect in another inmate. The first is strength, which is not always a physical thing. A person's reputation can give him an aura that goes far beyond bulging pecs and deltoids. The second is knowledge. If you have some basic skill or intelligence which others deem valuable, this can also elevate you.

Some guys, they couldn't read or write. They needed a guy like me to sit down with them, read out loud a letter from their girl or family back home. If they wanted to write back, I was there to offer my services.

What really worked on you after years of incarceration were the lack of options or freedom. You didn't make your own schedule. You got shifted from here to there, got counted, got shifted and counted again, ate the food you were given and did the tasks you were assigned. Special permission was needed for anything else. You watched your back like a man on the battlefield while being treated like a kid in preschool.

As if that weren't enough, I was drug-tested out the ass. Way more than most. I was put in a holding cell, given water to drink, then told to piss in a cup. Only later did I realize I was their poster boy for clean drug tests.

"You're helping our numbers," the captain told me. "You make us look good."

Determined to survive this place, I tried to make a few decisions for myself by focusing on a job and a hustle.

My job was working on the prison newspaper. Somewhere in my years of job-hopping I'd done a short stint at a printing press, so I could already typeset and write. The cliche about child molesters facing the worst treatment in prison didn't seem to be the case, because the editor of our paper was in for just that and he fared okay. I was paid sixty-five cents an hour, money usable at the commissary for cigarettes, new socks, and any soap other than the bars of sandpaper the prison provided. My work was light compared to the manual-labor jobs. The welders, they got paid the best, putting stuff together, such as metal picnic tables for state parks.

My hustle was where I earned extra money, since I was getting no assistance from my family. Many inmates spent time in the neighboring law library, writing appeals and paying others well-versed in legal matters to write motions for them. Every once in awhile, a guy was granted a new trial or full pardon. Whether successful or not, inmates needed copies of their paperwork, sometimes hundreds of pages. Using a copier only available to me as newspaper staff, I charged a dime a page, almost half of what the prison charged. I collected each week by giving each customer a list of commissary items I wanted delivered to my office. If you failed to deliver, you were cut off.

My next hustle was stocking my desk and cell with my "payments." Once I had a stash, I let it be known I was a "store man." Inmates visited my "store" to get cupcakes, candy bars, Zoo-zoos and Wham-whams, coffee, sugar, and tobacco. I had it all. Some even bought hotplates to cook ramen noodles. Credit wasn't cheap in prison. The payback was three for one. If you got a bag of coffee on credit, you gave me three bags back. If you didn't, your credit rating tanked. You were S.O.L. Just like in the real world.

My last hustle was something I knew how to do really well. I ran a football and NASCAR pool. The bet was two packs of cigarettes. For every three packs bet, I kept one, and the winners got the rest. Let's just say, I smoked well. And the great thing was, even some of the guards were players, so getting busted wasn't a fear.

I stopped by the chapel some evenings. Not for any spiritual benefit. No, the chapel was a relatively safe, quiet place for inmates to get word out about drug deals, gang activities, and for me to conduct business. Plus, chapel visits looked good on your jacket. They implied you were repentant and contrite.

Yeah, right.

My communication with family was limited. Mom visited once or twice, but wouldn't accept collect calls from me. While Dad never visited, he still wrote at times. I noticed his words were looking shakier, his health affecting his penmanship, and I could tell the effort took a toll on him. He also spoke to me a time or two on the phone.

"Why haven't you written lately?" he wanted to know.

"Mom told me not to."

"Do what?"

"Something about the envelopes being marked and it not being a good look. I don't know."

"Son," he said, "you write anytime you want to write. You put my name on it."

I couldn't see his face, but it was the first time I ever heard him say "I love you." Those words were a long time coming and they meant a lot, considering I would never see my father again. Dad just raised me the way he was raised, meting out discipline for bad behavior, real or perceived. There wasn't usually a lot of guidance or instruction to go along with it. Crime and punishment, pure and simple.

If I did have any motivation to toe the family or legal lines, it was to avoid pain.

Yet, pain was the problem in the first place.

The gambling, the sleeping around, the swinging, the burglarizing, all of them were forms of managing, or at least numbing, the deep pain within. My misguided attempts at dealing with the inner turmoil only led to harsher punishment. A downward spiral. A cycle of emotional sickness and daily survival.

Behind bars, I was forced to spend a lot of time with myself. Moments of reflection swung from crippling shame to repressed rage. The chains of the past had grown heavier over the years. They cut through skin and bone. They bound my heart.

I knew I wasn't the only one. All I had to do was look around the prison yard and realize there were hundreds just like me. Inmates fueled by anger, guilt, insecurity, fear. Some guys, it was obvious why they were locked up. They would gut you like a fish without an ounce of remorse. Others were smart, well-mannered, stuck in here because they lost their cool during a lover's quarrel or got greedy with department funds.

Where was God in the midst of it all?

Far as I was concerned, He was hiding over in the chapel after evening chow. He was nowhere to be seen amidst the grime of my daily routine.

35

WASTED YEARS

When you spend your days running from yesterday, tomorrow doesn't exist. Why think about what lies ahead when nothing awaits you but more of the same?

The nightmares which haunted me as a child and beyond were now joined by the smells of burnt flesh and images of flashing knives and blood-red bubbles. My past and present formed a collage of terror I could not escape. I kept my head down, avoided conflict, and counted the days. It was all about surviving. Little did I know I was learning a valuable lesson which would serve me well down the road.

It was 1999, the end of an age.

As the turn of the century approached, millions of people worried over Y2K and whether computers would reset their calenders to year zero, throwing systems into chaos. As for me, I was leaving Tennessee after three long years, and all I could think about was converting my commissary dollars so I'd have cash on me at the next prison.

A sheriff's deputy came down from Kentucky and picked me up from Turney Center. We stopped at a fast-food joint along the way and he let me get out, with no handcuffs, to share a meal indoors. All around us, life carried on at warp speed. I felt both conspicuous and invisible. Children's laughter produced an ache in my chest.

Where was Josh these days? Was he ashamed of his father the felon?

The deputy drove us north into Kentucky, where I would serve two years for my next prison term. Here in the Bluegrass State, I was told, I would be allowed to wear my own clothing. Already, this sounded better than where I'd just come from.

When I arrived at the facility, I found inmates rolling dice on a table. They had real money up for grabs, and none of the authorities seemed to take issue with it. No prison garb? Gambling in the open? Clearly, things were run differently in Kentucky.

Blame it on politics, I guess. Turns out being a jailer was an elected position here, and Bill Perkins was ever mindful of the fact. His inmates were mostly local, and each of them had friends and relatives who went to the polls. Since Mr. Bill liked his job, he aimed to keep it by providing good treatment to those in his care. Instead of the dollar-per-minute calls in Tennessee, here we had free ten-minute phone calls twice weekly, free access to a VCR and videos—nothing X-rated, of course—and free coffee-cart visits three times a day.

"Every vote counts," as Mr. Bill liked to say.

It seemed to work. If guys got out of line, he simply stripped away all of our privileges. The pressure to do the right thing came from within. Nobody wanted to be blamed for making everybody else pay the price.

My father had cancer. I'd heard the news. On the bright side, he had responded well to chemo and his doctors were optimistic. On December 23, 1999, with Dad turning eighty-five the next day, I told a female sergeant that I hoped he stayed well long enough for me to go back and see him. It had been years since we spoke face to face.

The sergeant squared her shoulders. Her face was expressionless. Across the room, I saw our kitchen director, a woman we all called Mom, turn and leave.

What was going on?

That evening, my brothers Robert and John appeared. Had Mr. Bill pulled some strings? Were they here to take me back to Nashville? Would I get to speak to Dad?

"Sorry, Steven," they told me. "Dad had a massive heart attack."

My blood ran cold. "What does that mean? Why are you here?"

"Dad died earlier today. We asked Mr. Bill and the staff not to say anything so we could come and tell you ourselves."

I lost it.

The mental and physical abuse, the secrets, the wasted years, the final "I love you" . . . It was all too much, and my chest felt clawed open by anguish and regret. Tears spilled down my cheeks, bitter and hot.

John shifted on his feet. "What're you crying for? He was an asshole."

As true as that was, I still loved the man on some level. He had given me life and my family name and now he was gone forever. I never even got a chance to say good-bye.

To his credit, Mr. Bill did everything in his power to get me to the funeral a few days later. However, I needed permission from both the Kentucky and Tennessee governors to cross state lines, and the latter was on Christmas vacation. No one could reach him. By the time any paperwork could be signed, the funeral date was upon us.

I sat up in my cell after a long, restless night.

Dad was gone.

How many times had our family met out at Poplar Hill Cemetery for Decoration Day, remembering those who had gone before? Today, my own father would be laid to rest beneath a tombstone bearing his name. Though cancer had tried to pull him under, he persevered. Then, just like that, a heart attack took him out one day before his birthday. When it was your time, it was your time. There was no cheating death.

Gone.

Mr. Bill popped his head in. "Steven, put on your good clothes."

I could barely lift my eyes to meet his. "What's going on?"

"If I can't get you down to Nashville today, at least I'll get you outta this jail. Now get yourself dressed."

What sort of jailer goes out of his way to cheer up one of his prisoners? I mean, if that wasn't God giving me glimpses of His love, I don't know what was. For the whole day, Mr. Bill drove me around in his own car, meandering through rolling farmlands, racing along country roads, taking me out to lunch, spending hours by my side when I was unable to go down and be by my dad's.

It was a kind and caring gesture I remember even now. Definitely not something I was used to. Let's just say, Mr. Bill made one of my worst days feel special and memorable.

36

JAILHOUSE ROCK

Once you find your happiness, you realize every tear you shed along the way was worth it. Beauty without contrast is muted, and the darkest days add texture to the sunny ones. When my dad died, I thought my tears exposed some weakness or flaw in me. Only years later did I start to appreciate their contribution to my story. Here's what I learned:

Don't fear your tears. Embrace them.

Don't fight them. Free them.

Don't get stuck in the pain they bring. Experience their relief as well.

There is healing in every teardrop that falls and there is hope on the other side of despair. I didn't know any of this then, but I'm telling you now from all that I went through. Keep holding on. There is light around the corner. Your days are not over yet.

In early 2000, after five months in a rundown jail facility, I and my fellow inmates were moved into a brand-new structure with open quads, nice showers, and an outdoor rec area featuring basketball hoops and picnic tables. We were allowed to roam out there until 11 p.m., and I sat beneath the stars on many a smoke break, listening to the insects, staring up into that inky expanse.

Was anybody out there?

Were we floating through this universe alone?

No one at home was taking my calls these days, and it pissed me off. In hindsight, however, I see how it was a good thing. A therapist assessed it correctly: "To survive, you had to leave what's out there, out there." Other guys, they made calls to their loved ones, got emotional, then went back to their bunks thinking of what they were missing. For me, psychologically, it was easier to shut it all out and accept my current reality.

Mr. Bill, after learning of my past restaurant experience, handed me the jail's kitchen operations. I ordered from Cisco, kept things under budget, and saved my jailer a lot of money—always a plus when it came to his canvassing for votes. Each day, I got up before dawn to serve breakfast. The woman we all knew as Mom oversaw daily cooking and cleanup, and the two of us made a good team.

In Kentucky, prisoners weren't paid a dime for their work. I needed money, so I ran my own laundry service for other inmates. By hand, I washed their soiled, stinky clothes in the shower and hung them to dry in my cell. I also assisted guys with their GED courses, charging cash or working in exchange for quality soap and shampoo.

Mr. Bill was an all-around good guy, and my freedom grew as I proved myself worthy of it. There would be life after prison, I could taste it.

So what did I do? I rushed headlong into yet another relationship, trusting my wounded, wayward heart to guide me. The woman was serving a few months for a minor drug offense. Yeah, I know. I can really pick 'em. We started talking as I delivered meals to the women's side. Soon, letters were being exchanged and one thing led to another. When Mr. Bill caught wind of what was going on, he called us into his office. She got there first, and when I walked in, I figured I was in trouble.

Mr. Bill said, "I hear this is serious, what you two have going."

"Yes," I admitted.

He looked dead in my eyes and told me she had something she wanted to say to me. Not sure what to expect, I turned her direction and waited. What came next was hard to even believe.

"Steven," she said, "I love you, and I want to marry you."

My mouth dropped.

Mr. Bill asked if I wanted this as well and I told him it was. Scripture tells us in Jeremiah 17:9, "The heart is deceitful above all things, and desperately wicked; who can know it?" Well, that's not what society tells us. It says to follow your heart, and that's exactly what I did.

Her family wasn't thrilled that we had a wedding in jail. We said our vows before a licensed officiant—of all people, it was the same Kentucky judge who had sentenced me—then consummated our marriage that night behind blankets strung up in a nook of the library. Talk about jailhouse rock!

For a short time it seemed I had rounded a corner. Life was looking up. Love—or at least sex—was in the air.

Then the marriage ended as quickly as it began, with an annulment.

You're not surprised?

Yeah, neither was I, though I took it as proof that happiness would never come my way and all those cuddly, smiling couples out there were just putting on a show. I knew the truth. We were all selfish creatures and true sacrificial love was just a fantasy.

37

THE KEYRING

After nearly two years, my time with Mr. Bill was over. The day I left, he told me if things didn't work out when I put all this behind me, he'd always have a job for me running his jail kitchen. I will never forget him and his positive impact on my life. Things had gone from bad to okay in the last two states. They would soon go from okay to much worse.

A private contractor came for me in Kentucky, cuffed my hands to a waist chain and shackles, then loaded me into a cargo van. A few hours down the road, I was moved onto a bus full of other inmates. We traveled from the Bluegrass State into Illinois, down into Arkansas, and deeper still into Louisiana. Guys were picked up and dropped off at various correctional facilities. For forty-seven hours, I rattled along on hard plastic seats, over cracked county roads and rural byways. Every pothole rattled my chains and seemed to loosen my teeth in their sockets. My empty stomach grumbled. I was lucky to finally get a McDonald's cheeseburger, no fries, and a cup of water.

By the time I reached my destination, my ass was sore, my mood dark, and my mind acknowledging the fact this would be nothing like my time with Mr. Bill.

I wasn't a name. I was a number.

A criminal who deserved everything he had coming to him.

Don't get me wrong. I was guilty. Guilty as sin. I certainly never counted on the Bible Belt doing me any favors, considering how deacons and youth leaders had behaved in my past, but the correctional system in the South was much closer to hell than anything in America ought to be.

I arrived sweaty, famished, and exhausted at a county jail in Mississippi. It was a prefab structure with iron floors, iron walls, iron doors, everything welded together on site. Guards' booted footsteps reverberated throughout this human cage. Voices echoed.

The noise was a form of torture. Though I had only to wait until I was sent off to a more permanent facility, I wasn't sure I could last that long.

For the first time in my prison experience, I thought seriously of escape.

As I waited in that iron structure, they made me a jail trustee, extending to me some responsibility because of my good behavior. My job history also helped. Not only had I managed bars, nightclubs, and restaurants in the past, I'd overseen a jail kitchen in Kentucky. They put me to work. Scrubbing dishes, flipping pancakes, mopping floors, I did it all. Just like in Kentucky, there was no pay for my long hours. No commissary dollars. Nothing.

Hard and hot as it was working in jeans and a T-shirt in that stifling kitchen, it sure beat waiting for classification in a crowded holding cell. Buses to various locations came on certain days. If a guy got called up, we knew just by the day where he was headed. I heard horror stories about the system down here. As I stood over the grill or sprayed off dirty pots with a metal flex hose, those stories did a number on me.

Four more years.

To me, it sounded like forever.

The lady who ran the kitchen, she drove up every day in her beat-up Buick. She hung her keyring on a hook by a small corner office. The only people back in this area were paid staff and other trustees.

That keyring dangled there, whispering my name.

One day, I dried my hands on my apron, untied it, and slung it over a mop handle. There was no one else around. I slipped those keys from the hook, nudged through the kitchen exit, and strolled to the driver's door of that ol' Buick. The car started up, the tank had gas, and traffic was minimal here on the outskirts of town. My heart hammered at my chest. If anyone asked, I was picking up supplies for the kitchen director.

I turned on the blinker and made my first turn out of the county-jail lot.

Just running an errand, relaxed as could be.

As that prefab structure shrunk in my mirror, I wondered how long until the director noticed her car missing? Probably not for awhile. She was a busy lady, her plate always full. And how long till they realized I wasn't in my cell or at evening meal?

If lucky, I had a two- or three-hour head start.

Following the rules of the road and the speed-limit signs, I steered north. My hands were at ten and two on the wheel, my eyes hopping from my rear-view to my side-view mirrors. Every odd engine sound spiked my pulse, but the director's Buick chugged along and carried me over the state line by sundown. Out-of-state plates wouldn't draw any attention here, and I doubted any APB would extend this far so soon. I would reach Nashville in time for the ten o'clock news. Would my escape already be an item in Tennessee? Probably not for another day or two.

I was free. Now what?

I had no plan. I had no money.

My family wouldn't want to see me, and even if they let me through the door, they'd press me to turn myself in before the cops came knocking. I'd burned my bridges with old coworkers, girlfriends, and wives.

Sure, the car could serve as my room for a night or two, but I ran the risk of a Metro officer identifying the tags and making the connection. My rumbling stomach reminded me I had already missed dinner, and if I didn't come up with a solution soon, I'd be resorting to steps two and six, just like in my youth: thievery and shoplifting.

What about the ringmaster?

If there was anyone I knew who wouldn't ask questions and wouldn't want any authorities involved, it was him. I'd done him more than a few favors in the past, helped earn him a bundle of money. Did he still live in the same place? With the nightlife heating up, I figured I might track him down at one of his clubs or adult bookstores.

Sure enough, he was still active about the city—and now married to a lady I'd introduced him to years ago, a former flame of mine. The moment Summer and I saw each other, I knew there were still embers burning. This could be trouble. Summer even cautioned her husband not to take me into their home.

Bless his heart, he welcomed me anyway.

Ditching the car I'd "borrowed," I moved into a spare room at his place just outside of Nashville. I did odd jobs for him, getting paid under the table. I was out of sight, not hurting anyone. I wasn't some armed murderer on the loose, and there was no public outcry on the news. I might actually pull this off.

Of course, I couldn't hide forever, and two of my brothers caught wind of my presence in the area.

Billy Dean, the oldest, he noticed the flowers I put on Dad's grave over at Poplar Hill Cemetery, near Watertown. I borrowed a vehicle and went there alone to pay my respects. I shed some tears and gave the farewell I wasn't able to do in person. The flowers, sure, they may have been a slip on my part, but they were a risk worth taking for the man who raised me and managed to say he loved me before the end.

If Billy Dean did report me, I never knew about it.

I ran into Byron, my second-oldest brother, while in Home Depot one morning. The ringmaster had a few projects that needed to be done around his place and he sent me out for hardware and supplies. Byron worked there, wearing a name tag and orange apron. We hadn't seen each other in years and he didn't recognize me as I passed by.

"Really?" I said to him. "You're not going to say hello?"

He did a double take. "Steven? Excuse me."

"How's the wife and kids?"

He lowered his voice and stepped closer. "You know they're looking for you, don't you? They've been asking around."

To his credit, though, Byron didn't say a word about me to anyone.

Months passed. Nearly a year. While I stayed away from cops in general—and still do to this day, that old fear stuck in the back of my head—I started to let down my guard. It was New Year's Day, 2002, and I was in the ringmaster's truck with two frisky females when a policeman pulled me over for expired tags. He ran the plate but not my name. He wrote me a ticket, unaware he had an escaped convict within reach.

I breathed a sigh of relief but knew it was only temporary. I could either spend the rest of my life running, or I could turn myself in and hope all I got was a court date for my ticket. Of course, the chances of that happening were extremely slim.

The ringmaster presented me one other option.

"Just say the word, buddy, and by tonight I'll have you out in Vegas. You can run my operations there. You know the ropes and I trust you. Plus, I feel bad about the expired tag on my truck."

"How long, though, before someone puts two and two together?"

"There's always that risk."

"Is that really what I want? To live on the run, looking over my shoulder?"

"Helluva way to live."

"I could just suck it up," I said. "A few more years and I'll be a free man."

"If that's how you want it," the ringmaster said.

Not long after I reached the courthouse, the wheels of justice started churning. A pair of detectives from Fugitive Division came in and informed me I was headed back to Mississippi. Instead of charging me with grand theft auto and other crimes, they would only hit me with a misdemeanor, for breach of trust by violating the opportunity given me in the county jail kitchen. It was a mercy I did not deserve.

Of course, my flight risk was now a factor during my classification in Mississippi. They wouldn't make the same mistake twice. When the bus rolled around on a particular day and I heard my number called, I knew exactly where I was headed and what it meant. I'd heard the rumors and imagined the place in my head. After nearly a year on the loose, I was going back to prison.

You can do this, I told myself.

I would spend all of 2002, 2003, and a portion of 2004, in Parchman.

38

COTTON, COFFEE, AND TOBACCO

Occupying nearly twenty-eight square miles in Sunflower County, Parchman is the state's oldest prison and its only maximum-security facility for men. Built in 1901 along Mississippi Delta bottomland, it features many aspects of an antebellum slave plantation. Though the cotton has been replaced by other crops, inmates over the past century have worked as free laborers, earning the state millions of dollars. The penitentiary has served as the background for films and crime novels, and has come under investigation on multiple occasions.

Even to this day, the prison is in serious neglect and woefully understaffed, with inmates roaming about freely. As recently as January 2020 a deadly riot broke out. Gangs have launched an all-out war on each other, and murder is not uncommon, by beatings, stabbings, and strangulation.

Parchman beds over 3,500 inmates, including those on death row in Unit 29. When I arrived in 2002, they started using a lethal injection table, and in winter of the following year, a prisoner escaped from Unit 24B, though he was recaptured in San Diego and returned three weeks later.

It's a massive prison farm, the size of multiple penitentiaries on a single property that runs flat for as far as the eye can see. The summer heat is brutal, with no air-conditioning in the units or pods. Prisoners labor for long, grueling hours in either the fields or in the workshops. The guards demand respect and address their charges as "inmate," "convict," or "number such-and-such." Any misbehavior results in a visit with the disciplinary board and a loss of in-house privileges. Any violence beyond a black eye or split lip can get you thrown into The Hole, doing solitary—and nobody wants that.

The prison is a haven for huge rats and mice. They wobble along the walls and skitter across old plumbing and metal stairs. Rodents were the least of my fears, though.

The one thing you can't show in prison is fear.

I knew that, of course, and my first night in Parchman I was approached in my cell by a Black guy with four others just behind him. Any advantage I had in height was more than compensated for by his size and by his buddies.

"Hey, Pops." He nodded his chin at me. "You got any coffee for me?"

"I don't have much of anything yet," I told him. "I just got here by way of a jail in Kentucky, and it'll be some time before my stuff's transferred over. Once I get some, we can share. You're more than welcome."

"Pops, are you listening? We can come take what we want."

"Be that as it may," I said without blinking an eye, "you'll just need to decide what price you're willing to pay for that coffee."

"What does that mean?"

"You guys might be able to take me, but the first two through that door might wind up in the hospital or morgue."

Our gazes locked and I remained as cool as possible. It was vital to convey calm mixed with a willingness to act. A nervous disposition gets you nowhere in prison.

"Well, Pops," he said at last, "what's your name?"

"First off, my name's not Pops. I don't know any of your mothers. My name's Steven, and I'll call each of you by your names."

"That's fair. Listen, Steven, do you smoke?"

"Yes, I do."

Just like that, he ordered one of his buddies to go up to his "house," his second-level cell, and grab me some coffee, papers, and tobacco. "I like you, Steven. You didn't break down. You stood up for yourself. As long as you're here, I got you covered. You're hands-off."

Unbelievable. The first people I met in one of America's most notorious prisons were gang members. But that was okay. Hands-off sounded good to me.

As in every prison I was in, we started our days early. Each pod had its own chow hall, with breakfast served before sunup—and Fridays were pancake days, just like in Tennessee. After mealtime and count, we were transported on flatbed trucks over rutted roads across acres and acres of fenced farmland.

I could've been in the 1950s for all I knew. Guards eyed us from horseback, shotguns resting across their laps, as we chopped cabbage and lettuce with hoes. We picked cucumbers, tomatoes, corn, and potatoes, bagging everything. All of the produce went to the processing plant, most of it readied for state prisons and public schools.

Eventually, I got moved to the plant, where we spent hours unloading bags of vegetables onto conveyor belts and sending them into huge steamers to be cleaned. Spiders, worms, dirt—most of it came out in the wash. Though it was hot, filthy work, it was better than my time in the fields.

We had very little recreation time, and I was usually too worn out as it was. If I got through an entire chapter of a book before falling asleep each night, I was good.

We did have weekends off, which you'd think was a blessing, right? Not so fast. Those unscheduled periods were the hardest for me, without any letters or phone calls or visitors. In the system, I was shuttered from society's daily judgment but could not escape my own. I was trapped with myself and my thoughts.

Just me, Steven Allen Young. The man in the mirror.

The convict, the liar, and the thief. The husband of three ex-wives. The stepfather of long-gone daughters and birth father of one distant son.

Outside these walls and these fences, I had constructed one facade after another. Whether in jobs, marriages, or friendships, I was always afraid of being exposed for who I really was. I even tried to hide that truth from myself. No such luxury in a prison cell.

Throughout my adult life, what had I done every time things went well? I took that loaded gun of success and shot holes in my thin facade before the spotlight could reveal my true nature. It was best to end things on my own terms and timetable.

Now I had nothing but time. Too much time. Month after month of backbreaking work in the fields and the plant. If I could've installed a shutoff switch to quiet my memories, I would have done it.

39

THE DAMAGE DONE

This is my book, right? My story?

So I'm about to share some things I have never told anyone, not until deep into this writing process. If you've made it this far, I hope you will stick with me, but you are more than welcome to skip ahead to the next chapter if it makes you more comfortable. That's up to you. I just figured I should warn you.

I was reading Grisham's *The Chamber*, still one of my favorite novels, when the pod locked down for nightly count. We had a female guard on duty. Considering her environment, she had to be tough if not tougher than her male compatriots. She mostly deflected the random harassment and catcalls.

But we had some sick, twisted puppies among us.

One prisoner, he called out a few inappropriate things and started masturbating by his cell door as she went by. I was disgusted and she didn't seem amused. If she thought ignoring his lewd behavior would discourage him, she was wrong. It became a regular occurrence.

Before breakfast a few days later, I heard the offender's cell door click open, controlled by an automated system in the guard booth. Four guys streamed into our section of the pod from another area, their access granted by another female officer. They entered the unlocked cell and beat the masturbator to within an inch of his life. The whole thing went down in less than two minutes. In and out, and they were gone.

Our warden was not happy.

What happened? Who was responsible?

I was clueless, same as everyone else. Self-preservation was the overriding urge in these situations, and I knew to keep myself out of the fray. Just as in Tennessee, there were guards bringing in drugs, cigarettes, and cell phones, and even the officer on duty claimed she hadn't seen a thing. Clearly, anyone who ratted her or the others out would be next in line for a beating.

I tried to always stay alert, avoiding confrontation while exuding confidence. If you didn't mess with me, I wouldn't mess with you. Thanks to my Black friend on the second level, I also had that extra layer of protection.

Hands-off, in his words.

Untouchable.

The problem is, other gangs didn't take kindly to him or his methods. They were looking to send him a message, and their opportunity came as we were in a prison-wide lockdown. This usually happened after an inmate escape or violence. My guess is this one had something to do with that guy who got loose in the winter of 2003.

Lockdowns pretty much sucked. We were locked in our cells, no privileges or outside movement. We ate meals in our bunks. We took showers one at a time, then went straight back to our cells.

At last it was my turn for a shower and a guard called out my number. He marched me to the bathrooms, where stained white tile and moldy grout prevailed. It was strange to be the only one in there, with nobody else to worry about, no need to watch my back. I was told I had thirty minutes, which sounded like a lifetime, and I peeled off my clothes.

Where did my attackers come from? Why weren't they in their cells? The guard, was he in on it?

I don't know.

They were members of a rival gang, this much is certain. Somehow they were on the loose, sent to pass on a message through me. A pillowcase came down over my head before I could even turn to see a face. There were three of them, I eventually determined, by the sounds of their voices. Their fists and feet landed hard and fast, pummeling my body. My lungs gasped for air. My ribs cried out in pain. Someone worked my head over until I was bleeding beneath the pillowcase.

If it had been just a beating, that might've been alright.

Message received.

Next, though, I was dropped to my knees and shoved facedown on the tiles. I was held there, naked, the weight of three men restraining me. My legs were kicked apart. My cheek was in a pool of water, the smell of soap and bleach in my nostrils. It mostly blocked out the stink of testosterone and lust. I suspected what was to come next and didn't even struggle or put up a fight. A dark cloud of acceptance rolled over me, years of shame and questions. Putting up any resistance would only make things worse. I was completely at their mercy.

No matter what I did, it couldn't have made things any worse. The pain was excruciating as they took turns raping me. Time crawled. Their grunts filled the long gaps between each second. They spit and uttered curses, ridiculing me.

I hardly made a sound.

The violation was so extreme, I would spend months in the hospital, physically and emotionally damaged. With my eyes swollen shut, it would be days before I could even see again. Virtually blind, I was locked in the black space of my memories—a prison worse than any built by human hands.

It wasn't the evil done to me that shook me to the core. Since childhood I had witnessed the beast that lives within each human. In Sunday School, they called it sin. Even if I wasn't exactly on speaking terms with God, I had no doubt there was a battle raging inside all of us. It certainly raged inside of me.

It wasn't even the shame of this latest degradation. This treatment didn't come as any real surprise. Like I said earlier, there were some real deviants behind bars, guys whose only thrill was to dominate and destroy.

What shook me so deeply was my own inaction.

How would others perceive me if they heard I just laid there on that cold, damp floor? How would the women in my life view me differently? What would my own father have thought if he learned his son went numb and did nothing?

Even to myself, I couldn't explain my response. I was a misfit toy. Something in me was broken beyond repair.

Why, Steven? Why the hell didn't you fight back?

What kind of man just lies there?

Later, I wrestled with these thoughts and tried to put them into words. Therapists have told me that writing things down can be cleansing for the soul and I believe they have a point, but my poetry at its best offered temporary relief.

SEASON IN HELL

The darkness fell with sudden haste
Its presence hard and cold
It gripped my very being
With an unforgiving hold
No longer free to pick and choose
The way which I would travel
I could only watch, with impending doom,
As my world unraveled
What I once had has slipped away
As each day remains the same
The "me" I knew just disappeared
Now a pawn within their game

The cuts were deep, the damage done
How much I cannot tell
I'll have to wait until the end
Of my season spent in hell

40

EVERY STEP FORWARD

The prison warden and state authorities wanted answers. They appeared at my hospital bedside feigning concern and empathy. The truth is, they were worried about potential lawsuits and public perception. This had occurred on their watch, and they already had enough headaches from recent gang incidents and escapes.

"We need names, Mr. Young."

Oh, now I was a mister and not just a number. This charade made me sick. "What about the guard?" I snapped. "Didn't he see anyone?"

"He went to grab a coffee, trying to give you a little privacy. He didn't even realize anything was wrong until he came back and found you."

Since when, I wondered, had anyone cared about my privacy?

"If you're worried about retaliation, we can protect you," they told me.

My bruising and stitches said otherwise.

"Help us out here."

I shook my head. I wasn't a snitch. "There were three of them, like I told you. That's all I know. I never saw their faces. Black, white, Hispanic, I couldn't even guess." This last part wasn't completely true, but what did it matter?

"Here's the deal, Mr. Young. We already have a good idea who they were, since there were three men signed out of their cells for cleaning duty during that time. You're our only witness. Identify them for us and we can prosecute."

That was a big fat no. I'd be signing my own death warrant.

Thanks to a sympathetic doctor, I spent twelve weeks recuperating in a hospital bed. He repaired the physical damage and took note of my fragile psyche. He made sure I received more than enough time and care, then arranged for my transfer to a private medical facility for inmates.

Before the transfer, someone passed on a message to me:

Hands-off meant hands-off. Yes, paybacks for my attack had been carried out.

While the private facility was a reprieve from my prison cell, it had some limitations. For example, there was no outdoor rec area. Though I could roam freely inside, the outer doors were always locked. I never stepped into the sunlight. After months in that place, I was a walking corpse, a ghost.

I still had time on my sentence and I worried about going back to Parchman. Thankfully, in view of an overloaded system, the state legislature signed off on a three-for-one deal, granting inmates three days off their prison terms for every day they worked. This was great news. To get "good time," all I needed was some sort of work, but work was hard to come by in my limited confines.

My counselor pulled me aside one morning. "Okay, Steven, I got you a job."

"In here? I'm all ears."

"You're going to be a wall washer."

Was this a joke? My eyes scanned the room with its muted colors and mostly bare walls. It might take me six or seven hours to go through the entire place and wash off any dead-spider smudges or rubber-soled scuff marks along the baseboards.

"Don't question it," my counselor said. "On paper, it's a job."

Not long after, I landed a more legitimate position as a teacher's assistant for inmate GED courses. With my body now mostly healed, my mind appreciated any sort of distraction from the flashbacks.

"Keep up the good work," my counselor told me. "We'll have you out of here before the end of the year, maybe even in time for the holidays. I bet you're excited."

"Sure." I shrugged. "I guess."

I knew, come wintertime, there wouldn't be anyone waiting for me. As pale as I was, if I showed up on the doorstep of a friend or relative, they would swear I was the Ghost of Christmas Past. In their minds and mine too, I'd never be free of my chains.

On December 6, 2004, the Mississippi Department of Corrections issued a Discharge Certificate for Inmate K5262, Steven Young, granting me an honorable discharge after four years served, with good time factored in, and remanding me to probationary supervision.

I walked out the door and lifted my face toward the sun. Its warm golden rays had never felt so amazing.

Now what? Since my family wasn't taking my calls, nobody knew of my discharge. There was nobody present to pick me up. Nobody serving up a home-cooked meal for the man who had done his time.

I called a Nashville woman I'd connected with during my period on the lam. She seemed less than thrilled, but agreed to come get me. We didn't say much to each other on the ride back, as Mississippi bottomland gave way to forests and rose into the hills of Tennessee. When we arrived at her condo, the woman and her teenaged kids acted weird around me. I got the impression she didn't want to be left alone with me. I went to bed close to midnight, and she didn't follow until a full hour had passed.

Two days later, an old club friend of mine stopped by. "You need to know something," he said. "Your lady friend has been living with another man. He's waiting at a nearby hotel till you two work this out, but he's none to happy about it."

"Is that true?" I asked the woman.

"I want to be with him," she admitted.

"So you want me to leave? Well, thanks for at least giving me a ride. That was good of you."

"I'm sorry, Steven. I didn't mean for it to be this way."

"Not your problem. You enjoy your life."

I gathered up my things in a sack and headed out the door. I called my mom. Since she didn't recognize the number, she actually picked up, though when she heard my voice, she registered neither joy nor relief. I was out, I told her. I was back in town. Since Dad's passing, my brothers had hosted Christmases on rotation and I asked whose house we were meeting at this year.

"Doesn't really matter." She cleared her throat. "It wouldn't be a good idea for you to show up."

I wished her a Merry Christmas and ended the call.

My club friend let me sleep on his couch, but I screwed that up a few days later when I lied to borrow his truck. Instead of running to the store like I told him, I headed over to work things out with my lady friend. Her boyfriend started running his mouth. Things got heated. The police rolled up.

Not my smartest move.

With Christmas just around the corner, Music City, USA, felt anything but festive. All I cared about was finding my next meal and a place to lay my head. Despite having my independence back, my past still lurked and my present demanded attention. Who had time to think of the future? To me, it stretched on ahead like a joyless wasteland.

There was one last person I could call: the ringmaster.

This time he offered me space in his downtown warehouse. I had a bathroom, shower, and office to use as a small apartment, which sure beat where I'd been the past nine years. I plopped down my bag of clothing, toiletries, poems, discharge papers, and paperbacks. This was it, everything I had to show for my forty-eight years on this earth.

I had no idea that only two years down the road I would be making more money than I knew what to do with. Or that even further down the road, a hazel-eyed woman who worked in a nearby bank building would come wandering back into my life. I couldn't even begin to picture any of that.

One step at a time, that's all I could handle.

And though I didn't yet believe it, every step forward was an opportunity.

Part Four

"I guess under the right circumstances,
a man will do just about anything."

—John Grisham, in *The Racketeer*

Mike Dotson and Steven on Nolensville Rd, at Steven's corner where they first met

Home Street Home Ministries team distributing food and supplies to Nashville's homeless community

Mississippi Department of Corrections

DISCHARGE CERTIFICATE

TO WHOM IT MAY CONCERN:

The undersigned, Director of Records of the Department of Corrections of the State of Mississippi, hereby certifies that:

DOC No. K5292 _____ NAME Young, Steven _____

Race White _____ Sex male _____ Date of Birth 5-20-56 _____ Ht. 6 _____ Ft. 3 _____ In. _____

Weight 240 _____ Hair grey _____ Eyes blue _____ Complexion fair _____ Build large _____

Marks and scars N/A _____

Who was convicted by the Circuit Court of _____ Tate _____ County

for grand larceny/burglary of a dwelling _____

and was sentenced to _____ 1 & 3 yrs. cs _____ Year(s) in the Mississippi Department of

Corrections with _____ 0 _____ Year(s) Suspended and _____ 4 & 3 yr. _____ Year(s) Probation.

THAT DOC No. K5292 _____ NAME Young, Steven _____ has

completed service of _____ 4 _____ Years in the Mississippi Department

of Corrections and is hereby honorable discharged therefrom because of expiration of sentence.

THAT, according to law, DOC No. K5292 _____ Name Young, Steven _____

is hereby remanded to the supervision of the Mississippi Probation and Parole Board to complete the suspended

portion of this sentence under the jurisdiction of the Court.

Witness my hand and seal, this the _____ 6th _____ day of December _____

A.D., 2004 _____

DIRECTOR OF RECORDS

Steven's discharge papers from the Mississippi State Department of Corrections

41

HARD KNOCKS

Of course, not every opportunity represents a step forward. Along life's journey, some of my opportunities pointed me in the right direction, while others diverted me toward sheer drop-offs and dangerous ravines.

So, how can you tell which opportunities to follow?

When your arms are open to God's guidance and your heart is expectant, that's when it is easiest to sense the difference. When your hands are clutching, desperate for anything, it's much harder to get it right.

My next opportunity came after a cheerless holiday in that lonely warehouse. It was now 2005. I was clutching, desperate.

And Summer was the ringmaster's wife.

Despite the ringmaster's promotion of casual sex and swingers clubs, he was more protective of this relationship than of his previous ones. He'd been with her ten years and probably thought it was the real deal. Nevertheless, she and I still had that connection from the past and she was looking for a way out. Soon, she had left him and moved into her own apartment in Gallatin. She needed her space. The circles she and the ringmaster mingled in were freewheeling and loose, but that lifestyle often hides a gnawing despair. I knew this firsthand from Kate's and my experimentation.

Summer was lean and long-legged, taller than other girls I had dated. We started chatting regularly and things rekindled between us. Within weeks, we were looking for opportunities—there's that word again—to be alone together.

I knew her husband's true colors. He was as bad as I had been, a snake, a sleazy peddler in temptation and adultery, so I felt no guilt in trying to connect with his ex.

Summer and I rendezvoused one afternoon outside Shoney's in Madison—yes, the same location where I once worked and got handcuffed and arrested. I tended to hover around familiar spots, comfortable in their shadows.

About that time, the ringmaster pulled up in his vehicle and all hell broke loose. There were accusations and threats. He told me he wanted me out of his warehouse that day. I had a car, a cheap runaround. I went straight to his building and removed my stuff. With nowhere else to go, it was inevitable I would move in with Summer.

Oh, he didn't like that, his estranged wife and his friend mixing it up.

A few weeks later, I waited in the parking lot as Summer retrieved her belongings from the ringmaster's offices. She seemed to be taking longer then expected in there, so I called her phone. She didn't answer. My fingers drummed on the steering wheel. Where was she? She should've been back out by now. I called again. Still no answer. This time, I dialed the ringmaster and he picked up.

"Where's Summer?" I demanded.

"We're talking, alright. She'll be down when we're finished."

"C'mon, don't make this harder than it has to be."

"She's not yours, Steven."

"Well, she doesn't want to be with you. Deal with it." In the background, Summer was squabbling about something. "Just let her get her things and go."

When Summer exited the building, she was disheveled and bleary-eyed. We loaded her things into the trunk and drove off in a plume of dust and exhaust. "He kept blocking the door," she said. "He wouldn't let me out of there."

"Hmm. Figures."

"What're you doing?" Summer asked as I redialed.

I ignored her question and let the phone ring two, three, four times. The moment the ringmaster answered, I roared at him, "You ever do that again, I'll kill you and put you somewhere they will never find you!"

I should have remembered I was dealing with a snake.

He recorded the call—of course, he did—and used it as evidence, going to the Metro Nashville Police Department to file an order of protection against me. It read in part: "Because of the threatening phone call on Monday, June 27, 2005, I am requesting that you refrain from visiting any properties/businesses that are owned/managed by me . . ." It listed addresses and carried his signature. He and I were finally through.

Soon after, I considered taking another stab at marriage. Why not? Summer and I got along. If my third marriage wasn't the charm, perhaps a fourth go-around would do the trick. It was my same old pattern:

Looking for family, approval, and love. Trying to create reality from fantasy.

Hoping for something I barely even believed in.

For the next year or two Summer and I went through all the motions, celebrating holidays with my mom and brothers, attending family reunions. We all drove out to Cumberland Mountain State Park, rented cabins for the weekend, and had some good times together.

Rarely did my time in prison come up in conversation, except when my brothers wanted to use it against me. Maybe they felt guilty for not staying in closer contact. Or maybe they just figured, hell, I deserved what I got.

Mom, though, she had no empathy at all. "Oh, it wasn't that bad," she would say. "You survived it. Get over it."

One day, the two of us were alone and I snapped. "You want me to get over it, Mom? Like you have any idea. I got raped at Parchman, did you know that? Do you give a damn? I bet you never heard about my three months in the hospital afterward. Most people, they think it's a cakewalk in prison—free food, showers, TV. They couldn't last forty-eight hours in there. They'd be wetting themselves and begging to go home. But yeah, Mom, you're right. It wasn't that bad. Oh, it was one helluva good time!"

She offered no apology. Neither did I.

I still had nightmares from my time in the Mississippi Department of Corrections, and MDOC wasn't done with me just yet. As I soon discovered, my parole officer was a real piece of work. He saw me as a pawn in their game, to be shifted around at will.

Summer and I were cooking up breakfast one Friday morning when a hard knock rattled our apartment door.

I knew it was the law. I just knew it. What could they possibly want? Three more knocks.

"Go look through the peephole," I whispered. "Tell me what you see."

Summer eased over to the door and came back with a description of two guys in suits. Detectives, that was my guess. What now? I'd kept my nose clean, toed the line. There was no reason for them to be hassling me, not that it'd ever stopped them before.

"Okay, Summer, I'm going to climb over the back balcony and hide. Go find out what they want and don't call my phone till you've watched them drive out of here."

Twenty minutes later, my cell rang. The men were federal marshals, Summer explained. They had a warrant saying I was in violation of parole down in Mississippi. Most people on parole have to show proof of a job and residence while reporting regularly to a P.O. Since I lived in another state, I had been granted a non-reporting parole agreement to go along with my discharge papers. As long as I stayed out of trouble, I had no obligations to MDOC.

Apparently, someone down there thought otherwise.

I called my attorney. "I don't know what's going on, but these guys are looking for me. It makes no sense."

"I'll look into it," he said. "But I might not have an answer for you till Monday."

With my mom in the hospital at the time, I figured I could lay low at her place a few nights. En route, I had Summer drop me off at Target for some cans of soup and weekend supplies. Hopefully, this whole misunderstanding would be cleared up by Monday afternoon. With bags in hand, I settled back into the car.

As we eased out of the parking lot, we were lit up from behind. The marshals, as fate would have it, had grabbed burgers just down the road. They spotted our vehicle, pulled us over, and soon I was headed south to a Mississippi jail. My attorney said there was no way around it. I would have to appear before a judge and explain my situation.

I was furious. This was why I didn't trust the system. They played games with people's lives and there wasn't a damn thing I could about it.

"What the hell is going on?" I asked my P.O. "I have signed documentation saying I don't have to report down here. It was part of my plea deal."

"We'll see about that. Do you have those papers with you?"

I then called Summer and had her FedEx them to me overnight, then made copies before letting the P.O. take them away. He said it would take some time to "look things over," then failed to show back up for two days. What was so difficult about this? When he sauntered in, he didn't seem the least bit bothered by the delay.

"There's only one thing holding you up," he said. "Your parole fees to the state."

"Fees for what? I live in Tennessee. You never even have to meet with me."

"Pay them and you're good to go."

What a hassle. Per my request, Summer drove down from Nashville the next morning with cash in hand. In an hour or two, we'd be headed back home.

"Not so quick," the P.O. told us.

"Now what?"

"You still have to go back in front of the judge."

"You lying S.O.B. You said if I paid the fees, I was done, I could walk."

He smirked. "That's the problem with you, Steven, you think you're above it all."

The two of us yelled back and forth, getting nowhere. Summer stepped in. She'd heard enough. Relax, she told me, just sit tight. She would handle the rest from here. Sure, I mean, what else could I do? I was stuck in this lousy place till someone with any sense did what was right.

Summer was a woman scorned. She didn't take kindly to her husband being lied to, disrespected, and locked up. She'd made the long drive south and wasn't going back unless she had me by her side.

Court was not yet in session when Summer marched up the courthouse steps, down the corridor, past a secretary, and straight into the judge's chambers. The secretary scrambled to apologize to the startled judge, but Summer was the picture of composed determination. She waved my documents in her hand and explained the whole situation.

To his credit, the judge heard her out, then studied my parole agreement. Wearing a frown, he picked up the phone and contacted my P.O. "I have a young lady here from Tennessee," he said, "who claims her husband is sitting this very moment in my jail. Would you like to explain this to me? Mm-hmm. Okay, well, here's what is going to happen. I'll handle the court costs with her through my secretary, then I'm going to send her back to the jail. When she gets there, her husband better be dressed, waiting, and ready to go. Once they're gone, I'd like to speak with you here in my chambers."

Summer reappeared at the jail with jaw set and eyes ablaze. My P.O. could barely look at her. She stepped up to him as we prepared to leave. "Lemme tell you something, you ever mess with me or my husband again, you'll have nothing to fear from him. I'm the one you should worry about. You have everything to fear from me."

Six days after the marshals first knocked at our door, we headed home.

"You hungry?" Summer asked. "You wanna stop for something to eat?"

"What I want is a cigarette," I said. "But not till we've crossed the state line."

42

NORTH IN THE NIGHT

An eBay order arrived at our apartment one afternoon, a pair of used women's jeans. As Summer slipped into them one leg at a time, I admired the fit from across the room but wondered aloud why she hadn't just gone and bought herself some new ones.

"You don't like these on me?"

"Oh, I like them alright. That's not what I said."

"With my height, it's hard finding clothes for my body type," she explained. "When it comes to the older styles and brands, I know the exact right ones for me."

"I suppose they're less expensive, anyway."

She tilted her head my direction. "You'd be surprised."

And I was. With one look at the amount she paid, I saw an opportunity. It led to a booming business as I learned to shop Goodwill, especially on red-tag days, and walk out with dozens of old Levi 501s and other styles which sold online at high margins.

It wasn't just jeans, either. People, I realized, would pay through the nose for a bit of nostalgia. My own interest in Mickey Mouse memorabilia was proof of this, with limited cartoon prints on my office walls and a Mickey phone on my desk. Together, Summer and I scoured thrift stores, estate sales, yard sales, and going-out-of-business sales.

There was money to be made from items of the past. If they held sentimental value, we could convert them into real-world dollars.

Speaking of conversion, I discovered a whole other avenue for generating income. In the mid-2000s, converting British pounds and German marks into US dollars often added to my profit. In England and throughout Europe, there was a demand for certain unattainable American toys, games, and even cold cereal brands. I had British customers buying Lucky Charms at three or four times the price, and I often increased my margins by shipping directly through a surplus supplier.

By 2006 and 2007, Summer and I were making a small fortune. You would think we'd be happy, but our marriage was on the rocks. The ringmaster was constantly stirring crap between us, using the daughter he and Summer had between them to rile Summer's guilt. This poisoned our relationship with discord and pain. Sick of it all, I turned to an old remedy:

Gambling.

Tunica welcomed me back like an old friend, dazzling me again with style, hypnotizing me with lights. Two or three times a week, I headed west into Mississippi and planted myself in front of the blackjack dealers. It was as though nothing had ever changed. The casinos still loved me and my money as much as ever.

As the addiction squeezed tighter, my marriage slipped through my fingers. There were other issues involved, of course, and the divorce was inevitable.

So long to number four.

I was alone again.

Then came the rumblings of a recession, even as Barack Obama and John McCain were ramping up their 2008 presidential campaigns. Not only did the dollar's value against foreign currencies drop, but the eBay market as a whole took a dive almost as deep as my addiction. Between the two, my money began evaporating.

On impulse, I cleaned out my bank accounts, packed my duffel bag, and hit the road, gambling down through Mississippi and Louisiana as I tried to figure things out. By figuring things out, I mostly mean throwing away the rest of my fortune.

Three months later, I was stranded on the outskirts of a Gulf-shore town. The salt air and gentle breeze gave all the hints of ease and luxury, but my tank was almost empty and I was out of money.

I wrote in large block letters on a piece of cardboard:

NEED GAS TO GET TO NASHVILLE.

For hours, I sat alongside the road with my beat-up Toyota Camry station wagon and my flimsy cardboard sign. Close to dusk, a gentleman pulled over and called out from the cab of his pickup. "How much you figure it'll cost ya to fill the tank?"

"Forty should do it," I said.

"Did you lose it all at the tables?"

I lowered my eyes, too despondent to lie. "Every last dime."

"You're not the first and you sure ain't gonna be the last. Well, here ya go. Forty even. Son, you be sure to head straight to the gas station and nowhere in between."

"I'll do that, sir. Thank you."

He checked the traffic over his shoulder, ready to drive off.

"Uh, sir . . . I don't know the area. Can you point me to the nearest station?"

He grinned. "You're in luck—and the right kind, this time. There's a place just down the road from here."

He pointed the way, then drove off. Those two twenties in my pocket stirred my thoughts with possibilities. Forty might earn me hundred, and a hundred might earn me a thousand. My bad luck had to end sometime, right? No, Steven, don't think that way, I scolded myself. You wouldn't be here in the first place if that was how it worked.

Gas. Nashville. Nowhere in between.

Ten minutes later, I was topping off the gas at the BP station when the gentleman eased alongside in his pickup. He gave me a nod of approval, then wished me well on my journey. I thanked him again and headed north in the night toward Tennessee.

I couldn't call my mom or brothers. That door was closed.

And I sure wasn't about to call the ringmaster.

As I rolled into Nashville, one other person came to mind, an old family friend, almost like a cousin to me. She might be kind enough to give me a meal and a bed—and in fact, she did. It was okay for awhile and I found a few paint jobs. Old habits die hard, though, and I was still Steven being Steven, a user of people. When her lease on the duplex came to an end, she began looking for a place across town. I wasn't invited.

Out of prison, out of money, and out of options, I wondered what to do.

My homeless years began as 2008 came to an end. I was fifty-two years old. Hungry and alone, I knew if I ever got truly desperate the Nashville Rescue Mission was open. I checked in for one night, but the place felt to me like self-imposed incarceration. I was just a number again. The noise was incessant. And, as with every mission, there were strings attached.

In this case, it meant mandatory chapel service.

No thanks. I'd rather starve and use a curb as my pillow.

I hadn't been to church in ages and nothing could get me back through those doors. Church? Oh, I'd had my fill of the fake smiles and hallelujahs. A particular deacon came to mind. And my parents. And a youth leader. In their own ways, they'd all turned me away.

And God?

He seemed conspicuously absent or weak. Where was He when I was facedown on a tile floor, violated, humiliated, degraded? After the fact, why hadn't He at least put an ounce of concern into my mother's churchgoing Baptist heart?

Instead of separating His truth from others' lies, I just blamed the Big Guy for it all and staggered off into the darkness, cutting myself off from my one true hope. I couldn't fathom there was a lesson to be learned here. I couldn't imagine anything such as healthy, godly discipline, administered out of tough love. The only discipline I'd ever received from a father was a good ass-whoopin' based on his fickle moods.

My Heavenly Father, I'm sure, was trying to get my attention. He still saw me as worthwhile and valuable. He would use my time on the streets the way a person might use a broom to pound a carpet, each firm whack clearing the dust and grit from its worn fabric.

Be that as it may, I wasn't about to lie down just yet.

Not for Him. No, not for anyone.

43

THE GAME

I hadn't yet accepted that I was homeless. My family friend's duplex had two days left on the lease, and she had already moved out. The place was empty. With my spare key, I let myself in to spend one night on the floor. It was cold but better than staying in my car. Assuming the door locks would be changed soon, I rigged the back window in hopes I could come back through there again. Who would even check it?

Someone checked it. The next night, it was locked.

As it got dark, I sat in my old station wagon, arms folded, hands tucked under my armpits, my breath freezing on the insides of the windows. I don't think I have ever felt more lost. In some ways, that first night in my car was more terrifying than my first night in prison. Behind bars, I had structure and stability. I had a schedule, a meal, and a bed. Here, in the thin, cold air of my car, I had nothing but questions.

Where was I going to go? What was I going to do? When the light of dawn woke me up, how would I spend the next sixteen waking hours of hopelessness, to be followed by more of the same the next day and the next?

I parked in the cul-de-sac. My eyes darted to the end of the street, waiting for a cop to pull up. Every sound made me jump. A fitful sleep overcame me, until a knock on my driver's-side window brought me bolt upright in my seat.

"Can't sleep here, sir." It was a vigilant neighbor. "You'll have to move on."

For two nights, I shifted my car about the area in an effort to remain unnoticed and get some rest. Now, though, food was becoming an issue. Hungry, weary, and emotionally raw, I applied for jobs and got no response. Could I work? Absolutely. Could I find a job? Not a one. We were now in a deep recession and there was no hiding my criminal past on applications. Even if I tried, it would turn up on background checks.

I had no income. I had no food. I had no home.

Really my homelessness had started forty years earlier, at age twelve, on the day I told Dad and Mom about the deacon's abuse. Whatever nurture and support should have been available fluttered away with those words uttered by my father: "What did you do to make him think that's what you wanted?"

With that as my childhood backdrop, the thought of home was a joke to me, and a house was just a box with a roof.

Now each morning was a sharp jab in my ribs, a frank appraisal of a life which no longer matched any of my clever fabrications. I wasn't a competent nightclub or restaurant manager. I wasn't the DJ everyone loved to hang out with. I wasn't the sharp-dressed gambler or the profitable online marketeer. I wasn't even a husband to any of my four ex-wives. Yes, I was a father, but certainly not a dad.

And I was a homeless person.

No amount of lying to myself could change this harsh truth.

Even in prison, I'd had my release date to look forward to and trusted there was something better for me out there. It helped me live the lie just a little longer. Not now, though. I couldn't live the lie here in my old Camry. I just felt paralyzed. Part of it was the shame, hoping no one would learn of my situation. Part of it was being stuck, just me and my demons—nowhere else to turn, nothing else to distract me.

Is this what I've come to? I asked myself as I got in line at The Contributor.

A local newspaper created to assist the needy, The Contributor was my last good option. I was joined by all types—teenagers in hoodies, old toothless ladies, men in wheelchairs, couples with puppies, business-looking types, and twentysomething women whose good looks were marred by weathered skin and the jitters.

"Here you go." My first ten papers were free. "That'll get you started."

From that point on, I worked as an independent contractor, purchasing papers at wholesale and selling them for retail. If I didn't sell off my supply, I was out that amount of money. It was as legitimate as any other sales I'd done, and some guys and gals spent ten, twelve, fourteen hours a day working their corners. They arrived before the morning traffic backed up and stayed till after evening rush hour.

As with real estate, the key was location, location, location. My first day out, I stood at the intersection of Donelson and Elm Hill Pike. The traffic was good, but the turn lane had short gaps between lights which didn't allow me much time to sell my papers. On my best day I pocketed $12, basically a dollar an hour. I spent it all on food, coffee, and a gallon or two of gas. Those first few nights, I found quiet corners of parking lots and sacked out in my car until some security cop or store manager asked me to move. I wasn't yet committed to this life. I was still shell-shocked by my circumstances.

Soon after, I tried a place down Murfreesboro Road. It wasn't much better.

Where next? The thought of setting up on a corner downtown horrified me. With all my years in Music City, I was bound to see someone I knew. Lord, I hoped that didn't happen. What if they realized I was living out of my car?

By selling the paper, I managed to eat on a regular basis. As spring, then summer, moved in, it turned warm enough that I could park in a corner lot or alleyway, unroll my sleeping bag under a nearby tree, and not worry about thieves targeting my empty ol' clunker. As humbling as it was, I also accepted food, drink, or clothing offered to me, but I never asked for money, not once in five years on the streets. It was one thing to receive the kindness of a stranger, and something else altogether to expect or beg for it.

Nevertheless, I was now labeled.

I was a beggar and a bum. An addict and an asshole.

Jobless, useless, clueless, a nuisance.

Poor and destitute. Mooching off those with actual jobs. Most likely mentally ill. Probably with a criminal past.

While there's no denying my gambling and burglarizing were part of my story, the rest of these labels had no bearing on my situation. I could dredge up more accurate labels for myself, but you've already heard enough about my past. You get the point.

In many ways, I was more vilified on the streets than in prison. During my incarceration, I was sheltered, even protected, from society's judgment. As convicts, we were all equal, following the same routine, doing our time. We existed in a realm of our own, oblivious to the world's opinions of us. Once I was discharged, I still had some dignity intact. I had paid my debt to society.

On the streets, however, society threw more debts in my face. I heard it all. I ought to clean up, get a job, go to church, stop smoking, drinking, using, get some counseling, get right with God. I faced judgment every day. It was public. It was constant. It was apparent in the faces that turned away as much as in the glares and bitter scowls. It ranged from pity to ridicule to degradation.

I also dealt with the fact that my family knew I was out here and they did nothing. As rotten as I'd been through the years, their apathy was still hard to swallow.

"Are you really homeless?" a guy once asked me. "You don't look homeless."

"Well," I said, "can you tell me what homeless looks like?"

Here's what I really wanted to say: "So lemme get this straight, if I take care of myself and maintain a little pride, then you can judge me as a moocher and not feel any need to do a thing. And if I look bedraggled and dirty, then you can judge me as a lazy-ass bum and simply walk on by. Seems to me, I'm S.O.L. either way."

The guy's comment made me face things more pragmatically. The truth was, I could stand on the corner with newspapers in hand, hair combed, clean-shaven, shirt tucked in, and get nothing, while the stumbling drunk on the sidewalk got handed a twenty-dollar bill. As much as I hated it, I would have to play the game. Not by any rules the homeless community had come up with, but by the rules society made.

I quit shaving, let my hair grow shaggy.

Put on a ball cap. Scuffed my shoes.

Bought matching T-shirts, pants, and shorts so I could change into clean clothes, while always appearing to be in the same tired outfit.

I did what was necessary, part of this sad, stupid game, and as you might have guessed, I started making more money. The game was rigged, that much was obvious. By these rules, did anyone ever escape homelessness? Did anyone ever win?

44

ACROSS THE FIELD

I was a free man. Even though I didn't have a place to live, at least I no longer answered to the Department of Corrections. I no longer wore handcuffs or waist chains. Was I really free, though? Hell, no.

The hardest chains to break were within.

Anger and hatred. Shame and self-pity.

They coiled and clanked about my chest, metallic serpents locking onto my heart and refusing to let go. They injected venomous memories into my blood. They fed off me, drained me of life, and left my heart pale. Doctors will tell you how emotional issues can contribute to physical ailments, just as bodily sickness can lead to depression and despair. For me, the cycle kept coiling back on itself.

How, some have asked, could I go hungry in the land of the free? How could a kid from the suburbs end up penniless on the streets?

It happens every day, believe me.

To commuters, I was a reminder of an America hurting more than it cares to admit. I was one of thousands who could no longer pay bills or deal with mental illness or reconcile hopes and dreams with the hypocrisy all around. We were on the bottom looking up. We saw this country's underbelly. And it wasn't always a pretty picture.

I needed another change in scenery. As a humid Tennessee summer segued into a a new school year, with leaves turning and evenings shortening, I shifted to a more affluent area on the other side of Nashville. Green Hills is home to many medical professionals, country music stars, and dozens upon dozens of churches. If not always friendly to those on the streets, it has at least the veneer of Southern good manners.

Early each day, I set up at an intersection on Hillsboro Road near one of the churches. With lights stopping cars from all directions, I had time to sell *The Contributor* to doctors, lawyers, landscapers, and soccer moms. Some resented my presence and stared straight ahead. Others smiled, waved, bought the paper, and offered a blessing.

This one guy who lived across the street, he started providing a hot drink for me every morning. I never even knew his name. With no judgment or expectation, he set the drink on his doorstep in an insulated container. "I left you a cup of coffee over there," he would say before carrying on with his day. His small effort meant a lot.

The nearby church operated a private school on its property. Though it had no playground, it did have a field, and daily the kids came out and ran three laps. By this time, I was a fixture, always on my corner, and they waved at me as they passed by. I waved back. I loved the joy in their distant voices. I missed the laughter of my nephews and stepdaughters. It made me wonder about my own son.

Where was Josh these days? How was he doing? Why, he must be in his twenties by now. There was so much of his life I had missed, so much of my own I had wasted.

As the students circled the field each day, they always had a chubby kid trailing behind. His schoolmates chided him to hurry, to stop dragging his feet. A nice kid, he seemed to take it all in stride, even as he came in last again and again.

Oftentimes, he glanced up at me as he huffed by. "Hey, mister," he called.

"Hey," I called back with a wave.

One day I couldn't help myself. I set down my papers, hopped the ditch, and jogged alongside him. "C'mon, buddy," I said. "You can make it."

Some of the others teased from a distance, and even though they weren't mean-spirited about it, it caused the boy's shoulders to sag.

"Don't worry, you got this," I said. "We'll finish this together."

His name was Charles, I found out. The next afternoon I did the same thing, joining him for his laps. Some of the others shrugged, cut across the field, and joined us. It got to a point where none of the students stopped running until Charles was done, with many encouraging him along the way. This didn't go unnoticed, of course, and parents and teachers began waving at me as they arrived and departed from the school.

A man in business attire pulled up beside me one morning. I never knew whether to expect a five-dollar bill, a middle finger, or an evangelistic tract. His window lowered, and he said, "You're Steven, is that correct?"

Cautious, I nodded.

"Well, thank you," he said, reaching through the window to shake my hand. "My son, Charles, he thinks you hung the moon. It hasn't always been easy for him, but his mother and I've seen a real difference in him lately."

"Charles is a good kid. You should be proud."

December, 2009. Decorations brightened the Mall at Green Hills, the Bluebird Cafe, and West Nashville's busy thoroughfares. Salvation Army bells rang outside Whole Foods Market as carols played from fancy stereo systems in Porsche Cayennes and BMWs. As a person selling papers on a corner, I felt sorely out of place. Sales had declined, and my Christmas mood was low to nonexistent.

At the nearby school, things were about to shut down for the holidays. I saw movement from that direction and turned. A group of teachers, parents, and students were floating my way across the field.

"Be careful," I cautioned them. "Don't cross the ditch."

They came anyway, arms bearing gifts. They handed me practical items, such as socks and gloves and fast-food gift cards—always appreciated! They also gave me cookies with red and green frosting, homemade Christmas cards, and a scarf crocheted in sections by a number of the kids—almost too much for my heart to bear!

I thanked them all, then realized someone was missing. Where was Charles?

"Charles," a teacher explained, "was absolutely heartbroken that he couldn't be here. His family's on Christmas vacation, and he really wanted to give you his card in person. You've really made an impact on him."

Me? The guy living out of his car?

Well, how about that for a Christmas miracle?

Choking back tears, I said, "Tell him I loved it. His card means the world to me."

45

GOLDEN ARCHES

I never did see Charles again. A week later, on Christmas Eve, I realized my Green Hills location wasn't going to cut it through the winter. With schools closed and the weather turning, my paper sales were down. Weekends were dismal. I couldn't make it if I stayed here much longer, so I loaded up, put a few gallons in my car, and headed across town.

On the south end of Metro Nashville, there was an available spot at McDonald's, near the intersection of Nolensville Pike and Old Hickory Boulevard. A homeless buddy was leaving the area and he said sales by the golden arches were steady all day, not just during morning and evening rush hours. As a rule, *The Contributor* mapped out a spot for its consistent salespeople, and they agreed to let me take over this particular one.

I parked nearby, then set up by a tree on a corner. I wasn't pushy. If you wanted a paper, it was yours for a dollar or two. If not, have a good day.

In 2010 and 2011, my sales climbed quickly, relying on traffic from a Lowe's hardware store, an Office Max, two fast-food places, and shops in the strip mall. Sometimes other homeless guys cut in on me with scrawled signs and obnoxious behavior, but I mostly let them be. Once they rounded up enough money, they usually took off to buy booze or cigarettes. I was in it for the long-term, not just for a quick fix.

With all the vehicles passing me each day, it was inevitable I would be recognized by someone from my past, even here, far from where I grew up on the other end of Davidson County. The first time it happened, though, I was mortified. I dropped my head, turned, and pretended to dig for something in my bag hanging from a tree branch.

Were they gone? Okay, good, they didn't see me.

Minutes later, they circled back. "Steven? Steven Young? I thought that was you. What're you doing out here?"

"I don't want to talk about it," I mumbled.

The shame was debilitating. I walked straight into McDonald's, locked myself in a bathroom stall, and stayed there for thirty minutes. Two days passed before I could return to my spot. No matter where I went, the chains inside still bound me.

I was a loner on the streets, just as I'd been in prison. Very territorial. Some of my homeless friends, they liked hanging out with each other. Misery loves company, and they drank and griped together. In the evenings, they filled a booth at McDonald's and often grew loud and belligerent. I wanted none of that. I didn't buddy up with anyone. I was on an island of my own making, in exile from society.

Bitterness ate at me. Distrust clouded every interaction with others. Though I could have saved up enough money to get a cheap room somewhere, I had no interest in that. I would still be trapped with myself and my issues. Money had never solved my problems. Marriage was a roller coast that always ended in disillusionment. My successes just propped me up for more failures. If getting off the streets meant going back to being the same person, no thank you.

Homelessness is hopelessness. It does a number on you. If a person is on the streets for over six months, their odds of returning to regular society drop drastically. It's easy to both resent the culture at large and to think it owes you something at the same time. I saw this with many of those around me.

One fellow named Rodney, he was as normal as you or I to start. Like me, he loved to cook, and he was known to serve up some fried seasoned tofu, which everyone swore was delicious. Being on the streets messed with Rodney's head, though. He shifted belief systems every few months, became a frequent pot-smoker, and spouted conspiracy theories. He went from being a friendly, open guy to being paranoid.

My years behind bars actually helped on the streets. I knew how to look after myself and how to do without. I also knew how to establish a routine.

There at Nolensville and Old Hickory, I entered McDonald's every morning after sunrise, washed my face, brushed my teeth, got a cup of coffee, then went to my spot by the tree as consistently as an employee punching a clock. Late in the afternoons, I headed to the Edmondson Pike Library and logged onto a public computer. At nightfall, I drove to Exxon for some cheap food, which I ate in my car while listening to sports-talk radio before going to sleep. Not only did these patterns help my days pass quicker, they kept me moderately sane.

I have to say, McDonald's treated me well. I came and went without ever making a fuss, and in turn, they stopped charging me for hot coffee and cold drinks. Customers weren't always as kind. They sometimes whispered or pointed as I walked in, and I can't say it didn't hurt.

The employees at Lowe's were also good to me. I always tidied up my spot by the tree, taking pride in it. They showed appreciation for this as they came and went from work, treating me with respect. Cultivating these relationships was important to me. I was Steven, the guy on the corner, a fellow human being, selling The Contributor and trying to survive the same as anyone else.

Over three or four years beneath those golden arches, I eked out a living. The same commuters passed each day, some never looking my way, others acknowledging me with a wave or a nod. A number became my regular customers.

Does it sound fun? It wasn't.

Here, lemme explain . . .

46

ALL THAT'S WRONG IN THE WORLD

You probably have a general idea of what an abusive childhood looks like. Perhaps you've seen it depicted in a documentary or in a film, or you yourself went through the same horrors I did. I don't pretend my experiences are unique.

You can probably also picture a day in prison, based on books you've read or movies you've seen. If you've heard the jokes about being someone's bitch, it's probably not something you worry about. As long as you obey the law, or at least avoid getting caught while bending the rules, it's doubtful you will ever get locked up.

Homelessness is harder to pin down.

How could people sink that low? Could it happen to you?

Many Americans live paycheck to paycheck, barely keeping their heads above water. They work hard to avoid ending up on the streets, and as long as they can make it month to month they feel justified eyeballing that grimy guy or gal on the corner and convincing themselves they will never end up like that.

As I've said from the start, though, everyone is somebody's kid. That guy, that gal, they matter. They too are created in God's image.

Are they helpless victims? Of course not.

Are they responsible for their choices? We all are.

The truth is, even if they are reaping consequences for their actions, they don't deserve to die of heat exhaustion or malnourishment. They don't deserve to be beat up in their sleeping bags or struck intentionally by passing vehicles in the dead of night. They don't deserve to have their out-of-sight tents bulldozed with no warning at the crack of dawn. No one is beyond the reach of God's love.

Daily, I felt like a man on display, my failures plain for all to see. For each friendly smile I received, I also got three or four scowls, rude gestures, or shouted slurs. For those hunting others to judge, the homeless are always in season. There are no regulations or game wardens. They're easy targets, open game. Go on, take a shot. Nobody will mind. You might even be cheered on for telling them like it is.

"How long've you been homeless?" I was asked more than once.

"Two or three years."

"So what was it, huh? Alcohol, drugs, or both?"

There was no room for conversation. Ninety percent of those passing by thought they had me figured out. I was an alcoholic, a crackhead, or a tweaker. End of discussion.

A guy stopped in his truck one afternoon, a smile on his face. "You hungry?"

"Sure," I said.

He handed me a pizza box through the window, then smiled as he drove away. He seemed in a good mood and I was thankful for a little variety in my diet. I peeled back the lid only to find some half-eaten pizza crusts.

Others threw drinks at me.

Or zinged their garbage at me like I was a target.

I'll never forget the elderly fellow who pulled up in his shiny, old, black Cadillac. "Son," he called, as he powered down his window, "I've been preaching the gospel forty-plus years. If you'll just give your life over to Jesus, He'll get you out of this."

"Thanks, Pastor. Can I ask you something, though?"

"Sure, you can ask me anything."

"What makes you think that I haven't?"

He was swift with his response. "If you had, you wouldn't be in this mess."

"Well, thank you for stopping by. Thanks for your words of wisdom."

"Now, you listen to what I'm telling you. You can get out of this situation, if you just heed the things I'm saying." The pastor's words, uttered without any personal concern or context, seemed simplistic if not downright cruel.

Most people, when asked, guess that summers are easier than winters for the homeless community. In some ways, yes. I'll tell you this, though, hot and cold are both miserable. Both extremes demand a toll. Nashville regularly reaches the 100-degree mark in June, July, and August, and the Cumberland Basin creates a pressure cooker of humidity. Sweat drips into your eyes, your ears. It magnifies the rays that burn your skin. Heat exhaustion depletes the body and brain of resources. Moods turn cranky. Feet blister on hot pavement. Body odor is unavoidable. The stench of exhaust and diesel fumes poison the lungs, and high pollen count leaves many of the homeless with watery eyes and swollen glands.

Since standing somewhere highly visible was my key to selling papers and earning a buck, I endured ten to twelve hours at a time in that sizzling heat. It was all part of the job, but it was tough. For a landscaper or roofer, there is the hope of a shower and a cold beer at the end of the day, a burger or pizza, an hour or two in front of the TV. For me, there was just another sweltering evening in my station wagon, windows down, mosquitoes buzzing, cicadas raking the night with their high-pitched calls.

I've always liked my blankets pulled up tight. As a kid, I hid under the covers to shut out my parents' shouting in the other room or their ominous footsteps in the hall. Sleeping in my car, I still wanted my blankets close and secure. I was torn between dripping sweat all night long or feeling physically and emotionally vulnerable.

In the winters, of course, I couldn't snuggle deep enough into my bedding. As temperatures dropped, nights in the car turned torturous. My feet became blocks of ice even in three pairs of socks. By four or five in the morning, I shivered uncontrollably. It was not enough to layer pants and sweatpants over long johns, or a heavy coat over shirts and sweatshirts. Ice crystals clung to my beard. Even with my sleeping bag and some hand warmers, there was no escaping the bitter cold.

I parked in various places, trying to avoid harassment by security officers and buffeting winds. A solid sixty minutes of sleep was rare. I bought a tent and tried that out, finding a hidden spot up in the woods. The conditions weren't any better, and the first heavy rains turned my shelter into a soggy disaster.

Dawn was always a welcome sight. Thank God for that free McDonald's coffee.

As spring returned, a woman pulled alongside me one morning. She barely acknowledged my existence. Though her windows were down, she didn't even attempt to lower her voice as she spoke to her daughters in the backseat. The girls were maybe ten and twelve.

"If you don't start behaving and doing better in school," she said, "if you don't start listening to your father and me, you are going to end up like that man right there, that worthless piece-of-trash bum. Is that what you want?"

I heard it all clearly.

Each word cut like a razor.

Two pretty little heads swiveled my way, examining this example of all that was wrong in the world. I found myself peering into round eyes fraught with fear. Their expressions were even more cutting than their mother's words. They saw me exactly as she had described me. I was what worthless looked like.

Living on the streets wasn't really living. It was drudgery. It was an existence full of questions, nightmares, and regrets. Home was dead to me, and even the family I did have was slipping away. My brother Byron passed on April 15, 2012. Mom followed on October 8, 2012. I heard the news through the grapevine, and I wasn't even invited to her memorial service.

Was I supposed to feel some profound sadness?

I didn't feel much of anything.

As the holidays came and went with zero connection to my own flesh and blood, I made a silent vow. This is it, I told myself. I can't do it anymore. I'll die before allowing myself to go through another Christmas alone.

47

TARGETED

Telling someone "I love you" should be more than just words and emotion. It should be a commitment to action. Though I'd accepted Jesus as a twelve-year-old boy, I had a skewed view of love and I've only lately realized that truly loving Jesus takes action. Actions can be seen and felt. Loving others requires the same thing. If someone doesn't feel loved, it takes more than trite phrases to fix that.

As I stood there at Nolensville Road through the hot summer, cooler autumn, and chilling winter of 2012, I experienced love in action from one person in particular.

Mike Dotson is a Bible-believing, Jesus-loving man. He is a husband and father. He serves on the council of his local church. He's fluent in Spanish and goes on regular outreach trips to Latin America. Of course, none of that mattered to me in my day-to-day existence. What mattered was that Mike stopped consistently to offer me food and ask how I was doing. He even waited around to hear my responses.

I didn't say much at first. I made it tough. What did this short guy with glasses want from me? Was I supposed to go to church with him? Did he want to parade me around as his trophy of good deeds?

Mike kept coming by. Didn't he see he was wasting his time? What if he knew the truth about me? I shot him down with snide remarks, ribbed him, and gave him the cold shoulder—still do sometimes—but none of it deterred him. He was the first person who refused to give up on me.

In snippets, I began sharing my story—the failed marriages, the gambling, the years in prison. He took it all in stride. I learned to spot from afar the real estate door magnets on his car and secretly looked forward to his visits.

Over the months that followed, Mike never tried feeding my soul until he was sure my stomach had been fed. He was forthright about his own faith without being pushy or manipulative. His concerns were genuine. He not only treated me as a fellow human being but as a friend. Where others had preyed upon my weaknesses, he prayed for God to give me strength. He told me I was worthy in God's sight.

I almost wanted to believe it. Was there any truth to what he was saying?

Careful now, I warned myself. In the past, any time I had cracked open the door of my heart for a whiff of kindness or forgiveness, there'd been someone to come along and slam that door back in my face. I'd slammed the door on others too. I wasn't some innocent victim here. It was all part of the pattern, dishing out and accepting mistreatment because I believed it was what I deserved.

What about now? What about Mike? Could I trust him?

I was wary. To trust was to become a target, and the homeless are targeted every day. Sure, I could converse with Mr. Mike Dotson and accept his tokens of friendship, but I still wasn't going to let him get too close.

For the homeless, predators come in all sorts of disguises. Whether it's a contractor looking for cheap labor, a church lady wanting to save a soul, or a sex fiend hoping to score, there is always trouble to avoid. A lone woman on the streets has it especially rough. Who's going to believe her if she calls for help or goes to the police? Will anyone care?

And men on the streets aren't treated much better. To many, they're just freeloading drunks and bums.

Since my corner was near an exit of the Lowe's parking lot, it wasn't uncommon for painters in panel vans or handymen in pickups to stop and ask if I wanted to make some extra cash. Nashville has typically been a resilient economy and construction is usually booming. There are always new homes, apartments, and condos going up somewhere. I'm a big guy, able-bodied, and contractors could pay me under the table, avoid taxes, and save a bundle by not hiring a professional.

When asked to help, I often said yes. I painted, hung drywall, did manual labor. More often than not, though, these guys took advantage and paid me less than promised.

"Hell, no," I would say. "That's not what we agreed upon."

"It is what it is, man. Just be grateful you got some work."

"But a deal's a deal. If you say something, I expect you to stick to it. This barely comes out to minimum wage."

"Listen, I could've paid a real painter and it would've been done hours ago. I'm doing you a favor, see? Be happy for the beer money."

"I don't even drink."

"Yeah, right."

This happened on more than one occasion. These contractors were well aware I had no legal recourse. And if I simply accepted their abuse, I lost yet another ounce of my dignity. It was a no-win situation, and I stopped responding to their offers of work.

As Nashville's homeless community expanded, with over three hundred selling *The Contributor* at intersections throughout the city, many citizens grew uncomfortable. The issues on society's underbelly were too painfully visible for some to tolerate. Public perception soured and politicians cracked down. Less people bought the paper, and *The Contributor* scaled back. Homeless men and women were attacked in sleeping bags, hovels, and alleyways. Teens raided homeless camps, slicing tents and setting things on fire, with little to no repercussions. Various churches and ministries showed concern, with some offering genuine help. Many, however, lacked any real follow-through.

I encountered this myself one Tuesday afternoon, when a lady pulled up beside me outside McDonald's. "Well, hello there, how're you doing?"

"Doing good, ma'am. How are you?"

"I see you out here most every day and I bet it gets awfully boring. Would you be interested in attending a Bible study this Thursday night at our church?"

Thanks to the sincerity I'd seen in Mike Dotson, I didn't reject this woman outright. Coming from a kind-faced stranger, her invitation sparked my interest. Whether or not God was involved, it sure felt nice to have someone reach out to me.

"Yes, I would," I said.

"Oh, great," she exclaimed. "And while you're there, we also have a shower and laundry you can use. Is that something you would enjoy?"

"That would be nice, ma'am. Thank you."

"Then I'll be here at five on Thursday."

For years, I had been focused on only today. Or on my past. Now, for the first time in ages, I dared to do something radical by living in anticipation. How long had it been since I enjoyed a hot shower? What would it be like to have clean clothes? And who knew, the Bible study might even provide some sorely needed hope.

The rest of Tuesday seemed to take forever.

Wednesday dragged.

At last, Thursday arrived, and even then the morning hours crawled by. Noon came and went. Four, four-thirty . . . five!

From my usual spot, I saw no sign of the church lady. Thirty minutes later I was still expectant, certain she had been delayed by rush hour traffic. Sixty minutes went by. Ninety. For three hours I waited before accepting the fact she was not coming. Well, good luck getting me to show up for another Bible study.

Fool me once, shame on you. Fool me twice, shame on me.

Oftentimes, the biggest lies spoken to the homeless are by Christians. They send out armies of Bible-toting do-gooders who preach at the rescue mission or in the camps or one-on-one, saying "God loves you and we love you" while ignoring empty stomachs, ailing hearts, fragile minds. Even if they're kind enough to hand out sandwiches, apples, and bags of chips, they rarely return. There is no long-term trust established.

Was I surprised? Hardly.

Curled up in my car with my sleeping bag pulled tight around my neck, I felt straight-line winds rock the chassis and wondered where the church lady was resting tonight. Wherever it was, she wouldn't have any cops knocking on her window and telling her she didn't belong there. She wouldn't be asked to move along. As she faded off into dreamland, the real surprise would be if she even had a thought of me in her head.

48

IN SHORT SUPPLY

People often want to know which was worse, my years in prison or my years on the streets. Neither was a picnic, lemme tell you, and they both did serious damage.

Prison is worse in regards to confinement, violence, and constant fear. Few places are safe. You have to worry about fists and knives. The experience turns you into a faceless pawn, moved here and there, barely capable of making decisions for yourself or exerting any autonomy. Once you are out, you have to live with it on your record for the rest of your days. It comes up in job interviews, silences you at election time, and limits you in other ways. It's a permanent scar.

The streets are worse in regards to mental welfare. You have no money, no means, and nowhere left to run. You are at the end of your rope, confronted with your own failures in relationships, the workplace, and society. You are stripped of everything. The unrelenting pressures to find a meal and a place to sleep shrink your entire world into a self-centered, self-pitying scramble for survival. On the other hand, the moment you shower, shave, and get a roof over your head, you're back to being viewed as a normal person. You don't carry some homeless mark on your official records.

I will say this: I don't fear being back in prison the way I fear being back on the streets. As long as I live, I'll dread the thought of ever winding up homeless again.

At times, my fears from prison and the streets collided. One winter afternoon in 2013, I was at my usual spot, selling *The Contributor,* when a patrol car pulled in off Nolensville Road and faced me from the Lowe's parking lot. A female officer sat watching me from behind her wheel and I felt distinctly uncomfortable. My criminal past could lead others to make rash judgments and assumptions about me, and cops sniffing around quickened my pulse. To this day the sight of a courthouse or courtroom stirs those old fears.

What did she want? I wondered. My area was spotless. I never left trash or made a scene or drank alcohol. Normally Metro police officers just said hi and left me alone. Maybe she was new to the job. Well, I still had work of my own to do.

She finally pulled up next to me, her window down.

"How're you doing today, officer?" I said.

"Do you have your permit?"

"What permit?"

"The city permit to sell the paper."

If this was supposed to intimidate me, it didn't work. "We are covered under the First Amendment, officer. I don't need one."

She mulled that over. "Well, do you have your vendor badge?"

"It's in my bag."

"Can you show it to me?"

I fetched it from my bag and dangled it from my fingers.

"Can you please hand it to me? And I would like to see your ID."

Heart still pounding, I complied. I was annoyed by this harassment which did neither of us any favors. She was interfering with my business. She ran my info through her on-board computer before handing everything back.

"Didn't find anything, did you?" I said. "No outstanding warrants."

She shrugged. "It'll be a cold one tonight, so I was just doing a welfare check."

Considering I'd had homeless friends die every year of exposure to extreme summer or winter conditions, it was a nice sentiment, but I knew she was full of it. My vendor badge and ID had nothing to do with where I would be sleeping when the temperatures dropped below freezing.

And this wouldn't be the last time she and I talked.

We'd run into each other again down the road.

On days such as this, with fingertips frozen and a nose like an icicle, my chains nearly brought me to my knees. Remorse was heavy around my neck. Even Mike Dotson, with his Christlike love and listening ears, didn't know the worst of my past. He didn't yet know about the deacon. Didn't know about the attack at Parchman. What would he think if he had all the facts? Would he stop coming by?

I still had no future and no destination. If faith is the substance of things hoped for, as it says in Hebrews 11:1, then I was in short supply. Each day was just more of the same to me. This hopelessness revealed itself in the monotony of a simple poem:

GOING NOWHERE

Going nowhere
Nowhere to go
Passing moments
Passing slow
Hear my heartache
Feel my pain
Nothing changes
All stays the same
Going nowhere
Nowhere to go
Going nowhere
Nowhere to go

Christmas was only weeks away and I was on my own. Where could I go to give and receive gifts, to share hugs and laughs, to toast loved ones on New Year's Eve? I'd ruined everything good in my life. I had no ties to my son Josh. And what about Andy, my one true love? Was she still alive? How had life treated her? Better than I had, I hoped.

A year ago I had made a silent vow. With that now in mind, I started hoarding and making plans. This Christmas would be my last.

49

OVER AND DONE

Over three decades earlier, I'd made headlines by nearly ending my life with a jump off the Shelby Avenue Bridge. The old bridge, now called the John Siegenthaler Pedestrian Bridge, is closed to automobiles and provides a beautiful view of the skyline for those on foot or bicycle. Spanning the Cumberland River, it connects the city to East Nashville and to Nissan Stadium where the Tennessee Titans play. On the west side, it dips down into SoBro—the South of Broadway district—where the Schermerhorn Symphony Center, Johnny Cash Museum, and Martin's BBQ offer a variety of local experiences.

Somewhere above this hodgepodge of activity sat Andrea.

Andy to me.

Though I didn't know it at the time, my first wife was still in Nashville and worked in an office overlooking the seedy downtown warehouse that once served as my apartment. As I questioned God and wrestled with my demons, my five-foot-two, hazel-eyed ex faced battles of her own. She would later recount them to me in person.

Andy, with coiffed blond hair, stared intensely out the window of her highrise office. A few blocks away, the iron girders of the former Shelby Avenue Bridge reminded her of our short marriage, my flagrant adultery, and the suicide scare. That was a lifetime ago. Past history. Yet still she wondered:

What had happened to me? Was I even alive still?

After Andy's and my divorce in 1981, she had gone numb. Though she kept her job at the law firm, she partied, drank, did recreational drugs, slept around. Her friends worried about her.

Over the next three years, she settled down and married a dependable, stable man. He was a good athlete, dancer, and father. She gained a stepson by marriage, and in 1990 birthed a son of her own. She loved both boys dearly. She got saved along the way, and as a family they were deeply involved in their local church and ballgames. The envy of all their friends.

After ten years of marriage, though, Andy was fed up. The constant target of her husband's putdowns and jokes, she sought help from a Christian therapist. During the first few sessions, Andy talked about her early years. Andy had already forgiven me for the past, but when she opened up about her first marriage to yours truly it took five weeks of sessions to cover all of the damage done.

Five weeks! Okay, I'm not proud of that.

Through the course of her counseling, Andy was advised to separate from her husband and take time to figure things out. Soon, she divorced the man. Her sweet boy, a toddler too young to understand, was heartbroken. As a result, Andy did what she thought was right at the time and remarried her husband. For awhile, all was well.

Andy also had rejection issues from childhood and from the discovery at age seventeen that her biological father worked nearby as a physician. After seven years of learning about him, she met him in person by making an appointment for a physical under a different name. Her father recognized her immediately, cleared his schedule, and spent two hours talking with her. It was the only time she would ever meet him in person, and despite his promises, he would call her but once after that. Years later, she would learn he had died of a heart attack.

That one day with him, while it lasted, had been the best day of her life.

In the mid-1990s, after fourteen years at a law firm, Andy reached a point of career burnout. She got a position at a nonprofit firm. She climbed the corporate ladder, garnered accolades, became the COO, and eventually earned six figures a year. In the midst of her success, her husband's old habits came roaring back—the verbal jabs, the belittling remarks. As the distance grew between them, Andy began drinking regularly with friends after work. Surrounded by sharp-dressed men, she cheated on her husband after nineteen years of marriage and numbed her guilt with even more alcohol. She was working late hours, taking cross-country flights, attending weekend conventions, and making regular jaunts to Puerto Rico.

Her husband, naturally, realized something was wrong, and once their youngest son headed off to college, she finally called it quits.

Her friends and church family were flabbergasted.

After twenty-five years? How could she divorce the man again?

For Andy, it was the end of the hypocrisy. She stopped going to church and threw herself into the partying life. She ate up all the attention as a successful, self-assured woman. Shame dissolved in the blur of the dance floor and the alcohol. She tried her best to suppress the rejection, guilt, and shame which triggered most of her behavior.

Soon after divorcing her husband for the second time, she lost both of her parents, one in 2011 and one in 2014. It was a tough time. She had her son and her job to hold onto, both of which gave her joy and purpose.

Alone one night in her rental home, she called out to God. She had always loved the worship songs at church, but in her current state she couldn't even recall a single word or melody. The Lord seemed so far away. Lying face-up on her bed, she felt her eyes brim with tears. She cried out in a prayer more desperate than human words, a groaning from the depths of her soul:

Oh, Jesus, hear my cry. Heal my heart. I need you!

In the midst of this prayer, she watched black creatures, almost bat-like, flutter from her body and dart toward the ceiling. Was it just her imagination? Were they actual spiritual entities or simply symbols of her guilty behaviors? Did it matter? Either way, she sensed an instant release from years of guilt and shame. God was here with her. Her trust was in Jesus. Her male rejection issues were also over and done with.

When she woke up the next morning, she felt light as a feather, and all those lyrics from the worship songs came bubbling up from her heart.

Then came a diagnosis of cancer.

Years earlier this might've crushed her, but where Andy would have once feared for her life, she was now able to handle the news with grace and faith, confident at last that her Heavenly Father was all she needed. He was enough.

50

MY TERMS

If God is love, and love makes the world go round, then the absence of love can be a fatal, cataclysmic event. It can occur with a single phone call, a two-minute conversation—or a lifetime of failed relationships.

There wasn't any exact earth-shattering moment for me.

I just knew I was done.

Aside from the efforts of a few individuals such as Mike Dotson, love was nowhere to be found in my life. I didn't fault anyone else for this. I was the one to blame. In all my failed attempts, I was the common element—not a good feeling, I assure you. I had rushed into marriages and affairs without weighing the consequences. I'd damaged others' hearts and lives.

Stephanie, Kate, Ashley, Summer.

My stepdaughters.

Josh.

And worst of all, Andy.

Andrea Thompson was my first love, and in one year of marriage I had cheated on her, attempted suicide, got sent to the psych ward, and been put in prison. If she was still around, I was the last person she would ever want to see. My face would be the bookmark in a horror story she'd rather forget.

I was now a fifty-seven-year-old homeless man, and as 2014 approached, I was one year closer to realizing my biggest fear of dying alone without ever experiencing a healthy, loving relationship. Before that realization could swallow me whole, I would put an end to my misery. On my own terms, remember? Always on my terms.

It was Christmas Eve. Dad's birthday.

He was gone. So was Mom.

Hmm, shouldn't the thought of them bring up some warm fuzzies or nostalgic memories? They were side by side out at Poplar Hill Cemetery. A good son might drive out there one last time and pay his respects, but I was past all that. I had never been the good son anyway.

I threw my unsold copies of *The Contributor* into the back of my car. There were cheap motels not far from here on the south end of Nolensville Road, but I had just enough gas to get up to Trinity Lane on the north end of Nashville. There, I would be close to Inglewood and Madison, Hendersonville and Goodlettsville, all my old stomping grounds. Something about that area drew me.

The car chugged along, drafty and loud. Semis and RVs roared past as I merged from I-24 onto I-65. A few exits later, I pulled off. I could see my destination. There was nothing special about this place. A room for the night would do.

At last I had come full circle, after decades away in cities such as Memphis, Tunica, and Vegas. With nobody around to mourn or memorialize me, I would end things where they had started—near my childhood houses, churches, schools, and jobs. For what they were worth, these places had formed the backdrop of my life. I'd been saved and baptized, then lost it all in a swimming pool. I'd survived a crossing-guard collision, a robbery at gunpoint, and multiple car accidents. I'd managed kitchen crews, spun discs on the radio, packed clubs with my DJ skills, and been top salesperson for a Chevy dealership. There were moments of grace along the way. Moments of mercy too.

What did I care?

In the end, my chains were my only constant companions. They were cold, hard, and biting. If there was no way of getting rid of them, I was left with only one solution.

Part Five

"I needed peace,
because I'd been at war my entire life."

—John Grisham, in *The Associate*

Steven with "the girls" of Miracle on 4th

Steven & Andrea's engagement

Andrea & Steven's first wedding

Andrea & Steven's forever wedding

Andy, the love of Steven's life

Mickey and Hondo, the family pets

Josh and Steven, son and dad

Steven's co-author, Eric Wilson

51

THE BEGINNING OF THE STORY

On December 24, 2013, I wandered back from my late meal at Waffle House and locked myself in my room at the Hallmark Inn. I drew the chain on the door. It wouldn't stop any cops or paramedics from finding me later, but it guaranteed me some privacy while I did what needed to be done.

Even now, in these last minutes, I was dealing with chains.

Locking myself in.

Locking others out.

Fully clothed, showered and fed, I closed the curtains against the walkway lights outside. I settled into a chair with no arms. The digital clock told me it was 8:27. At fifty-seven years old, I had come to the end of the road. It was time. Time to complete this journey into darkness that began forty-five years ago at a church camp and included an assault decades later in a penitentiary. Every step in between had been mired in shadows and secrets.

Mom: "We will never bring this up again."

Dad: "What did you do that made him think that's what you wanted?"

Oh, I could blame it on a whole list of people, from a deacon to my parents to a youth leader to a vengeful district manager to a trio of guys in a prison bathroom. I could even throw it all in the Big Guy's face, but why give Him that much credit. As far as I was concerned, He'd forgotten my name and fallen silent ages ago.

I was done.

Beaten and bleeding on those damp Parchman tiles, I had lost the will to survive. It all felt inevitable. Felt deserved. The fight in me was gone.

Propped now in the motel-room chair, I pulled a container from my pocket, removed the childproof cap, and poured over a hundred pain pills onto a small table. For days I'd been hoarding them. As an ex-convict I wasn't allowed to own a firearm, and a death by gunshot wasn't my choice anyway. Clean and neat, that's how I liked things— no burden, no fuss. As long as I always appeared to have things under control, you might not guess the troubles lurking within. You might not see my demons, my chains.

One by one, I lined up the capsules beneath the lamplight.

More than enough.

From outside came the hum of traffic and the arguing of a couple on the walkway. This Christmas Eve, the chains of anger, bitterness, and shame coiled tight in my gut and there was nothing left to feel. I was alone. Aside from the woman at the front desk, nobody knew where I was and nobody cared. I'd pushed away anyone who meant a thing to me and the resulting emptiness was big enough to swallow me whole.

I glanced at the pills, heard their promises. If all went as planned, I would never wake up. The motel staff would find my body, the police would investigate, and my surviving brothers would get the news of my suicide. I doubted they would even grieve.

Which was my fault as much as anyone's.

First, a final courtesy.

I smoothed out sheets of motel stationary and scribbled a few lines to Robert and John. They deserved this much, at least. Then I penned letters to my exes, briefly explaining my past, my regrets, and my decision to end it all. I wasn't crazy, just weary and worn out. They weren't to blame. I hoped they would understand.

My last letter was to Andrea.

Oh, Andy!

I thought of our wedding day over three decades ago when she had tossed the bouquet and I'd tossed her lacy garter belt. Bursting with excitement, we had ridden off together, our whole lives ahead of us. Had she since found happiness, despite all the pain I caused her? I sure hoped so. I truly did.

I fanned out the letters. Though they bore no addresses, I was confident the authorities would distribute them accordingly. My entire world had dwindled to this table, these letters, these capsules.

The clock read 9:01.

"Okay," I muttered. "Let's do this."

A knock at the door startled me and I almost fell out of my chair. There was no grogginess on my part, just confusion. Who could it be on this night before Christmas? Nobody knew I was here. They must have the wrong room number.

Another knock, louder this time.

My confusion deepened and my eyes shot to the clock. It now said 11:00. Surely, I hadn't nodded off. I was still upright, even without any chair arms to hold me in place. The pills were still waiting in nice, tidy rows. Had two hours passed? Was that possible?

A female voice at the door: "Housekeeping. Are you staying or checking out?"

Since when did motels clean rooms after dark? There was a dim glow at my curtains, which I assumed was from the walkway lights. Nevertheless, I peeked outside. I blinked against the sunlight, blinked again. What the hell? It was daytime out there, people on the sidewalk, a car rumbling past. Well, in that case, it wasn't eleven at night. It was eleven in the morning.

Fourteen hours had passed.

It was Christmas Day!

Everything stopped in that moment. While I had no explanation for the huge gap in time, I couldn't deny it, and the housekeeping woman was still waiting for a reply. I counted the money left in my pocket and called out, "I'm going to stay. I'll come pay in just a minute."

How can I even describe what happened next? A calmness settled over me as soothing as a warm blanket. The peace was unbelievable. It was unlike anything I'd ever known in my childhood, teens, or adulthood. It was beyond my understanding, yet for some reason it felt real and personal. No, I couldn't explain it, just like I couldn't explain how I knew everything would be okay.

But I did.

I'd love to tell you it was my come-to-Jesus moment, with a sudden blossoming of faith in God, but it wasn't that defined. The knock on the door minutes earlier had filled my mind with confusion, and I would wonder for days why any of this had taken place. However, in the weeks to come, it would all become clear:

God had come looking for me. God had wanted me all along.

When nobody else seemed to care, God still did.

Who else!

There in the Hallmark Inn, instead of ending my story, I was suddenly ready to begin again. I flushed the pills down the toilet. I tore up the letters. I paid for another night and counted my remaining money. I had $8.32. Don't ask why that number's still in my head, but that's exactly what I had. After a visit to the MAPCO mart across the street, I plopped down on my motel-room bed with candy, chips, and cold Cokes.

Traditionally, this was the time millions celebrated the birth of Jesus, the Savior of the world, the Prince of Peace. To this day, I believe if you go seeking for God, you will find Him. He reveals Himself to those who thirst after Him and His righteousness. Floundering in rage and rebellion, I wasn't doing any of that, so why did He come to me? Clearly, it had nothing to do with my own good works or intentions. I deserved nothing. I deserved the death waiting in those rows of pills.

This is where God's grace stepped in, a grace both amazing and humbling. He states in Isaiah 65:1, in the NIV translation, "I revealed myself to those who did not ask for me; I was found by those who did not seek me."

That's what He did. He revealed Himself, even when I wasn't asking.

Seven years later, it still brings this grown man to tears!

That December day, I kicked back on the bed, watched Christmas movies, and snacked my way through the day, celebrating in the best way I knew how. I had never in my life felt so at peace.

52

ALTERNATE ROUTES

Did my homelessness magically end? Did a furnished home suddenly appear? No, that's not the way it went down.

I did return to my corner beneath the golden arches on Nolensville Road, selling the paper through January and February of 2014. Mike Dotson still stopped by with sandwiches and friendly conversation. He kept telling me God had a plan for my life, and now I even believed it—sort of. Another guy who passed on foot every day also became a friend. His name was Eddie, and Eddie would play a large role in what was to come.

To the commuters on Nolensville Road and to customers streaming from Lowe's and the McDonald's drive-thru, I was still the guy on the corner with newspapers in hand and a duffel bag hanging from the nearby tree. To them, nothing had changed.

Inside, though, I knew this wouldn't be my life forever. I couldn't explain it. I didn't know how. And it happened quicker than I could've ever imagined.

This chapter was almost over.

During our time on this earth, we all make life-altering decisions. They seem good at the time, but they're only temporary fixes. Altering a schedule doesn't change where you work, just as altering a suit or a dress doesn't change what you're wearing. These decisions might provide an alternate route that eventually ends up at the same location. Or simply leads from one bad relationship to another.

Life-changing decisions are entirely different. They take you to new jobs, dress you in different clothes, and give you a new mindset. They don't just alter a location, they change your destination. They change the way you approach relationships.

Yes, the landscape of my life was altered by my Christmas Day experience, and healing and forgiveness began to grow in me.

I hadn't yet been fully changed, though. Not at the root.

"Look at you, Steven," Mike would tell me. "God's working on you. I can see it in your eyes. When He does that, it means He is preparing you for something."

"We'll see," I said.

Those were my two favorite words: We'll see. I still had unresolved issues, the main one being my trigger of pain at age twelve. As time went by, I found the courage to bring that childhood abuse into the open by sharing it with Mike and his wife Carol. Even as chains of shame tried to weigh me down, the Dotsons prayed with me and spoke of forgiveness. I felt lighter just shedding those memories. I did not have to carry this alone, and eventually I could stop carrying it altogether.

Each Thursday at dawn, Mike and four other men from his church met at McDonald's for coffee and a Bible study. He introduced them to me and they started calling me by name.

Mike pulled me aside one day. "Listen, Steven, I talked to my guys and told them I wanted to get you off the street. We all pooled our money together." He handed me an envelope. "There's enough in here for a month at the Stay Lodge, over off I-24."

Was there a catch? Did he expect me to start showing up at his church?

"It's yours," Mike insisted. "Remember, God's not finished with you yet."

Thanking him, I tucked the money into my billfold. It was more generosity than I knew how to handle. I finished selling my papers, then drove toward I-24. With hundreds of dollars pressed against my thigh, I heard a familiar voice calling my name. Instead of turning off at Harding to check into the Stay Lodge, I continued northwest through Paducah, Kentucky, to the casino across the river in Metropolis, Illinois.

That old addiction was as demanding as ever and by midnight I'd lost it all.

I rolled back into Nashville at 3 a.m. Shivering, I slept in my car.

"Did you get checked in?" Mike wanted to know the next morning at my corner.

"The thing is, I . . ." The truth was too embarrassing to admit, so I spun a lie. "I went to do my laundry before heading to the Stay Lodge, and stupid me, Mike, you know how I can be, I set down my billfold in the laundromat. Well, when I came back from the restroom, it was gone along with all the money."

He mumbled something about being sorry, being careful next time He stood there like he wanted me to say more and I kept looking off over his shoulder.

Two days later, Mike was back. "You wanna tell me what really happened?"

I came clean.

Hearing that I had betrayed his trust, Mike had every right to cut me off. Instead, he showed me just how far God's grace will reach. He went back to each of those men in his Bible study and personally repaid them. Then in March of 2014, he told me to meet him at the Stay Lodge. I stood beside him at the front desk as he covered my first month's stay. I could barely speak a word.

Such grace and mercy bolstered my faith. Through Mike, I saw a Heavenly Father who wasn't looking for opportunities to beat the hell out of me, but to hug the hell out of me. It was God's kindness that led to repentance, according to Romans 2:4, and once again I had the faith of a child.

Mike was learning too. "That was a lesson for me," he said. "You're not ready to be handed money yet. That's okay. We'll get there. And I'm still going to help you."

You would think at this point I had learned my own lesson.

But, no. I fell off the wagon more than once.

Even as I stumbled, Mike stuck by me. He drove me to my first Gamblers Anonymous meeting and waited outside. As forgiving as he was, he wasn't a fool. He made sure I saw this through. He wasn't doing this just to brag to his church buddies. He never introduced me as that homeless guy he knew. No, he just called me his friend.

I'll tell you this: If it weren't for Mike Dotson, I wouldn't be where I am today.

"God's not done writing your story," he told me more than once. "He has a hope and a plan for you, Steven. He will complete what He has started."

I was beginning to see the light.

Mike caught a glimpse of this a few weeks later when I walked for the first time through the doors of his church. It wasn't an easy decision for me, considering my past experiences. I had no idea what to expect. Mike introduced me to Pastor Cummings, who seemed like a straight shooter.

At one point, Pastor Cummings asked me, "So, Steven, what's your story?"

I raised an eyebrow. "You sure you want to hear it?"

"Tell it to me," he said, "and don't bullshit me."

I knew right then we would get along.

Going to that church was the first step of a year-and-a-half-long journey, which at times moved me closer to God and at other times caused me to question Him. Regardless, I knew this was where I was supposed to be.

"It's where God wants you," Pastor Cummings agreed. "But only for a season."

Mike told me the same thing.

Their words struck me as odd. I mean, I was happy here. Didn't they realize what a miracle this was? I was a former God-hater. Just months earlier, I would have said you were crazy for even thinking I'd show up at a Sunday morning service. As it turned out, though, their prediction eventually came true.

53

MIKE AND EDDIE

Even though I was off the streets, finding a job wasn't easy. I continued selling papers from my corner. When we could, Mike, Eddie, and I met for coffee at my "office"—a table in McDonald's. My defenses were up and I often held Mike and Eddie at bay. Sometimes Mike called me on it. Other times he just glanced away. Eddie was a good-sized guy, closer to my body build, his arms bronzed by walking outdoors every day. He was generally soft-spoken, often balancing Mike's responses with quiet comments.

We talked about God's grace, His power, and His work in our lives. We shot the breeze, kidded each other, and debated the Tennessee Titans' chances of reaching the playoffs. As you might guess, the homeless were also brought up.

We discussed the real homeless situation, the one I knew firsthand. Not the one churches, government, and society like to paint. From there, it wasn't long till the idea of us doing something about it came up. I would love to tell you I jumped up, shouted hallelujah, and said let's do it. But no, that was a world I was trying to leave behind.

"You know," Mike observed, "we all care about our homeless friends here in Nashville. Steven, you know what it's like out there."

I knew what it was like, alright. And I didn't want to go back there.

Mike noted my reluctance. "I've got your back," he told me. "You can help people who are stuck where you were, but you'll have to overcome your fear."

Easier said than done.

Mike kept working on me. "Well, what do you think they need?"

"Who knows better than you?" Eddie chipped in.

Neither of them understood how wounded I still was. I'd been pulled from the pit and the very thought of edging up to it again scared the hell out of me. As I worked through my doubts, a battle raged within me. God was calling me toward the very thing I thought He had rescued me from. What was wrong with just going back to a normal life of barbecues and football games and lazy Saturday afternoons?

Mike and Eddie never gave up on me, though.

Or on God's calling for me.

"This is what He's prepared you to do," Mike challenged me.

I'd run out of excuses. Mike had proven his commitment to me, as a friend and as a brother in the Lord, and I appreciated our relationship. If it got to be too much, I knew he was that one person in my life who would stand beside me as I caught my breath. This gave me the courage to take a chance.

"Okay," I said. "Let's do it."

The first time in a homeless encampment, we took only pen and paper. We introduced ourselves and asked how we could help. When we showed back up four days later with everything on our list, our homeless friends were shocked.

"We didn't think you'd ever be back," they said. "That's how it usually works."

I knew what they meant. Sure, people make lots of promises, but there's very little follow-up. It's no wonder most homeless people live in the moment. It's all about survival for one more day, and they'll take advantage if you show any weakness. While I wanted to be liked as much as the next person, I understood how things were on the streets.

What we needed from the homeless community was to be trusted first and foremost. Respect would follow.

"We have to do what we tell them we'll do," I explained to Mike. "We have to follow through. But we can't let them play the homeless card. Being homeless doesn't give them the right to disrespect or try to play us."

"Like me taking you to GA?"

"Alright, wise guy. Touché. Seriously, though, they have to know actions have consequences. If someone asks for a sleeping bag this week, then again next week and the next, there's a reason. It's called laziness. That sleeping bag, it's their responsibility. They can't let that thing get wet or go sell it or whatever."

That was our launching pad. Once we had earned respect and established some ground rules, we could help in positive and practical ways.

For months Mike, Eddie, and I made our rounds in ever-widening circles. We found people living out of sight in plywood huts, cardboard-lined hovels, carved-out bushes, alley doorways, and abandoned vehicles. Some were only yards from major thoroughfares. Others were out in the forest.

They came from all ethnicities and backgrounds.

Men, women, children.

Couples. Loners. Addicts, alcoholics.

Families bankrupted by medical bills. Discouraged businessmen. Divorcées. Widows and widowers. Mothers who had lost children. Soldiers who had lost an arm, a leg, or both. Women escaping the sex industry. Teens just getting into it.

The day starting an official outreach ministry was brought up is emblazoned in my mind. Mike broached it first and Eddie jumped on board immediately.

Me? Not so much.

I came up with reason after reason it wouldn't work. In reality, my reasons were just excuses. At the root of these excuses was my old friend fear.

These guys were crazy if they thought I'd go along with this. Nevertheless, Mike and Eddie spent weeks discussing the idea with me. There was no denying my experience could be a plus. I knew what was being done to help those on the streets and, more importantly, what wasn't being done. But who was I, in my current condition, to be leading anything? Together, we weighed the pros and cons.

Cons. Kind of appropriate, don't you think?

I mean, who would give money to an organization run by someone who spent years in prison for grand larceny, theft, and burglary? If those details came out, we were done before we started. And I didn't want to head up a nonprofit that constantly required me to relive a past I'd only recently left behind. Until a few months ago, I was still sleeping in my car. Even now, I was still selling The Contributor and doing interior paint jobs three times a month.

Bottom line: I wasn't ready yet. Deep at my core, I still doubted I was worthy.

Well, even if I wasn't ready, God was.

"There are hundreds out there," Mike said, "not being reached by the current ministries. We need to leave the ninety-nine and go find the one lost lamb."

"We could call it Handshakes and Hugs," Eddie suggested.

Hmm. While that described some of what we were doing, it didn't capture the full sense of hope I wanted to convey. We needed something catchy, clever, and relevant. When I was on the streets, I hadn't wanted pity or even charity. I'd craved dignity. I'd needed to know I mattered to someone. Deep within, I'd longed for a place I had never really known. A place called home.

Maybe we could use home in the name somehow. Or maybe—

Stop, Steven! What're you doing? If you play along, Mike and Eddie will have you running this thing before you know it. You know what success has done to you in the past. Hold your horses, buddy. This is a dangerous path you're going down.

"Are you saying you'll do this?" Mike asked me.

"We'll see," was all I could say. "We'll see."

54

A MADNESS TO MY METHOD

Even Steven Allen Young couldn't stand in God's way. I'd spent a life-time trying to do just that—and look where that got me! I was beginning to love the Big Guy like never before, and as He worked in and through me, a love I'd never thought would be mine was starting to fill me. I went to church. I had Christian brothers I prayed with. I read my Bible.

As 2014 eased into 2015, Mike, Eddie, and I continued visiting camps and handing out supplies. It was exhausting, physically and emotionally. Our hearts were torn open by the needs all around. Personally, I faced fears of being homeless again every time we hit the pavement. It was a space I had just escaped.

I couldn't turn away, though. I could not do it.

This was where God had found me.

This was where He was working.

As my friends and I plugged along, the need for assistance became increasingly evident, and Mike and Eddie started with a full-court press again. I knew it was time for a serious meeting. We gathered at my office, my home away from home, and sipped piping-hot McDonald's coffee. I told them, yes, okay, I would move forward as the leader of a nonprofit, but I had stipulations they needed to hear.

"I've been waiting for this," Mike said. "I just knew God was working on you."

"Aw, shut up, Mike. For once, just lemme talk."

"Are you kidding? Letting you talk is all Eddie and I do around here." Mike and Eddie exchanged grins. "It's just a question of whether anyone's listening."

"Are you finished?"

My two partners in ministry weren't making any promises.

"So here's the deal." My eyes roved around the dining area. There were a few old guys sipping drinks and chewing on apple pies. A mother was wiping her child's nose in the playground area. This was a strange place to be forming a new nonprofit, but then again I had never done things the usual way. "If we do this," I continued, "I'm not going to hide the junk in my background. I have a credit score of four hundred and a rap sheet a mile long. We'll just have to put it all out there, be transparent, and hope for the best."

No disagreement so far.

"And to be successful," I added, "some of my old gifts will have to come into play. You'll see sides of me you haven't seen before. There is a madness to my method and a method to my madness."

Mike's eyebrows furrowed. "Should I be worried?"

"I used to be good at sales. I know how to motivate people, how to market things. In restaurants and nightclubs, I took inventory, ordered supplies, and made sure things ran smoothly. I can use all of these skills, but in the past it was all about money, money, money. My manufactured ego and success had a way of taking me down. Fair warning: these skills could lead me in the wrong direction and take others down too."

"They're also what we need to make this ministry work," Eddie noted.

"We'll have your back," Mike said. "If I see something wrong, I won't cut you any slack. We all need each other."

"But you'll lemme do things the way I know how to?"

"If you're good at them, then God's clearly given you a gift. It's all about how you use your gifts, whether for good or for evil."

"Is that a yes?"

Mike and Eddie gave me verbal affirmations.

"Okay, then," I said, "let's do this."

In the McDonald's dining area, we celebrated the moment, though I still wasn't 100 percent on board. In fact, I was scared to death. My plans for transparency weren't just intended to fend off any attempts at discrediting the ministry, but also to give myself a way out if things failed. Oh well, I could say, I warned you guys. No wonder we're not getting any donations, considering I told the truth about my past. Guess it's time for me to move on. Least we gave it a shot.

"To be incorporated, we need a name and a bank account," Mike said. "We'll need the name before the IRS will allow us to form an official public-benefit or religious corporation. Any ideas?"

"Let's each write down a name on a napkin, then vote on which we think is best," Eddie ventured. "What do you say, Steven?"

"Works for me."

With napkins in hand, we mulled things over. I contemplated my lifelong desire for home. How could we work that into a name? So many on the streets had lost that connection—or never even had it—and we wanted to take that sense of care and belonging to them.

Mike, Eddie, and I turned over our napkins, ready to vote.

My suggestion won.

In early February, Home Street Home Ministries started a Facebook page and a GoFundMe as a means of raising money to purchase food, bottled water, tents, sleeping bags, blankets, shoes, socks, and other supplies. There were generous souls who invested early on. Those who were struggling themselves were usually the least likely to turn a blind eye. How could they ignore the homeless when they themselves could so easily slide into the same predicament? One bad month. A missed paycheck or two. A doctor bill. A car repair. These were real fears and possibilities.

Together, we looked into starting a 501(c)(3) nonprofit, but we needed thousands of dollars to complete that process. For now, it was a hope and a prayer and nothing more.

Through the bone-numbing winter, into the scorching months of June, July, and August, we distributed supplies. Mike and I put thousands of miles on our cars. Gas was not cheap. While we couldn't imagine stopping, we didn't see how we could continue.

Lord, we needed help.

Then, out of the blue, we got a phone call. Apparently, a woman had spotted us ministering on the streets and recognized the real estate magnet on Mike's car. She called the realty owner's wife, a friend of hers, and told her what one of his agents was up to. The owner, co-incidentally named Steven Dotson—yes, another Steven and another Dotson—called Mike in and wanted to hear the details.

"Well, we want to help," Steven informed Mike afterward. "What can we do?"

"Our next big hurdle is becoming a nonprofit."

Steven set up a lunch with Mike, Eddie, and me. He had me tell my story, then describe the needs I saw and the costs involved. When it was all said and done, he stepped up and covered the fees for establishing a nonprofit. He is the reason Home Street Home is where it is today.

On October 28, 2015, the IRS granted us nonprofit status, and the state of Tennessee gave us a charter as a nonprofit corporation. In accordance with legal requirements, we listed an address—my place at the Stay Lodge, where I would live until 2018. We appointed board members—who gathered for our first meeting at Mike's place. We opened a ministry bank account—with $600 put up by Mike himself. And we came up with a logo—which we later updated, thanks to the skills of a graphic designer.

Nineteen months after my own homelessness ended, we were official.

Of course, it wasn't all smooth sailing from there. Public apathy is widespread: "Hey, if I can pull myself up by my bootstraps, why can't they?" "How about being productive members of society instead of begging for booze on the corners?" "Aren't we just encouraging these bums? I'm scared to even walk from my car into the store?"

It was a learning process, and I had to confront my own insecurities. Was I even deserving of the grace I'd been shown?

I still remember the day Home Street Home got its first $100 donation. I was so excited, I called Mike to share the good news. Over the first year as a nonprofit, we barely made $12,000. While it wasn't enough to put much of a dent in the problem, we were humbled and grateful. At least we were doing something. It was a start.

55

SURVIVAL GAMES

It's impossible to come off the streets—or prison, for that matter—all on your own. You need help along the way and that help is hard to find.

Oftentimes, bridges have already been burned with family and friends. A criminal record makes employment a challenge. Zero savings and bad credit limit your options. Few people understand the damage done to the psyche, and the practical obstacles are very real. Even if you try to end your homelessness—usually in that early six-month window—it's more difficult than it seems. You're stuck waiting two weeks for a first paycheck while you wonder what to eat. To move into your own place, you'll need a deposit and probably first and last month's rent. As you save up, you'll be sleeping in a tent or vehicle or clump of roadside bushes.

Do any of these qualify as excuses for bad behavior?

Absolutely not. Just the realities people face.

Some reach a point of acceptance about their circumstances and come up with a con. They build a story. They become survivors. They learn to play the game of manipulation, theft, and lies. If someone stops to help them, they don't know if they'll ever see that person again, so they take everything they can get and they stockpile.

I was there. Oh, I played the game too. That survival instinct is almost primal, and until you find yourself that low, it's difficult to understand how persistent it becomes.

But how'd they get there in the first place?

That's a question I am often asked.

Lemme just say, how they got there isn't important. The answers are as varied as the day is long, and they're often nothing more than clever deceptions, mishmashes of the truth, or complete breaks from reality.

Why are they still homeless? That's what really matters.

What's keeping them from moving forward?

Living on the streets, your hope and belief are destroyed by the discouragement and the treatment you receive from others. You've tried everything you know to try, and one day you wake up and just reach that point of acceptance. Instead of trying to find a job or patch up relationships with family, to no avail, you accept that this is your life. You'll have to make the best of it.

That is when the games begin. It becomes all about survival.

Now is when the drugs and alcohol usually start, not before.

I'll say that again. Despite what many people think, less than 10 percent of the homeless end up on the streets because of addiction. They do not start that way. They end up that way. The drinking and drugs are the result, not the cause, of homelessness. As survival mode kicks in, you seek ways to numb the pain.

This is why it's so important to catch people before that hopelessness takes over, to help them move forward before they're permanently stuck. It's one of the main things we try to do as a ministry.

Eddie and I met one guy living on the streets who looked clear-eyed, well-groomed, and intelligent. He didn't match the usual profile. I took a drag on my cigarette, dropped it, and stomped it out with my toe, then asked, "What the hell are you doing out here?"

"I used to be an attorney," he said.

"That doesn't surprise me."

"I had a moderately successful practice before a car accident got me hooked on pain pills. I had it bad. When my doctor stopped prescribing them to me, I started buying off the streets. I got caught in a drug sting, ended up in jail. That was it. Soon I was disbarred." His voice caught as he told the story. "All I ever wanted to do was practice law, and now that's gone."

See, how he got there didn't really matter. Why he was still there was the issue. As crushed and hopeless as he felt, he had no motivation to get back up.

"I was in prison," I told him. "I knew guys in there, smart guys like you, who did paralegal work. They didn't need a license for it. I bet you could walk into some law office downtown and find a low-paying research job. Just work your way up from there."

Whether my words sunk in, I had no idea. A week later, though, the guy called to inform me he was off the streets and getting paid as a paralegal.

"I'm doing like you said," he shared. "I'm literally living again."

Another time, we spotted a tent by the railroad tracks. The occupant didn't have any obvious addiction issues. He was a young Black guy, level-headed and polite. I couldn't figure out how he had ended up down here. Why hadn't he rejoined the parade of life? His shoulders were slumped, his eyes down, even as I tried to encourage him.

Six months later, I received a call from Dallas, Texas.

"You probably don't remember me," the caller said, "but you stopped and spoke to me down by the tracks outside of Nashville. Something clicked that day. Something you said, I guess. An hour later, I packed my stuff, hiked up to the interstate, and hitchhiked all the way back to Dallas."

"Young guy? Living in a tent? Yep, I remember you."

"I knocked on my parents' door and told them I wanted to come home. I'm not gonna say it was easy. In fact, things were pretty rocky at first. But we worked through it. I decided I wasn't gonna run no more."

"Those first steps are tough. Good job."

"You know, things're starting to work out for me. I have my life back, man. Just wanted to tell you thanks."

Of course, not all of the stories are victorious. I can't tell you how many times we've helped people get off the streets into their own apartments, thanks to cooperative local partners, only to have them die of health-related or withdrawal issues. For the person ending years of alcohol abuse, the shock to the system can be deadly. The body no longer knows how to function properly.

It's often different for the drug addict. For a person hooked on heroin, the only life-threatening danger is an overdose, so medical professionals don't often invest in trying to end the addiction. The drug itself is a painkiller, and without it things turn brutal. The ones who do try to come off heroin go through withdrawals so intense, they feel like they're going to die.

As Home Street Home grew, I tried to communicate the situation to donors. I saw early on how my transparency about my past was a strength instead of a weakness. It earned respect and opened doors. God turned my negatives into positives, and we saw increasing interest from individuals, businesses, churches, and ministries.

My experiences also helped in dealing with the homeless. I could be both tough and understanding. I didn't let them play their survival games.

Finding that balance was critical yet often difficult. It led to some heartbreaking decisions that didn't always give me the feel-goods. Our bottom line, though, was doing the most we could for the homeless as an entire community and not just for one or two struggling individuals. We were in this for the long haul.

56

MEANS OF DESTRUCTION

Why, I wondered, does this woman look familiar? I swear I've seen her before.

We were on the same aisle in the store and that profile jogged my memory. As she spun and faced me, my thoughts turned bitter. It was the female cop who'd once pestered me from her patrol car, demanding to see my ID and permit.

"Hi, there," she said. "Aren't you the guy who used to be out on the corner?"

"Aren't you the cop who thought you'd nail me for something?"

She let that slide. "Haven't seen you for a while. What're you up to these days?"

"You really want to know?" I said. "I run a ministry helping others who are stuck in the same place I was."

"Wow, that's great news." She wore a genuine smile. "What's it called?"

"Home Street Home."

"I like the sound of that. Seriously, we need people like you. While on duty, I deal with the homeless every day. Most times, they just need a dry tent and some gloves or maybe a place to sober up. I hate to take them downtown, but with local business owners putting pressure on us, I don't always have good alternatives."

"Listen," I said, handing her a card, "we've usually got some supplies and resources. That's what we do. Gimme a call and we'll come to you, day or night. Most of these guys and gals don't need to be on your radar. They just need a little help."

"I'll do that." She took the card. "Steven, is it? Thank you. You're looking good."

True to her word, she still calls me to this day—one more reminder of how God can redeem even strained relationships.

Since boyhood, I had maintained my wardrobe not only to impress those around me but to cover my faults. There's a reason I love Mickey Mouse with his sharp and clean image, always dressed for the part. I was constantly looking for confirmation, affirmation, someone to tell me I was good enough.

One day the receptionist at the Stay Lodge said to me, "You do realize, don't you, that we can see you on the security cameras when you're in the laundry room?"

"Okay." I wasn't sure where this was going.

"We've never seen anyone so meticulous. You fold each and every item, crease your pants and shirts. Pair your socks. I mean, that's just not the norm around here."

These days, the clothes don't matter as much to me. I'm now a jeans, T-shirt, and shorts guy. And if you think my sixty-five T-shirts are more than enough, I must politely disagree. Don't even get me started on ball caps. Nowadays I splurge on my Skechers and my socks. Yes, socks. Why? It all goes back to my time on the streets, when I had one or two pairs. They were poor quality, rarely soft or warm. I often wore the same ones for days at a time. Well, I don't ever want to go back to that, so I have over four hundred pairs in dresser drawers and in bins beneath my bed.

Gotta be prepared.

Back in 2016, I was struggling despite my clean appearance, GA meetings, and church attendance. As ministry donations increased, so did the pressure to succeed. We had responsibilities to the IRS and the state. We needed more foodstuff and a vehicle for distribution. I didn't want to disappoint Mike, Eddie, or our board members, and I did my best to tame my tongue and my moods. I needed to look and act the part, I told myself, though my old insecurities were clawing at me. More than anything, I wanted to be the change we worked so hard to achieve in others.

But I wasn't changed. No, not completely. I was only an altered version of my earlier self. There was still a battle going on between God's will and my own.

And that battle would get worse.

How many times do we read about CEOs, pro athletes, politicians, or world-famous actors who seem to steer their lives off ledges? Such stories are in the news every week. My guess is, they fear success as much as I did. If they reach the top, they might be recognized as frauds and brought toppling down. Before others can do that to them, they allow their own doubts and addictions to undercut them. Chased by that monster of pride, they cycle toward self-sabotage.

As Home Street Home grew, I let my old insecurities wreak havoc. If this boat really got rocking, it might flip over and drown me. If I got up on this horse, it might just buck me off. Choose your metaphor, I envisioned a means of destruction.

So, I pocketed money from a paint job and made another trip to the casino.

Yep, you read that right.

I was a walking miracle and a walking disaster zone.

57

PANDORA'S BOX

To this day, I don't receive paychecks from Home Street Home Ministries. If we ever get to the point where I can be paid without taking away a sleeping bag, can of chili, or pack of water from a homeless friend, then I'll think about it. Understandably, though, my personal mistakes invited scrutiny. People close to me raised eyebrows. There were whispers of funds being misused. Though these weren't true, my behavior raised suspicions. Guilty till proven innocent. Here I was again, about to decimate the one good thing in my life. I was tired of traveling this dusty road.

I then made one of the most difficult decisions I've ever made, a decision to do something the old Steven would have never done. I went to Mike and a few others and fessed up. Yes, I'd hit the blackjack tables again. I'd gambled away the money I made painting. My money, not the ministry's. That was God's honest truth.

In the past, Mike had demanded accountability from me.

"Our books are open," I'd told him. "Do you see any red flags in there, anything that seems out of line? If you notice a problem, tell me."

"No, Steven, you're right. It's not a you problem. It's a me problem."

As faithless as I was in personal areas, I had never taken a dime from Home Street Home. Both Mike and I had fears to deal with here, and I give him credit for recognizing that. The questions persisted, though, and when someone confronted me rudely and publicly, spouting rumors that my personal problems were bleeding over into the ministry, it took everything in me to keep my cool.

Following up on the incident, Pastor Cummings asked me, "Have you and the ministry ever had to say no to someone, to turn them away from receiving help? Have you ever not fulfilled a promise?"

"No."

"Then that's what you say to those who ask. They need to get off your back."

My issues went deep, and I knew it was time to figure out these problems once and for all. Feelings of being unworthy and distrusted kept pushing me back toward the gambling's momentary glow. I could sit through all of my GA meetings and do everything others wanted me to do, but it still wasn't going to be enough to stop me.

Something had to change.

This required a radical step, an unconventional approach.

"Mike," I said, "I'm going to lock myself away in my hotel room for a while. It might be two days, might be two months, I don't know. I just need some time to figure things out in my own way. I won't come out till I see the way through this."

"I'll stop by and check on you. I'll—"

"You're not listening. No. Don't call, text, or knock on my door. You mean well, Mike, but I've got to do this in my own way and my own time."

He mulled it over.

"It's not up for debate," I added. "A madness to my method, remember?"

When I entered that room, I realized this was it. I would open Pandora's box, face whatever beasts appeared, and either defeat them or die in the process. I wasn't stepping back outside until this battle was decided. With God's help, it was time to cast off these chains once and for all.

Did Mike stay away? Well, what do you think? Mike is too loving, too loyal, and too annoying to leave well enough alone. He knocked on my door within a day or two, asking how was I doing, offering to get me supplies, and assuring me I could tell him anything. I told him no, he could leave, there was nothing to talk about.

For over a week, I stayed in that room. I could either worry until it hurt or pray until it felt good. Spending time alone with God, humbly and honestly, was the best medicine I could think of, directing my prayers to Him. Jeremiah 29:12 says, "Then you will call on me and come and pray to me, and I will listen to you." Psalm 73:26 adds, "My flesh and my heart may fail, but God is the strength of my heart and my portion forever."

Alone for that long gave me time to think. I'd jumped through others' hoops and tried their remedies, but I knew myself better than anyone else. Spinning my wheels to please others was futile. Trying to appear as someone I wasn't just wasted my time and energy. I even resented the GA meetings, doing them not for me but for my friend. I had to quit worrying about what others thought. With God's help, I would use the things He had put in me to seal up the cracks, repair the brokenness, and build something new.

In the process, I tapped into those same skills which helped me survive five years on the streets and over eight years in prison. Where I had once lied, dodged, and hidden, to avoid my memories, I now directed my steps straight into the shadows. Clinging to God's Word, I faced the pain and the nightmares. It was scary, but there was no more avoiding it. I had to go through it. For too long, I'd had one foot in the past and one in the present. Even when I tried to move forward, people's questions and judgments forced me to step back again. I could never work one foot free to step into the future.

It was time. God's love, I knew, was deep enough to reach me, wide enough to embrace me, and strong enough to carry me. He was with me every step of the way. If He was going to truly change my circumstances, first, I would have to let Him change me.

I'm Yours, Lord. Who did You create me to be?

Discovering His answer would be an adventure. Instead of fearing the unknown, I would embrace it. Only as I was willing to go where I had never been would I find what I'd never had but always looked for.

Life-altering versus life-changing . . .

In that hotel room, I gave my past and future to Jesus, and He didn't just alter my life. Falling off the wagon had altered my life. Attending meetings had altered my life.

He now changed my life.

He changed the way I dealt with the past.

He changed the way I saw myself and convinced me I was worthy.

He helped me think before opening my big mouth. He taught me to consult with Him and His Word before reacting. He gave me faith in Him where I'd once lacked trust in others. He, alone, was my salvation.

I heard God whisper to me: Yes, that was Me beside you when those ladies ran through the stop sign and t-boned your car. That was Me who kept the robber's gun from going off in your face. That was Me who grabbed you before you jumped off that bridge. When you heard that knock on your motel-room door and realized fourteen hours had flashed by, that was Me. I was that peace beyond all understanding. You can trust Me, Steven. I am with you.

Imbued with fresh courage, I stared down the monster.

THE BEAST

A gentle breeze, the blowing snow,
Invade the thoughts I've come to know
From peaceful slumber I awake
With awesome wonder a breath I take
The beast now stirs from deep within
In fiery frame and molten skin
Desires take form I've never felt
One step beyond the flames I knelt
Engulfed by knotted shades of dark

And so I pray one single spark
Light scattered down on fields below
I see the life that I let go
Then given strength I face the beast
And ask my God for my release

Eleven days after locking myself in, I stepped out of that room.
I was free.

I had decided it would be better to walk this world alone than spend the rest of my days trying to live down my past. I would live with one foot in the present and one foot in the future. I would no longer let others—not even old Steven—pull me back.

58

GOING TO THE WELL

There's not a problem on this earth God doesn't have an answer to. I believe that. I know it for myself. Stubborn as I am, I had spent so much energy looking everywhere else for answers, running to addiction, distraction, and temporary pleasure. It took a reckoning at the Stay Lodge for me to finally relinquish control.

I was changed. I was ready to take the next steps.

Of course, it wouldn't be easy. I knew that. When you make life changes, they come with consequences. I had to change my environment, meaning those doubters who spoke constant fear and guilt. I needed to surround myself with people who believed in me, trusted me, and would let me move forward. I lost some dear friends when I gave them that ultimatum. Since I no longer lived for their approval, they no longer had a hold on me, and some just faded away. Others left in a huff.

My approval comes from the Lord, but yes, those losses hurt. I still miss some of those people.

Here's the thing, though. For every relationship I lost in the process, I gained two or three more. Instead of it becoming a matter of subtraction, it became a multiplication. Where some people had once limited me, I now found others who didn't care about my past. Their love was unconditional.

I discovered there was beauty on the other side of the ugliness. The mirror, which had long been my enemy, was now an ally. In reflection, I saw myself as a child of God. I had a purpose. In the midst of my weakness, He was strong.

And the Lord had even bigger surprises ahead.

Mike and Pastor Cummings had predicted it, and I knew it was now time to move on from their church. In the early months of 2016, I floated around, searching for the place I could call my church home. I'd been in touch with my brothers, Robert and John, and it was Robert's wife, Peggy, who suggested I come visit Well House Church.

Where was it? I wanted to know.

At the RiverGate Skate Center, she told me.

Talk about a small world. The church was there in my old stomping grounds, minutes from where I'd gone to school and been in a deadly collision and later sold cars. And they met in a skating rink, of all places.

Oh, I had to see this for myself.

In March of 2016, I started attending Well House. The pastoral staff had hung curtains as a backdrop, rolled out some carpet, and turned the concession area into a small cafe. Instead of serving kids on skates, they served churchgoers. The congregation was a casual assortment of all ages, colors, and vocations. Even though they were a friendly crowd, I always showed up as service started and left as it ended. Aside from saying hi to Peggy, I wasn't interested in talking with anyone. My heart told me this was where I was supposed to be, yet I still had walls up.

"What's his story?" a few people inquired of my sister-in-law.

"If you want to know Steven's story," Peggy said, "then you'll have to ask him."

By early summer, I decided it was time to take the next step. I called Jason, the pastor, and told him I'd like to chat sometime. We met for coffee soon after at Portland Brew in East Nashville.

"God's called me to be at Well House," I explained to him. "The thing is, I'm not one to just fill a chair. I want to be active and do things. Now before you say, 'Oh, that's great,' you need to hear about me, and I'm warning you, I'm going to be fully honest."

"Go ahead," Jason said. "More honest the better."

I laid it all out for him, the good, the bad, and the ugly. He heard about my years in prison, my abuse, my gambling. He got an earful. The one thing I didn't mention was Home Street Home. I wasn't looking for financial backing. I needed Well House for my own spiritual growth.

As I wrapped up, I wondered what Jason's reaction would be. So far, he had listened without saying much.

His first question will always stick with me: "Is that all you got, Steven?"

"Is that not enough?"

Jason proceeded to tell me about Well House Church's philosophy. He believed in Jesus' ability to redeem anyone, and he claimed there were people in the congregation and on staff with pasts even darker than mine. He shared a few stories to prove it. "Listen," he said, "I don't expect you to leave your baggage at the door. I want you to bring it in and set it next to ours. Welcome home."

Those words meant the world to me. I'd been looking for home my entire life and didn't think it existed for me. Who could accept me for who I was and who I'd been? Well, now I had the answer.

A month or two later, Jason pulled me aside. "I hear you run a homeless ministry. Why didn't you tell me? Man, we'd love to be a part of that."

Taken aback, I said okay.

Well House proved their desire to help was sincere. It wasn't just lip service, as I'd found from many other places. The DNA of this church was to serve. They were already reaching out to the community in big ways and small. They built wheelchair ramps for individual homes. They did yard work for those too ill or old to manage things on their own. They even sent out Quarter Patrols, showing up at laundromats with rolls of quarters for those who needed help. They didn't mention the church unless someone asked. It was about showing Jesus' love in tangible ways.

In this caring environment, my heart healed and enlarged.

Right after Thanksgiving that year, Jason came over to me and said, "Christmas is on a Sunday this year. Here's my idea. Instead of a regular church service, what if we all went to a homeless camp? Is there one we could go to? We'd take them breakfast. No preaching or anything. We'd just sing and spend time with them. Whaddya think?"

"Well, it's never been done in this city."

"How many people would there be? We'd like to buy them gifts."

"Forty or so," I guessed.

"How about fifty dollars per person? Just tell me what you need."

I was blown away, expecting Jason to suggest maybe five to ten bucks a person. Instead of tossing them scraps, he wanted to treat our homeless friends like royalty. I loved his enthusiasm, though I wasn't sure how many churchgoers would actually show up on a Christmas morn. They'd be giving up time with family to hit the streets and mingle in the cold with penniless strangers.

I shrugged. "Listen, Jason, if even twenty show up, I'll be happy."

On Christmas Day, I pulled into the skate center's parking lot and found dozens of cars already filling spots. Gathered inside, a hundred or so people were ready to get going. The worship pastor and his wife had even dressed up as Santa and Mrs. Claus. I could barely hold back tears.

At a homeless encampment that morning, we served up sausage, ham, biscuits, and pastries. Cups of coffee and hot chocolate were passed around as we sang carols and upbeat tunes. Good to his word, Jason made sure there was no Bible-thumping or preaching. The time passed quickly. All around, I spotted my church friends chatting with my homeless friends. When noon came around, hardly anyone had left.

"What're we gonna do?" Jason asked me. "It's already lunchtime. We've got to feed these people. You think they'd like barbecue?"

It was a Christmas to remember, unlike any I'd ever experienced.

And it was only the first of many such times with Well House.

59

WHAT IS TRUTH?

I still had my struggles. After decades of erecting defense mechanisms, I slipped into old patterns every now and then. Maybe like some of you, I had to get my head out of my ass and out of my past. For decades I had used other people, with deceit just being part of the package. Back in 1980, Andy's brother had known I was trouble. He'd even tried to warn her before my first of four failed marriages.

Smart guy.

Me? Not so much.

As my work with Home Street Home took me into 2017, I started a new romantic relationship. I really liked this girl. I didn't want to just alter my previous behaviors but radically change them. My old tools of manipulation were no longer an option.

I tried to do things differently, I did. Yet I still screwed it up. As Valentine's Day swung around in 2018, I knew things were disintegrating between my girlfriend and me. This time I was the one who felt manipulated, as she told me she didn't really see me as a part of her life but as an escape from her life.

Ouch. The relationship screeched to a halt.

The romance had sure felt real to me at the time, but this obviously wasn't the surprise God had in store for me. What was going on?

Then in two separate conversations in one day, I heard this statement:

"Feelings aren't truth."

The words were simple yet profound and jarred me from my emotional quagmire. Clearly, God was speaking to me. He may have to repeat things to get my attention, but once He has my ear, I listen.

My emotions, I realized, had been dictating my feelings.

And my feelings had dictated my truth.

Now don't go thinking I'm some neurological savant. The psychology behind emotions and feelings is beyond me, and even experts on behavioral science disagree on where the two meet and overlap. Please hear me out, though.

Emotions are intense yet temporary.

Feelings, generally, are more firm and sustained.

Where we get into trouble is when we allow intense, temporary emotions to harden into sustained feelings. This is seldom positive. It usually happens when we are at our weakest and most vulnerable. A rush of negative emotions, maybe fear or worry or anger, turn into feelings which become our truth.

Intense emotions + Sustained feelings = Your "truth."

But what is truth?

That depends on whether we rely on our ego-wounded selves or on God to determine it for us. If we want the real answer, we must allow fact to enter the equation.

Well, of course, Steven. Fact is truth, right?

Actually, fact and truth are slightly different. Here's a fact: God loves you and always will. And here's something you might believe is truth: Nobody loves me, I'm not worthy, and I'm too messed up to ever be loved.

Our perception of facts can be affected by the emotions we let control our lives. These emotions, influenced by people, experiences, and events, become our feelings. They distort the mirror of truth. It had happened to me weeks earlier when someone said to me, "I'm sorry, but the bad you've done voids all of the good."

That hit me hard. In a flash, I forgot who I was, who God was shaping me to be. From my past, the old hurts, loneliness, guilt, and shame came rushing back, and I doubted my worthiness all over again. By dwelling on these emotions, I let them become feelings which defined my perception of self. This perception became more powerful than the actual truth.

Feelings aren't truth. I had to remind myself of this more than once. More than ever, the Bible has become my source for answers. To truly experience God's truth, I must realign my feelings with what He says in His Word:

"So God created man in His own image; in the image of God He created him; male and female He created them."
—Genesis 1:27

"I will praise You, for I am fearfully and wonderfully made; marvelous are your works, and that my souls knows very well."
—Psalms 139:14

"He chose us . . . having predestined us to adoption as sons by Jesus Christ to Himself, according to the good pleasure of His will."
—Ephesians 1:4-5

"But you are a chosen generation, a royal priesthood, a holy nation, His own special people, that you may proclaim the praises of Him who called you out of darkness into His marvelous light."
—I Peter 2:9

"For God so loved the world that He gave His only begotten Son, that whoever believes in Him should not perish but have everlasting life."
—John 3:16

Even on those days when my emotions are low and my feelings stray from the wisdom found in these verses, I still know they are the facts. They do not change. They alone define my truth.

On my journey to health, there were still steps I needed to take. One of those steps was participating in a Celebrate Recovery program. Another was meeting with two male therapists who helped me see that merely dealing with the past was not really healing from it. I couldn't keep running, passing blame, and trying to justify. They told me I had been the Wizard of Oz, trying not to let anyone see behind the curtain. It was time to drop that defense mechanism and take a hard look at myself in the mirror.

I learned a lot, pinpointing places where I had veered off-course. Step by step, I'd reached this spot in life. Step by step, with the Lord's help, I could retrace and reroute to find His true direction for me.

Sure, I got discouraged. Some days it seemed I would never learn. Was healing even possible? I had to constantly sidestep Satan's attempts at tripping me up with old memories, guilt, and sin. I reminded myself I was God's child, a member of royalty. I was fearfully and wonderfully made.

As followers of Jesus, just because we've been forgiven doesn't mean our enemy forgets. He'll do everything he can to use our pasts against us. We have to be vigilant. Hyper-vigilant. It's a skill I honed in prison and on the streets, a means of daily survival.

Survival? Am I kidding?

No, sometimes it's a matter of literally staying alive.

Even on those days when things seem to be going smoothly, I tell myself to stay alert. I'm not just punching a time clock as a Christian, I'm fighting a war. When there's no resistance or attack, I have to wonder if I'm actually engaged in today's battle. Or am I growing complacent, ineffective, and lukewarm? One of my favorite sayings is: "If the devil's not doing everything he can to make your life a living hell, you need to get on your knees and ask God why."

Talking to God goes much deeper than just rattling off needs and desires. Prayer should be a loving conversation with our Heavenly Father. We're not giving a monologue. We're listening. His mercies are new every morning, and we should rest in His presence before getting our next marching orders.

As much as I still wanted a special woman in my world, I decided it was better to be four times divorced and alone than spend a lifetime living a lie with one person.

Would love ever happen for me?

Maybe not. And I had to be okay with that. My acceptance and strength would have to come from Jesus Himself. He was my source of comfort, hope, and truth. If this seems like I'm rambling, I apologize. It's important, though, because if I'd failed to embrace this reality, I would have never been ready for what happened next.

60

AS PASSIONATE AS EVER

It was mid-May, 2018. Home Street Home was keeping me busy with a team of volunteers and regular forays into hovels and camps. Nashville was expanding faster than ever—the latest "it" city, said the New York Times—and our homeless community was also growing.

Since our beginning, Home Street Home had put together various fundraisers and events. In 2015 and 2016, we'd had our Faith, Freedom, and Friends Fourth of July Celebrations at a church downtown on Green Street. Hundreds came for good barbecue, cold drinks, music, and a talent show featuring our homeless friends. There was laughter, applause, and cheers. Afterward, many stayed and watched fireworks light up the Nashville skyline.

In 2017, we had moved the event to St. John's Lutheran Church, and this year we expected an even bigger turnout. I also wanted to add something different to our calendar, a September fundraiser in Goodlettsville, called the Sound of Hope Benefit Concert. We would provide free live music, home-baked goodies for sale, and items donated for auction by local restaurants, sports venues, and music stars.

I had high hopes. If all went as planned, the benefit would help us do more for the many hundreds of homeless across Davidson County. While most ministries waited for the homeless to come to them, we went out and found those in need. We were making an impact in unique ways.

Remember, the homeless were more than just numbers to us. They were friends. Regardless of age, race, gender, nationality, or religion, they could use handshakes and hugs and listening ears. We took them water, Gatorade, Vienna sausages, sandwiches, and ramen noodles. We hand-delivered green metal containers of cooking propane, personal hygiene kits, weather-appropriate clothing, four-man tents, sleeping bags, blankets, and tarps.

Daily, I got calls from potential donors. Most of them expected me to come rushing their way, as though darting from one end of the city to the other was the only thing I had to do. Sadly, the donations were often sacks of hand-me-downs, threadbare jackets, worn-out tennis shoes. I was thankful for the majority who gave so generously and sacrificially, but sometimes wondered what others were thinking. Just because people are homeless does not mean they deserve junk. I opened one bag and found a shower curtain still wet. Another contained twenty-seven pairs of stiletto heels.

Oftentimes, when receiving a donation of mediocre quality, I hear these words: "I know it's not great, but it's better than nothing."

Really?

When you say that, you're telling the person receiving it that they are nothing and you just made them better.

From the beginning, it's been my policy to provide the best to our friends on the streets. The shepherds and wise men who showed up in Bethlehem brought the best of what they had to the baby Jesus, and everything we do is as unto Him. No matter how society, churches, businesses, or politicians view them, the homeless are fellow human beings. Investing in them is not just throwing money down a black hole. It is planting seeds, watering and watching them grow. Apart from God's grace, that could still be me, sunburned and sweaty on the corner or hunkered down and freezing in my car.

To me, homeless ministry is all about taking home out to the streets, providing something they do not have. We're there to serve, help, love, and do it all over and over again. Whether or not they're able to get a job. Whether or not they ever show up at a church service.

"But how are you getting them saved?" I've been asked.

As far as I can tell, you and I aren't in the saving business. Only one person does that and His name is Jesus.

"But isn't it just wasting money?"

Newsflash! It's not my money and it's not yours either. We should spend it wisely and responsibly, but the results are not up to us. We are simply told to give.

In the Gospel of Luke, there are numerous references to helping the poor. Jesus says in Luke 14:13-14, "But when you give a feast, invite the poor, the maimed, the lame, the blind. And you will be blessed, because they cannot repay you; for you shall be repaid at the resurrection of the just." Jesus admonishes the religious leaders in Luke 11:39-42, "Your inward part is full of greed and wickedness . . . Rather give alms of such things as you have . . . But woe to you Pharisees! . . . you pass by justice and the love of God." And Jesus proclaims in Luke 6:20-21, "Blessed are you poor, for yours is the kingdom of God. Blessed are you who hunger now, for you shall be filled."

Hey, these are the words of Jesus, straight from the Word of God.

If I'm not going to let the homeless play games or cut corners, you can bet I won't go easy on those who have beds to sleep in tonight. Go read for yourself about God's concern for the poor. Nowhere does He let us off the hook. If we give even a drink of water, we do it as unto Him.

In 2018, with our Faith, Freedom, and Friends event just six weeks away, I was ready to answer the naysayers. I was as passionate as ever about the homeless—and for good reasons, biblically and personally.

On May 20, amidst all the planning and activity going on, my birthday was a mere afterthought. As evening came around at the Stay

Lodge, I went online to thank some of my well-wishers on Facebook, but it was really just another day to me.

Until the latest greeting pinged me in Messenger.

The sender's name was Andrea.

Andy?

Logic said that was highly unlikely. I mean, how weird would that be? We'd first met, married, and divorced nearly four decades ago and hadn't lain eyes on each other since. Could it really be her? I opened the message.

61

BETTER THAN WAFFLE HOUSE

As you know, my history of romantic and relational love was pretty dismal. The common element in each failed attempt was me. One of my biggest fears was dying alone, never having known what it was like to love and be loved in a vibrant, healthy relationship.

And now here on my laptop, I had a message from Andy. Yep, that Andy.

My one true love.

Her message was to the point. She had found my blog online, read about my past, and learned about my work through Home Street Home. She was glad to see God ministering through me and she wished me all the best.

Pulse pounding, I decided to check out her profile. In her photos, Andy still looked petite and full of energy, short hair framing hazel eyes and a thin face. All these years she'd been living in the Nashville area.

I'd love to tell you my heart soared and I was thrilled to hear from her. The truth was completely different. Caught off-guard, I felt the walls go up. Hesitating, I wrote her back. We went back and forth on Messenger, and to this day I have those texts saved, but I was still guarded and in protection mode.

The next day I called Mike for guidance. What should I do?

In his wisdom, he said, "You no longer have to do anything. You responded to her, Steven. You apologized. From here, it's not about what you have to do, but what you want to do."

That gave me the freedom to move forward.

Over the next week or so, Andy and I messaged regularly and conversed for hours on the phone. One night we talked straight through till dawn. She had forgiven me, she said, and as much as I found that hard to fathom, her voice carried no traces of bitterness. She was a self-assured woman, her heart given to the Lord, and she explained how God had helped her let go of those hurtful rejections.

One night she invited me over for dinner at her house. Was she sure about this? We could meet in public somewhere. No, she later explained, she was worried she might get emotional. She would rather see me face to face, without any concerns about who was watching.

I showered, trimmed my beard, and dressed casually. My heart was in my throat as I knocked at her door. When she opened it to let me in, I tried to keep my jaw from dropping. She was even more beautiful than I remembered.

"And as soon as I saw you," she confided in the days to come, "I knew I still had those feelings for you."

Back in 1980, God had brought us together, but at the time only one of us was mature enough for a relationship—and it sure as hell wasn't me. Due to my insecurities and fears, I'd sought out other women and destroyed the best thing that ever happened to me. Bit by bit, God now pieced our relationship back together. Andy and I cooked and ate meals together. Played with her dog Hondo. Watched movies. Put our feet up by the fire. Laughed. The decades apart disappeared, and it was like we'd been together the whole time.

When the Lord is the one involved, He works on His own timetable. That timetable had taken thirty-six years to bring us back together.

And now, He united us as one in a matter of months.

In June, as our relationship was heating up, we watched I Can Only Imagine on-demand, a movie portraying the life of a Christian musician who penned a hit song of the same name. His childhood was similar to mine and certain scenes reopened my emotional wounds. While he and his parents found some reconciliation, I could only imagine what that might have looked like with my own. They were both gone now. I never did get that closure.

What if I had spoken years earlier with Dad and Mom instead of harboring so much anger toward them? Would they have softened? Would things have been better between us? Even if they hadn't been receptive, I might have been stronger for trying.

And what if I had let God work on me sooner, instead of running from Him?

What if?

I shared with Andy some of my longstanding issues of pain. Thanks to the Lord in my life, I was getting better by the day. Rather than letting emotions dictate my truth, I was letting God peel back layers to reveal what was real. As He healed the damage in me, I became less damaging to others, verbally and emotionally. Andy expressed that she actually felt safe with me.

One afternoon, she sent me out for cigarettes. She smoked Winstons. I smoked Marlboros. She handed me her debit card and told me her PIN number. Blinking, I stared at the card. Was something wrong? No. I just couldn't believe she used that PIN, a number dating all the way back to our earliest days together.

"Is that intentional?" I asked.

"Maybe just subliminal. I guess our connection never really ended."

Being this comfortable around each other, I knew exactly where I wanted our relationship to go. Perhaps it was premature, but at a Waffle House one morning I suggested to Andy that we get married. It was really my way of fishing, wanting to be sure of her feelings for me.

Andy raised an eyebrow. "Are you popping the question?"

"Yes."

"Sorry, Steven," she said. "You'll have to do way better than Waffle House."

Hey, at least she didn't say no.

It was a bright sunny day when we kicked off our 2018 Faith, Freedom, and Friends event. Andy was fully behind what I was doing with the ministry, and the two of us met with Home Street Home volunteers outside St. John's. The Fourth of July picnic went smoothly. Meals were served, supplies distributed, and friendships made. Then I took the stage to address our two hundred homeless friends and volunteers. With everyone watching and microphone in hand, I called Andy up, introduced her, and gave a brief history of our past and reconnection.

I then looked over at her and said into the mic, "Is this way better?"

Confused, she scrunched her eyebrows at me.

"Way better than Waffle House?" I added.

She finally got it and her eyes misted over. In front of everyone I asked her to marry me, and this time she said the word I longed to hear:

"Yes."

The crowd went wild.

When September 23rd rolled around, ticket sales for our Sound of Hope Benefit Concert were dismal. Despite a ton of time and energy invested in the event, we had less than a hundred show up—and most of them were volunteers and people from Well House Church. Many of our donated auction items didn't even have a minimum bid.

What did this mean for us?

Put bluntly, Home Street Home would not have the means to minister effectively through the coming winter.

Thanks to a few generous bids by people from Well House, we covered the costs of the event and put some money in the bank—"We weren't going to let you fail," Jason told me—but the night was a huge disappointment to me. I knew in the months ahead we would have to turn some people away. Three years ago I had been one of those people. Just the thought of saying no hurt.

Of course, I was happier than ever with Andy by my side. We were planning a wedding and a honeymoon, and we would live together in a house on the eastern fringe of Davidson County. I was starting all over again with the woman of my dreams, and this time we were building on a much firmer foundation.

Clearly, the Lord was leading me into a new season.

Did this mean the ministry had run its course?

I kept this thought to myself and pressed ahead. Our HSH outreach team kept hitting the streets daily. We fed those we could and got tents to those who needed them. What other option was there? The days were already getting cooler.

My brother Robert called on a Friday night in late October. He and I now talked regularly, as did John and I. We were the last of the Young family. All three of us had gone through ups and downs, but at least we were on speaking terms again.

"So, Steven, how're you feeling?" Robert asked. "Tomorrow's the big day."

"Yep, my fifth marriage. But this time I get a do-over on the first."

"You nervous?"

I didn't even hesitate. "No, Robert, I'm not."

He seemed surprised by this, and even my wife-to-be found it hard to believe I wasn't jittery. The thing is, I only get nervous when I don't know the outcome of something or when there are questions or doubts. None of those applied here. I had never been more sure of anything in my life.

Humbled? Yes.

Amazed? Very.

Blessed? Beyond words.

The past five months had been indescribable, with Andy's and my relationship growing by leaps and bounds. If only I had been wiser the first time around, just think of where we could've been. Though we both had sons from other relationships, we could have had our own children together and even been grandparents by now. Well, we still had lots of life to enjoy.

And you better believe we would enjoy it. This time the love was planted in good, rich soil. It was rooted firmly, sprouting quickly, blossoming gloriously. Tomorrow I would marry the most incredible woman I knew. She possessed a beauty inside and out which was hard to put into words. We were best friends. She filled my life with joy. Because of her, I was already a better person in every way.

Nervous? Are you kidding?

I couldn't wait!

62

LIFTING OFF

It was the wedding day. The start of a new life together. At sixty-two years old, I stood before the mirror, no longer afraid to face myself, and adjusted my tie. As I did, I was reminded of a few tidbits of wisdom picked up along my journey.

First, love is about taking chances—and I mean chances plural. If you put up your defenses at the first cold word or run away at the first sign of trouble, you'll be doomed from the start. Love is and always will be a risk/reward proposition. Fear of losing control and fear of losing love will only drive you further from it. You'll either try to take the reins or get trampled underfoot. Neither does you any good in the long run. Your goal is to ride along together. You'll hit some rough patches, but just hold on.

Second, love is about number one—and number one will never be you. You must always consider your partner and not just think of yourself. If one person or the other becomes the largest part of the equation, there won't be equality or balance, and love will shrivel into selfishness. That's not to say you shouldn't ever speak up or fight for what is right, but the door of compromise must remain unlocked. Ask yourself, How do my needs or desires affect my partner? Is it really that important to get what I want? Giving up isn't always giving in. It can also be a way of showing your true love. When you both make it all about giving, you'll be amazed at what you get in return.

Third, love is about forgiveness—and not just when it's easy. There is no room for keeping score. There's no time for looking for red flags based on past experiences. Be willing to give and receive forgiveness, even when your partner doesn't think they've done anything wrong. You'll both make mistakes. Neither of you can stay on that pedestal forever. So override the emotions of the moment and hold onto the truth of your love for each other. No grudges. No paybacks. No "you did this, so I get to do that." Of course no one should become a door-mat, but unwillingness to forgive can be as big a mistake as the thing needing to be forgiven. Give each other an opportunity to start fresh each day, just as God's mercies for you are new every morning.

"You ready, Steven?" a groomsman called to me.

"I sure am," I said. It was time to put the lessons into action, and from here on out, I'd just have to learn as I go.

On Saturday, October 27, 2018, our outdoor wedding took place at the Buchanan Log House on Elm Hill Pike. We asked for casual dress. We wanted our homeless friends to feel welcome too. The ceremony started at four o'clock. This time around, Andy and I gazed into each other's eyes without any lies or shame between us. I said "I do" and kissed my bride, not a worry in the world.

A reception followed. Andy's son gave a short speech. With emo-tion in his voice, he met his mom's gaze and said, "I'm glad you finally made a decision for you."

We cut the cake and then the party really got started. There were plenty of non-alcoholic beverages and mixers available, and we'd told attendees they could BYOB. At the mobile dance floor, a DJ turned up the music and dancing commenced. Andy and I were right in the middle of it, living it up. The celebration lasted for hours.

You know, for old times' sake, I hope we paid that DJ well.

When it came to honeymoon plans, Andy and I had created a fund on our online wedding site. The generosity of others was unbelievable, and soon we were headed for Puerto Rico. As Andy fed me descriptions of sandy beaches and ocean vistas, we lifted off from Nashville International Airport into vast blue skies. With her hand in mine, I watched the greenery fade below and my heart swelled to overflowing.

God, what am I even doing here? You are too good!

Only a few years ago, even a few months ago, I would have thought this was impossible. Now look at me, on the trip of a lifetime with the love of my life.

What a journey this had been so far. With so much yet to come.

63

THE BIGGEST NIGHT

By the time November rolled around, the honeymoon was over.

Well, not exactly. Andy and I were two lovebirds, doing great.

However, when it came to Home Street Home, we had some tough decisions to make. The Sound of Hope event had failed to meet expectations and our funds were running low. While the holidays are usually big donation times, we were struggling. I was under constant pressure, pounding Facebook daily for contributions. Men and women on the streets needed food, clothing, and shelter. They needed to know they were not forgotten. We didn't want to just alter their situations, we wanted to radically change their lives.

A GED could help. Or a reading course.

What about cooking courses? Paralegal training? Or data-entry skills?

I had hopes of taking over an abandoned strip mall or warehouse and converting it into a homeless center with personal housing, kitchen facilities, job training, tutoring, and even on-site vegetable and herb gardens. We would be rigorous in our approach while leaving room for grace, so that men and women could move ahead.

Hold on, though. We couldn't even stock up on sleeping bags.

In mid-November, a TV reporter requested to do an interview with me about the work of HSH. It would air on Channel Two, on the late edition of the nightly news. I was still feeling inadequate, but with Thanksgiving around the corner I agreed to do it.

The interview aired on November 14th, following the 52nd Annual CMA Awards, the biggest night in country music. Brad Paisley and Carrie Underwood hosted the awards with their usual banter and wit.

I had no idea the awards were on that night. In fact, I didn't even watch.

Unbeknownst to me, April Tomlin was watching. April is an interior designer who works with many country music stars, and several of her clients were up for awards. Though she doesn't normally watch the news, the TV was still on after the CMAs. Doing business on her laptop, she caught my interview.

"Had to be a God thing," she later said. "I knew I was supposed to watch it."

As soon as the interview was over, she started tapping away on her computer, jumping from website to website, checking prices and availability.

Her husband was seated next to her. "What're you doing?" he asked.

"Ordering tents and sleeping bags. I can't just sit here after watching that."

April personally knew someone on the brink of homelessness, and this was an issue that mattered to her. She knew God was leading her to act. As I've since learned, when April sets her mind on something, nothing stands in her way. Right away, she contacted Lauren Akins, the wife of Thomas Rhett. Then they got a hold of Ellie, wife of Roman Josi, captain of the Nashville Predators hockey team. That led to Taylin, wife of Taylor Lewan, Pro-Bowl left guard for the Tennessee Titans. Though constantly asked to support local causes, as luminaries in Nashville, they felt responsible to be there for the community.

"People fall on hard times," Taylor Lewan later stated. "It's not our job to ask why or how, but to ask how we can help this person get to the next step to be successful in their life."

Thomas Rhett agreed. "I feel like it's our responsibility as Nashville to dive in hard and not just make it a one-time thing, but really invest in these people's lives."

Within days, a phone call was made to Natalie, our ministry's president, who arranged a dinner meeting. Next thing I knew, I was sitting in Nashville's Whiskey Kitchen, on Eighth Avenue, answering questions about myself and the ministry over a meal with Andy, Natalie, April Tomlin, and Lauren Akins. My mind was put at ease by the fact Jason from Well House had once been the youth pastor of both Lauren and her husband Thomas. They all vouched for each other.

After hearing my story, Lauren said to me, "What're your immediate needs?"

"Well, we have the worst months of the year coming up. I'd really like to not have to say no to anyone."

"What's your monthly budget?"

I told her.

"Okay," she said, "we'll make sure that's taken care of for the next four months."

I hardly knew how to respond. This whole thing was unreal.

"So, Steven," April asked, "what're your long-term goals for Home Street Home?"

"We need work done on Natalie's van, to start with. We're out driving every day, going to our homeless friends. Transportation is vital." I explained some of our other practical issues and my hopes of warehousing supplies to meet the growing demands.

"I have some stuff to give you right now," April said. She loaded up my vehicle with all the supplies she had purchased online. "And listen, we know a mechanic who can fix Natalie's van."

"That would be amazing."

"We're gonna talk to our husbands," Lauren added, "but we really want to help."

"You already have. Thank you."

Several days later I received a follow-up call from April and Lauren. They had spoken to friends and spouses and come up with a plan, pulling together a team that would become known affectionately as "the girls." They told me, "We're going to have a fundraiser in a few weeks. Invitation only. Don't you worry about a thing, Steven. We'll take care of every detail." From that point, things really got rolling.

A few days later I was introduced to Catherine Nail, or Cat, as we lovingly called her. She became the glue that held it all together, and in short time became a dear friend.

Cat is a dynamo, and from the first time I met her I knew we were in good hands. She poured not only her talent into Miracle on 4th, but her heart and soul as well. She's that person who remains calm when everyone else, namely me, is freaking out. She's a planner, organizer, and implementer extraordinaire. Without her, Miracle on 4th would not be an annual success.

Little did Cat know that her husband's music had helped me survive some of my darkest moments. David Nail is a singer, songwriter, and country music star. On the streets, music was my only constant companion, and several of David's songs had touched me when I needed it most.

On Monday, December 17, 2018, the first Miracle on 4th event was held downtown on Fourth Avenue, at the Bell Tower. Mondays are usually a day off for pro athletes and entertainers. Hosted by Roman Josi, Taylor Lewan, and Thomas Rhett, this evening proved to be a game-changer for helping the homeless in Nashville.

To say I was overwhelmed would be an understatement.

Intimidated was more like it.

The Bell Tower is a beautiful venue of old timbers, towering windows, and sparkling glass. Security was tight. As Andy and I walked through the door, April gave us hugs, then took me around the crowded room and made introductions. It was a star-studded evening with

NFL, NBA, and NHL athletes in attendance. The PA announcer for the Nashville Predators was there. Country musicians mingled with other movers and shakers in this city. Top songwriters performed on-stage. Of course, our HSH outreach team and volunteers were also there. They are key to all that we do.

"It's such an honor to meet you," various celebrities said to me. "God bless you."

Calling upon my old skills, I did my best to seem confident and at ease, but inside I was trembling. What was I doing here? I didn't feel I deserved any of this.

At the heart of the event, the girls held the whole thing together. They provided beautiful decorations, hors d'oeuvres, and an open bar.

When I finally located my table and my place next to Andy, I realized we were seated beside Jason Aldean and his wife Brittany. In a few minutes, I would have to get up in front of them and everyone else and share about myself and the ministry.

Nope, no pressure.

I slipped back to the glassed-in area, where items for the silent auction were displayed. I was trying to calm my nerves. Alongside me came Art Rich, the man who coordinates all logistics at Nissan Stadium for the CMA Fest each year.

"Little overwhelmed, are you?" he said to me.

"More than a little."

"Steven, don't forget that everyone of these people are here tonight because of you. You've earned it. Take it all in and enjoy it."

His words helped ease my nerves, and when it was my turn to take the stage, I had Mike Dotson, Jason, Natalie, members of my outreach team, and a group from Well House there as a safety net. As I talked about Home Street Home, I glanced their direction, knowing I had their acceptance and support.

Even more important, I had my wife in the room.

Andy later told me she cried as I spoke. She had never heard me talk publicly about my past and she knew how uncomfortable it was for me. She was 100 percent supportive. She was my anchor. She had a love, forgiveness, and understanding of me like nobody else. I could've made a complete idiot of myself that night and she would have still been proud of me.

I've got to tell you, God's timing was incredible. Considering the makeup of the crowd, I felt out of place, and years before, even months before, this night would've done me in. The pressure would've been too much. Now, with my wife, friends, and church family surrounding me, I was able to do it.

After I had shared, Charles Kelley, singer and songwriter for Lady A, weaved through the crowd and introduced himself. "Man," he said, shaking my hand, "I want you to know you're such an inspiration."

Feeling awkward, I nodded and thanked him.

"It's a lot to take in, isn't it?" he said. "Well, there's a lot of people in this room, and sure, we might be doing well now, but many of us were only a step or two away from being where you were. You belong here, Steven, same as everyone else."

His words couldn't have come at a better time.

In the days after Miracle on 4th, Andy and I were in a state of shock as the financial numbers came in. I could've never planned for something like this. In times past, Mike and Eddie had challenged me to go bigger with the ministry, but I never felt comfortable with doing that. My response was always, what we needed to do we were already doing, and if God wanted to do more, He would make it happen. And He did!

For Home Street Home, Christmas came early in 2018. It was truly a miracle, one I'd hoped and prayed for over the past few years. It took us to a new level. It was proof to me that God's hand was in this and always had been. This wasn't just Steven's show.

With the funds raised, the ministry was now able to do more for more. We had greater exposure and greater responsibility. As a non-profit organization, we needed to account for and spend each dollar wisely, but at least we wouldn't have to say no anymore—though I still have to say no, when necessary. We were also able to purchase a new truck and van, allowing us to serve more people than ever. Instead of chewing up time and gas with multiple runs to Walmart, we could now load everything in one trip.

Miracle on 4th changed the course of the ministry forevermore. It not only touched and changed lives, it literally saved lives as well.

64

MORE MIRACLES

According to the Harvard Public Health Review, suicide rates are nine times higher among the homeless. Despair is a killer as vicious as sub-zero weather. This is one of the reasons we go out daily to connect and build relationships.

Are there some rough days in the ministry? You bet.

One day did a real number on me, as we walked into an encampment and found one of our homeless friends facedown and dead in the dirt. Rigor mortis had set in. He'd been there for hours, victim of a heart attack. He died alone, with no one at his side. Well, that hit me hard. It could've been me. It would've been me. I had to go home early that day, and I didn't revisit that particular camp for months.

On the good side, Home Street Home has bought Greyhound tickets for people who went back to their families after years apart. We've moved couples into apartments. Bought used cars for families. Arranged new work attire for those getting jobs. Checked men into rehab facilities. Coordinated transportation for women going to night college courses. Reunited single mothers with their children. Taken hobbled, frostbitten people to hospitals. Called authorities when our homeless friends have been struck in hit-and-runs or attacked under overpasses or at the railway tracks.

We've also had people trash hotel rooms we booked for them.

Run off and begin drinking again.

Lie. Steal. Use.

Take their own lives.

I don't play games with the homeless community. You don't try pulling any stunts with me. That'll lead to trouble. On the other hand, I won't shut someone out because of a mistake. I made more than my share, as you know. Yet by God's grace, I also learned that I deserved so much more. Each person is created in His image, and distortions of that image are never part of His plan. The way back to wholeness and truth always begins and ends with His kindness.

On our HSH Facebook page, I have shared story after story of our friends on the streets. Many are no longer homeless. Many have jobs and are saving to get into a place. Some have disappeared. Others are dead by their own hand or by the hand of another. As with love, this ministry is a risk/reward proposition. Tragedy and joy come with the territory.

I never give up hope, though. Never.

When it comes to hope, I didn't have much for my son's and my relationship. Josh was now in his mid-thirties, we hadn't talked in ten years, and I deserved any hard feelings he had toward me. I knew that.

On a Saturday in March of 2019, Josh's mother called while I was out distributing goods to our homeless friends. She said Josh was struggling and needed some answers. By his permission, she gave me his number and I called him. Since he was on his way to Nashville for his mother's birthday, we arranged a meeting at O'Charley's restaurant.

Josh and I, we spent an hour or so over a meal, but it wasn't really the place for all that needed to be said. We finished our food and headed back to my house, where we sat out back and talked for hours. It got heated. Feelings were vented. And who was I to question his perception of reality? I admitted to him I hadn't been a good father. I didn't even know how to be. That was no excuse. It was just the truth.

I'd been so caught up in my own crap, I hadn't been capable of being what I needed to be for my own son.

The anguished look on Josh's face confirmed what I was saying.

"I'm sorry," I told him. "I can't change any of that. All I can tell you is, I'm no longer that person. You have every right to your anger and pain, but I love you, Josh. I've always loved you. Whether or not you'll lemme back into your life is up to you, but I'd love it if that could happen. From now on, I will always be here for you."

After that discussion, we began calling and chatting consistently. We met up when we could and slowly rebuilt trust. It was good for him. For me too. By reaching out to my son, I was able to repair some of the damage done to me by my father. Hopefully, Josh could take it a step further whenever he had a son or daughter of his own.

It was July 4, 2019 when I first met a skinny girl with big brown eyes and short-cropped hair. At five-foot-seven, Jayme weighed only 97 lb, clearly in poor health, with a horrible cough. She played the piano in the talent show at our fifth annual Faith, Freedom, and Friends event. Her music moved everyone in St. John's and I called her up on stage after the performance to find out more about her.

"That was amazing," I said. "What's your name?"

"Jayme," she responded.

"Can you tell us a little about yourself? Where did you learn to play like that?"

As she told us about her past in a matter-of-fact manner, I discovered she was in her early thirties, old enough to be my daughter. Jayme's story was raw. She ran away from home at an early age, ending up in several abusive relationships. She got caught up in the drug world and did things no one should have to do to survive. Eventually, she ended up here, living in a homeless encampment off Trinity Lane with her boyfriend—whom I'd already noticed was controlling and abusive.

Through the years, I've had people ask why we do these picnics and Fourth of July events. Well, this is why. We meet people. We build relationships. It's an important part of what we do.

That day, there were cash prizes for the top acts in the talent show. Whether or not the judges gave Jayme a prize, I knew we needed to help her, and announced to everyone that we were giving her some money as a special prize. The audience applauded.

Over the next two days, my heart ached each time I thought about Jayme, and I told Andy I had to go find out more about her.

When I tracked her down at her ramshackle tent, she didn't look good. Her boyfriend was out of the picture, due to an arrest, and I saw this as our window of opportunity. I spoke with some people at Teen Challenge and they agreed to enroll Jayme for a yearlong program at their facility in Knoxville. Since it would be a few days before they could receive her, I called Andy and asked her what we should do. I had this overwhelming feeling that I could not leave Jayme here. I just couldn't do it.

"Bring her home with you," Andy suggested.

Lemme tell you, that was a strict no-no. I always counseled my team and volunteers not to do this. However, I knew Jayme's life depended on it.

"Okay," I said. "We'll be there in half an hour."

Not only did Andy welcome Jayme into our home, she also took her shopping for new clothes. Which made Jayme ecstatic. We figured this was a temporary arrangement until I took Jayme to East Tennessee, just one of many people we get involved with as a ministry. Andy and I had absolutely no clue how much we would change Jayme's life.

On Monday, I drove Jayme a few hours east to the Teen Challenge facility. I dropped her off and figured I was done. She had clothes, luggage, and a small fund in her name. Only later did we find out she was now looking out the window of her new dwelling at an old crack house she had frequented. Not the best of circumstances.

On Tuesday, I got the call that Jayme had been to an ER in Knoxville. The Teen Challenge director told me she had been diagnosed with pneumonia and they couldn't keep her. They weren't set up as a healthcare facility.

On Wednesday, I drove east again to get Jayme. The director promised they would hold her place until she got healthy.

By Saturday, back in Nashville, Jayme was deathly ill and I rushed her to TriStar Summit Medical Center. Ninety minutes later, a doctor came out wearing a grim expression and asked if I was the father.

"No," I said. "But I'm all she's got right now."

"Are you in this for the long haul then?"

I didn't even hesitate. Yes, I told him. Andy and I were committed to this.

"Well, if she ever walks out of this hospital, it'll be months from now." He went on to explain that Jayme not only had pneumonia, she had double pneumonia. She also had a highly resistant strain of staph infection called MRSA, an infected heart wall, and full-blown AIDS. We had rescued her just in time to say good-bye.

No way! No, we weren't ready for that.

I told Jayme we weren't going to leave her, and told the doctors to do whatever needed to be done. Then Andy and I called on God to step in.

During that period, Andy bonded deeply with Jayme and prayed with her to accept Jesus as Lord and Savior. With spiritual eyes now opened, Jayme saw inky shadows creeping about her hospital bed whenever we left her alone, but they hid themselves whenever we came in. Scared, she told Andy, who knew all about those little black critters. Andy and Jayme prayed together and the torment stopped.

Soon, Jayme's coughing lessened and the healing began. As the doctors fought for her, she fought hard too. We gave her all the spiritual and emotional support we could. We believed for healing, still assuming she would return to Teen Challenge once she was able. In the meantime, she had an outpouring of love from well-wishers—

cards, flowers, crayon drawings, and stuffed animals. Both Well House Church and the Soul Revival Bikers Church stepped up for her in a big way.

Ten days later, instead of winding up in a casket, Jayme was released from TriStar and the doctors were amazed. Her primary-care physician said it was truly a miracle. She was still alive, rescued by God's grace. Her future would be her own to decide.

On Monday, November 18, 2019, we held our second Miracle on 4th fundraiser. Since Andy's and my wedding a year earlier, God had poured out His blessings on the ministry. This time, even more of Nashville's prominent names took part in the activities.

The guys from Florida Georgia Line were the headliners, performing an acoustic version of their song "Blessings." The decorations were tasteful and gorgeous. Jason and Brittany Aldean were there again. Radio, TV, and ESPN personalities talked amongst themselves. I handed the mic over to our MCs, Roman Josi, Taylor Lewan, and Thomas Rhett. The girls had worked hard on arranging security, catering, and items for the auction. Of course, Mike, Jason, and our HSH team were also in attendance.

Before Miracle on 4th ended, we still had a surprise for everyone.

We announced that Eric and I were now writing my memoir together. Eric, not realizing the type of event this would be, had shown up with uncombed hair, faded jeans, and a stubbly face. So what was new?

It was an incredible evening. Again, I was so moved by this show of support for my homeless brothers and sisters. The money would go straight to them through our boots-on-the-ground approach. Our mission has always been to be R.E.A.L., through Respect, Encouragement, Acceptance, and Love. In the previous year, we had delivered over two and half tons of goods, and we'd already doubled it this year. Now, with the ability to obtain warehouse and office space, we were poised for even bigger and better things in the year ahead.

Which was good. Because none of us knew what was to come in 2020, with its overwhelming hardships and needs.

God knew, though. God knew.

When we weren't out pounding the pavement and coordinating volunteers that holiday season, Andy and I sat around the fire pit in our backyard. We warmed our hands, told jokes, read books, and played with Hondo. He's a big white Goldendoodle who has no idea he's not a puppy anymore. If he's not knocking over my coffee or ashtray, he's bounding into our laps with muddy feet.

Go big or go home, I always say, and in the days before Christmas we had a get-together with relatives at Hermitage Steak House. I hadn't experienced such a meal in ages. It felt good to laugh and dine with family. A day or two later, Andy, Josh, and I went to the Nashville Sounds stadium for the GLOW Christmas experience, a major spectacle which drew thousands of people. It was magical.

By the time Christmas day arrived, Santa had stacked gifts all around our tree. I was already a blessed man, but a limited edition Mickey Mouse watch from my dear wife only added to that blessing. She knew me all too well. I was equally blessed by a Mickey Mouse ornament from my son Josh. It was a symbol of forgiveness, healing, and love. Along the top, three letters gave me a name I didn't ever think would be mine:

DAD.

I'll forfeit my man card if you want, but that brought tears to my eyes.

We added another another member of the family, a companion for Hondo, a German shepherd puppy. We named him Mickey. Yep, there was a running theme here.

Since Andy came back into my life, all of the missing puzzle pieces had been falling into place. Everything I'd lost was replaced tenfold—my friendships, my connection with my brothers, and my church family. Everything I'd destroyed was being repaired, even better than ever—my marriage, my relationship with my son, a home, and a ministry growing by leaps and bounds.

I felt hugely blessed!

If God called me home tomorrow, I could say honestly I've had more love, laughter, and dreams come true than many people experience in a lifetime.

It's a profound thing for me. It really is. After I finally stopped gambling and started trusting God, He turned me into the winner I had never been. I can tell you this, He always provides, if we'll just get out of His way. Look at me. I'm that person who had nothing and has now been given it all.

65

START MOVING

While no place was safe in 2020, Nashville experienced a unique set of hardships. On March 2nd and 3rd, the sixth costliest tornado in U.S. history ravaged the northern edges of Nashville, destroyed businesses, houses, and lives, and added to the homeless population. Two weeks later, another freak weather event left thousands without power for days on end.

Then the real force of COVID-19 hit. All across Davidson County, family, friends, neighbors, and strangers struggled to work, eat, pay bills, and keep their heads up. Nashville is a resilient and compassionate community, as we all experienced during the 2010 flood, and again we came together to heal and rebuild.

There's a reason Tennessee is called the Volunteer State.

I'm so proud to live here.

During that time many ministries had to back off due to storm damage and to COVID, but Home Street Home worked ceaselessly to help our hard-hit homeless friends. Since our offices are our vehicles, we were out in the field day and night.

We ran into single mothers who had lost their homes in the tornado. They had no money and nowhere to go, so we provided emergency housing. We sought medical aid for injured men and women. We distributed supplies as never before, thanks to the generosity of restaurants, barbecue joints, stores, schools, and countless individuals. Girl Scout Troops participated. Country music artists and professional athletes played a part. Families drove up from Alabama with trunks full of quilts and clothing. Sporting goods stores donated camping supplies. The Soul Revival Bikers Church got involved.

Beyond the practical help, we also offered emotional and spiritual support. Prayer is a constant on our HSH team, which consists of recovering addicts, ordained ministers, and others with unique skills and experiences for outreach. While they may not always understand the decisions I make as the head of a nonprofit corporation, they serve sacrificially. I don't like my face or name being all over everything for the ministry. I like my team to be out front. They are amazingly dedicated, loving people.

Looking back, I remember those early days when Mike, Eddie, and I had to pool our money together to buy a single tent. We were operating on a wing and a prayer.

Since those humble beginnings, we have answered approximately 22,000 calls for assistance, spent 45,000 volunteer hours in the field, handed out 2,300 tents, 2,700 sleeping bags, 2,100 camp stoves, 19,000 canisters of propane, 4,600 tarps, 3,000 blankets, and 10,000 pairs of socks, along with untold amounts of clothing, personal-hygiene items, and so much more. We've delivered over 46 tons of food, equaling 92,750 meals, and over 300,000 bottles of water. To our friends struggling to survive on the streets, we've provided more food, water, and supplies than all the other local organizations combined. God has truly blessed this ministry in ways we never imagined. We love what we do and those whom we do it for.

Of course, we haven't done it alone.

God has sent plenty of angels our way. From little children to senior citizens, so many have stepped up to help us continue our mission. They come from every background, race, and belief. Some are wealthy. Some are barely scraping by. Some are believers. Others not so much. What they all have in common is a love and compassion for our homeless friends. And to us, they are all heroes and angels.

Over the years, we have seen thousands of lives touched, blessed, and literally saved—more than we like to have to count. Honestly, though, I think we're the ones who experience the biggest blessings and are touched in the most profound ways. And as for being literally saved, you can count me in that number.

Unfortunately, not everyone in our community is quite so friendly.

One day I stopped for a bottle of water at a convenience store. As I walked back out to my vehicle, with its Home Street Home Ministries decals, I found a handwritten note under the windshield wiper that read: STOP HELPING & THEY MIGHT GET OFF THEIR LAZY ASSES & GET A JOB!

"Would you give them a job?" is a question I often ask.

Another time, with a hand on my truck's door handle, I was stopped by a casual male voice. I looked back and saw a man in a new, very nice, black Ford pickup. He looked to be in his mid-fifties, well-groomed and wearing a fleece pullover.

"If we're lucky," he called out his window, "maybe this virus will thin out that homeless herd. Then you can get yourself a real job doing something productive."

I was stunned. My blood boiled.

Shaking, I experienced flashbacks to the verbal abuse I'd endured during my years on the streets. I'd been labeled. Called names. But never, ever, had anyone told me they hoped I would die. With testosterone boiling, I wanted to march over and give this guy a piece of my mind, as well as a few hard, swift blows.

Before I could react, God intervened and helped me tame my tongue. Instead of cursing at the man as I might have done in times past, I said, "I'm sorry you feel that way. I'll pray for you, that you are spared from the virus and that your friends and loved ones are also spared. God bless you."

He scoffed at that, gestured dismissively, and drove off.

Emotions still churning inside, I climbed into my vehicle and angled toward an adjacent parking lot. I needed to calm down. And I also needed to follow through on my promise. The old Steven, he might have ended up back in prison with an assault charge to add to his jacket. Instead, I prayed for the man and his family, and I thanked God for being here with me, for loving me day in and day out.

My blessings are many. I have family and relatives close by. I have friends such as Mike Dotson who stuck by me even when I failed him over and over. I have godly examples such as Thomas Rhett who inspire me to be a better person, husband, and father. I have Jason at Well House Church, who's been my pastor and been real with me since the day I walked through those doors. That little church that started in a skating rink has done more for Home Street Home than all of the other churches in Nashville combined.

God cares about us and wants us to enjoy this life He's given us. He frees us to create, love, eat, drink, and laugh. Just as any good father, our Heavenly Father delights in seeing us smile. What matters isn't who others say you are, but who God knows you are. It's about being part of His family on this earth and beyond.

As busy as I am with church and ministry, I still cheer for the Titans and the Predators, getting even louder if Taylor or Roman make a good play. I read some serious books but still speed through John Grisham thrillers every now and then. I drink hot coffee and cold sparkling water—instead of Coke, after the discovery that I am diabetic. I listen to worship music, country music, and some 1970s and '80s hits. I like golf. I love camping. And what could be better than going out for dinner and a movie with my lovely bride?

Though my therapists are just a call away, they tell me I have all the tools necessary to move on. I credit Andy for my not needing to use those lifelines. She says I'm still a closed book at times, and yes, I tend to hold things in and try to manage on my own. Even so, when she's not around I feel like a lost pup.

We are never lost from God's sight.

Our Heavenly Father loves us more than we can imagine.

When all else fails and others abandon you, when the lights fade and the laughter stops, when love eludes you and pain sets in, hold onto His promise in Deuteronomy 31:6 that "He will never leave you nor forsake you."

He found me.

And I know He can find you.

This isn't just my story or your story. It's God's story. He is the Author of Life, He's still writing chapters, and there are plenty of good plot twists ahead. So how about it? Are you ready to start moving from chains to change?

Sign Off

HEADPHONES, SOUNDTRACKS, AND RADIO DIALS

It's the middle of the night, January 29, 2021. The sun is still hours away from rising, and as I sit in my office writing this, I'm reminded of my early days in radio. You are my "listeners" and I hope I've communicated with you in ways that have informed, encouraged, entertained, inspired, provided hope, and maybe, just maybe, helped some of you begin breaking your own chains and start healing.

I no longer hide behind my air name. Steven Michaels doesn't exist anymore. I'm Steven Allen Young, and like so many, I am broken, fearful, imperfect, and still battling my demons. The dark of night could overwhelm the promise of morning, but I won't let it. I choose to put these things behind me and move forward. With every dawn of a new day comes hope, promise, and opportunity. It's up to us to take advantage.

Easy? No. Worth it? Yes!

We each have a chance to do our own "radio show." You and I determine the soundtrack of our own lives.

I remember those boyhood nights in bed, the covers pulled over my head, listening through headphones to my little AM/FM transistor radio. I felt safe. The music and soothing voice of the DJ temporarily drowned out my guilt and pain. That soundtrack was only a dream, though. It had nothing to do with reality. It would be decades before that dream became my reality and the pain became a thing of the past.

If you're listening, maybe you're one of those who need to change the radio dial and the soundtrack of your life. I pray you've heard something here that will help you do just that. Like I said, it won't be easy. I struggle often. While I am no longer the person I used to be, who I was will always impact who I am. I was a thief, a con. I lied, cheated, and used people. I was abused and I abused. What counts now is how I handle those things in my past. When I was as far gone as I could get, ready to end my miserable existence in a seedy motel room, I found out we are never too far gone in God's eyes.

He has no limits. He has no boundaries.

He is always there, always ready and waiting to help us change the radio dial. To rewrite the soundtracks of our lives.

I'm living proof. This man behind the mic is a new man. Thank You, Lord, for Your mercy and love. Thank You for Your grace, which grows even brighter in the darkest places. Thank You for removing my shame, breaking my chains, and healing my pain.

Thank You for helping me change that dial.

Wow, what a journey. When I contacted Eric a year and a half ago and said, "I'm ready, let's do this," it wasn't an easy decision. I knew old wounds would be reopened. Pain and heartache would be revisited. My old companions of doubt and fear would raise their ugly faces, and my demons would be lurking, ready to pounce. Those old chains would rattle again, forcing me to bear their weight, if only one more time.

No, the decision wasn't easy. But I'm glad I made it.

I have a beautiful family now: Andy, both of her sons, my son, and—here's the latest—two grandkids on the way! Josh and his girlfriend are expecting, as are Andy's son and his wife. Of course, I can't leave out Hondo and Mickey. Life wouldn't be the same without all of the chaos, joy, and love they bring.

I also have my family of friends on the streets. I love what I do and those we do it for.

There's still work to do, lots of it, but for now I'm going to sign off the air, kick back under our pergola by the fire, sip some coffee, have a smoke, and watch the sun's rays break over the tree-line while I enjoy being home.

Home . . .

Oh, how I love that word!

Thank you for tuning in. I'm truly humbled, honored, and blessed that you did. So long from Nashville. Be blessed and, as always, much love!

Extras

ANDY'S CORNER

On May 20, 2018, I was cleaning and playing with Hondo, when out of the blue, Steven crossed my mind for the first time in quite a while. My laptop was fired up for work that Sunday afternoon, and without really expecting much, I thought I'd just check to see if Steven was on Facebook. Lo and behold, there he was!

I read all his posts, which lead to Home Street Home's website and then to his blog at the time, *Chains to Change*. I was saddened that he spent so much of his life the way he did and for the reasons he did, but also astonished at what God was doing in and through him now. As Steven says in these pages, "It is never too late and you are never too far gone . . ."

That tug to reach out to Steven was strong, Holy-Spirit strong. I wanted to let him know I had found him and was oh, so delighted that God was now a driving force in his life. I somehow forgot that nearly forty years had passed and I forged right ahead. I didn't really have any expectations, but his response to my first message made me think, Gosh, after all he's been through, maybe he doesn't even know who I am. He did, though.

I had truly forgiven Steven years earlier, in obedience to my Father. Forgiveness, I've realized, is not for the benefit of the person you forgive. It is for you. Until you take that action, you can't grow and embrace God's love, mercy, and grace for you, let alone extend it to others. Still, if you had asked me on that day or any day prior, I would have said there was no way Steven and I would get back together. No way!

That Sunday afternoon, though, God was talking and moving, and His reasons soon became clear. HE is truly the reason this book has been written. Hopefully, it brings honor and glory to His kingdom!

Steven and I have been married two and half years now. Ninety-seven percent of the time, we laugh together, and every day is a good, sweet, blessed day. But it's not always peaches and cream, if you get my drift. Some things have happened that admittedly hurt me deeply and gave me reason to pause. When confronted, Steven has at times gone into defensive mode and threatened to leave. See, he still to this day has his demons to deal with—and likely always will. Under the circumstances, who wouldn't?

Of course, I have my own baggage as well. At times, I'm no picnic to live with either. I've had to pray and pray. Without God, I can tell you, I could not deal. I must daily seek Him and His will. If I do not, I end up doing things my own way and screwing up God's way.

The end of 2019 and the year 2020 did a number on me. A layoff from the company I'd worked at for twenty-five years left me reeling. What looked like depression to Steven was really me grieving the loss of significant friendships with coworkers and clients built for over two decades. And as I agreed to take some time off, a tornado hit and COVID hit. In June of 2020, the virus left me with some of my own permanent, unexpected health issues, which I now take medication for. There were also more cancer scares, which always loom after you've gone through it, and small skin-cancer surgeries. Through all of it, Steven was supportive and caring.

You might think it's easy for us now that God has brought us back together, but it takes work for us, just like it takes works for you in your marriage or relationships. It is WORTH it, if you stick with it.

Some of Steven's past he had never shared with me until Eric provided the drafts of these chapters, all of which I read and proofed. When Eric completed the horrific scene at Parchman, Steven gave me the pages and said, "Andy, once you read this, I DO NOT want to talk about it, okay?" I said, "Got it." As I read it that morning, tears flowed. Was I shocked? No. But the details made my heart ache. "Steven," I said to him after reading, "do you think I had not figured most of this out? I do sleep with you every night. I hear the nightmares. It changes nothing between us." He thanked me, and the relief on his face said more than anything.

Reading this book brought about many a-ha moments for me. Steven, for most of his life, did not experience lasting, unconditional love. As soon as something negative happens, he can have one foot in the door and one foot out, thinking I won't stick with him and his baggage. Honestly, I've wondered that myself a few times. But here's what God has taught me through His Word, through spending time with Him: MERCY, COMPASSION, GRACE, FORGIVENESS are what He calls us to show to those we love, to those who are hard to love sometimes, and even to those we do not love at all. Does this mean I'm a doormat? Absolutely not. These days, though, I can discern when Steven does things in direct correlation to his past. It's not me. I'm enough and often need to realize that. Steven must also believe he is enough. He loves God, no doubt. He could not do what he does if he didn't. But in his humanness, he questions whether the Lord will still love him when he fails or takes a back-step. You know that dance. We all do. As God promises all of His children, He will complete the plan He started in Steven, in whole, in His time—and I know now I'm a tiny part of that plan for both of us.

I share this in the hope of encouraging others. Forgive one another as God has forgiven us, do not give up on each other, and do not give up on God. It seems the easier road at times, but wait it out. He is still in the miracle-making business. I love Steven with all my heart and so does our Father. I wouldn't trade this journey for anything.

From our brief courtship to this day, I've had a crash course in homelessness. I had worked in downtown Nashville most of my adult life and even lived there for a few years, passing homeless people by the dozens every day. They were a part of the city's fabric, a fabric I often just walked right by. I befriended and talked to a few but not many. Oftentimes, I sped up out of fear of being bothered or, heaven forbid, hurt. I hear people ask Steven, "Well, why don't they just get a real job?" He fires back, "Would you give them a job?" But that was my way of thinking too. I figured if I gave them money, they'd just spend it on booze. After going out with him and his volunteer team one Saturday, it all changed. I was beside myself with sorrow. For the first time, I really saw and got to know some of the people on the streets. Steven educated me on how to approach each situation on an individual basis. I witnessed such appreciation, genuine appreciation, for things we all take for granted: water, food, clothing, and a roof overhead. I most of all experienced LOVE from these people, and I LOVED them right back.

Working alongside Steven and witnessing what he does every day, seven days a week, on behalf of the homeless is one of the most humbling experiences of my life. He has an amazing volunteer team, and even though their names and faces change over time, they go out every Saturday to do the work of Home Street Home and serve our homeless friends. We thank God for our volunteers, because physically Steven can no longer do the type of work required on Saturdays, but he is "there," and by the time each weekend rolls around, he has already put in forty, fifty, sometimes sixty hours a week, with few exceptions. Our volunteers don't get to witness that. I do. The phone never stops ringing or dinging. If there's a need to me be met, he goes out at 9 p.m., or 10 p.m., or even when it's raining so hard he cannot see to drive.

Steven doesn't boast about himself. Never. You might have noticed that through this book. He does so many things others never know about—and that's fine. But I'm going to boast a little.

This past Christmas, a well-known country artist and his wife provided gifts for a single mother and her children in need. Steven met the artist and they loaded up Steven's truck, with presents stuffed inside and piled high in the bed. Steven was told to leave the gifts with the young mother's neighbor, a police officer. As Steven and the kind policeman made trips back and forth from the truck, Steven noticed there were no signs of Christmas in the officer's home. No tree, decorations, or gifts. When asked about it, the policeman said, "Man, my wife and I, we don't have the money this year and decided to skip it." Steven, very humbly, took out some cash and tried to give it to the man. "Here, you go get you and your wife a tree and some gifts." Moved to tears by this generosity, the officer declined the money. Steven would not hear of it. He insisted the man take it, and as a result I imagine they celebrated the holiday a little more than they otherwise could have. This story brought tears to my eyes, but I only learned of it while listening to Steven talk to someone else on the phone. He would not have thought to tell it to me.

Another single mother of a three-year-old boy called crying one night before the holiday. Home Street Home was, and still is, helping put a roof over their heads, but she couldn't afford anything for Christmas. Her son had been asking, "Where's our tree, Mama?" Steven told her to sit tight and he'd be right there. He helped her get a tree, decorations, and enough food to make a good Christmas meal. We were also able to provide gifts for the two of them—which made MY entire Christmas. Giving in every way is so much more than receiving. The young mother sent us videos of her son coming into the hotel room after she'd decorated. Priceless! And there are SO many more stories like these that you'll never hear from Steven.

If Steven had not experienced homelessness himself for five years, there would be no Home Street Home Ministries. I'm humbled to be a tiny part of that, and even more blessed to be sharing this season of life with my first and last love here on earth.

This wife and mama's heart is so, so full. This year, 2021, will soon bring a granddaughter to Steven and a grandson to me, another season of life I've so been looking forward to. Our future is bright.

In His love, I leave you with this passage of Scripture, which puts into a fresh light the way we should view ourselves and those around us:

"Oh, yes, you shaped me first inside, then out; you formed me in my mother's womb. I thank you, High God—you are breathtaking! Body and soul, I am marvelously made! I worship in adoration— what a creation! You know me inside and out; You know every bone in my body; You know exactly how I was made, bit by bit, how I was sculpted from nothing into something. Like an open book, you watched me grow from conception to birth; all the stages of my life were spread out before you. The days of my life all prepared before I'd even lived on day."
—Psalm 139-13-16 (*The Message*)

I pray you are encouraged and blessed. I pray you will better understand the plight of our homeless friends and extend a hand when the opportunity arises. Really SEE them. They are God's creation too. Lastly, I pray Steven's story gives you hope, encouragement, and compassion, and awakens you in some small way.

MIKE'S THOUGHTS

My mom used to say my relationship with Steven started with a biscuit. He was selling a homeless newspaper, and I, being cheap, bought whatever McDonald's had on special. I ate one and gave him one. If I couldn't help every homeless person, I could at least try to help one of them. As I began dropping off biscuits, I tried to reach the person behind the sign. I had no master plan and no real understanding of homelessness, but Steven and I could at least talk, right? I soon discovered he liked discussing non-homeless stuff, just like everyone else.

I was jaded at the start. Could I trust him? I didn't realize he was looking back at me, thinking, Why should I ever trust you? You're one of those religious types—the worst.

Yes, Steven did eventually break my trust and give me every reason to stop coming around. In the process, I wrestled with my ego and judgmental heart. However, I refused to walk away, half out of stubbornness and half out of a God-called-me-to-him realization.

I learned so much in that first year on why homeless people are typically shut off from family and society. I learned to avoid probing conversations about Steven's past, his childhood, and the pain from it all. I learned the path to homelessness starts for most people at a young age when they suffer abuse and trauma. Steven was no different.

One time I bought him a Little Caesar's pizza. Whereas I took pizza for granted, he told me he hadn't had pizza in a long time, and my compassion for him grew. He began lowering his armor just a little before jerking it back up. We continued to talk and laugh. I didn't call Steven my homeless friend. I just called him Steven. Labels were unfair to him.

Good things started happening. Steven was able to move into an extended-stay hotel. I was the naive outsider and soon learned it was filled with dirty and questionable people who were easy for me to pass judgment on. After visiting I always grabbed hand sanitizer, even before sanitizing was in vogue. Yes, this place was home sweet home for Steven, but in my comfortable suburban heart, I thought, No way, not for me!

I never bargained for a friend when I gave Steven a biscuit. I wasn't looking for someone to help me deal with my own junk, let alone a homeless guy!He needed help. I didn't. I pretended I had it all together. At the beginning, did I even think a homeless man could really change? NO! I did not have enough faith.

I had to be broken of my own pride to see that God never called Steven homeless. A lost prodigal son, yes, but never homeless. I had to see that God never saw in me an insecure stubborn son, full of anxiety. He hadn't sent me to Steven Young. He had sent Steven to me. To rescue me from my own world.

Steve grew to have a passion—a passion for rescuing others, mostly from themselves, by doing whatever it takes. It's that passion that drives him daily to work on changing the face of homelessness "one person at a time." It's that passion that leads him back to the streets, not to live, but to rescue.

Things have changed for both of us, mostly for good. The ministry has grown and God has blessed it in ways neither of us could have imagined. While we both stay busy with our own stuff, our connection is as strong as ever. Though we may struggle to remember in what year such and such happened, and may go weeks or months without seeing each other, we continue to do what we've always done. We talk.

ERIC'S FINAL NOTE

I know what it's like to go hungry, Years ago, I scavenged for day-old bread off garbage cans in Amsterdam just to fill my own belly, so I have a big heart for the homeless. In early 2013, Steven was still home-less and visiting the library the first time our mutual friend Eddie in-troduced us. Steven was sarcastic, his defenses up, his one-liners flow-ing. I threw some sarcasm right back, and from that point forward we seemed to hit it off.

A year and a half later, he was off the streets and turning his life around. He loved God, but didn't feel comfortable with the typical church lingo—another connection between us. Then I found out he, Eddie, and Mike Dotson were going out to Nashville's homeless camps. My heart jumped. I wanted to know more. In 2015, Home Street Home Ministries formed, and my wife and I were humbled to be part of the original board.

In the eight years since first meeting Steven, I have seen him grow in his relationship with God, soften in his relationship with others, and step up in a big way for the homeless in our city. He amazes me every day. We've laughed together. Cried together. Prayed together. I trust him around my wife and daughters. I would trust him with my grandchildren. I have given to the ministry without ever wondering if the money was well-spent. I've seen for myself the hard work put in by him and his volunteers.

Though I'm the author of numerous books, this book, in many ways, has been my most challenging and most rewarding. I wanted so badly to get it right, because I care about this man who is not only my friend and brother but a true man of God. Every week for a year, Steven and I got together and he told me about his journey. As I tried putting it down on paper, though, I kept hitting a wall. Why was I struggling?

"Next week," Steven said during one of our sessions, "I need to tell you something I've never told anyone. Not even Andy. Not even Mike. I think it needs to be in the book."

We both cried that following week as he opened up his heart to me like never before. From that point forward, the writing flowed quickly. I knew the whole arc of the story now, and as I much as I dreaded writing some parts, I couldn't wait to bring this incredible memoir to life. It moved and shaped me. I hope it does the same for you.

Throughout the process, I pushed Steven. I wanted the truth. I challenged him at points to describe in greater detail what had happened. And he also challenged me. We are both better for it, and I can say without an ounce of doubt that I trust this man, I love this man, and I can't wait to spend eternity in heaven with him. Of course, we won't have anyone to clothe or feed there, so I guess we'll just laugh a lot and enjoy every single moment with Jesus.

We will truly be home.

Thanks

TO SOME SPECIAL PEOPLE IN OUR LIVES

FROM STEVEN

Thank you, *Andy*. Your input during the writing process, your support, and your comforting presence beside me as I recounted and relived some exceedingly difficult moments gave me the strength to do this.

Thanks to my brothers, *Robert and John*, for taking me back and understanding this was something I needed to do.

Josh, thank you for giving our part of this story a happy ending.

Hondo and Mickey, thanks for the love and comedic relief when I needed it most.

Thank you, *Carolyn Wilson*, for sharing your husband with me.

Finally, *Eric*, thanks for letting me tap your incredible talent. For the education. For not letting me look like a fool. But most importantly, for your love.

FROM ERIC

Thank you, *Dad and Dee Dee,* for the cozy, creative nook at your place. The real writing of this book began there. You are always so open, warm, and encouraging!

Thanks, as always, to *Carolyn Rose,* my wife of thirty-one years. Your love, prayers, and support helped me complete my twentieth book! And you even caught some mistakes none of the rest of us caught.

Andy Young, what would I do without your editorial eye? You are amazing! You read this manuscript in numerous forms, to the point of being sick of it, but you never complained or let off. You pressed us to make it better at every turn.

Of course, none of this project would've been possible without my incredible friendship with you, *Steven.* You bring tears to my eyes. You make me laugh. And you inspire and encourage me every time we talk.

Most of all, I thank You, *Jesus,* for Your daily love, mercy, and grace. Without You, I'd be just another story with a tragic ending.

About the Authors

SOME STUFF YOU MIGHT NOT KNOW

STEVEN ALLEN YOUNG

You've read this book. You know Steven's story from childhood to the present. You also picked up on his poetic heart, birthed from lots of pain. He has blogged and shared extensively on social media. He spends hours each week on the streets and in the homeless camps of Nashville. Did you know he hopes to shed new hope and light on the things he has seen through a book of his collected poems?

Steven's story is not yet over. Like any great adventure, it will have more ups, downs, plot twists, and moments of glorious redemption.

ERIC WILSON

As a young boy, Eric lived overseas with his parents who smuggled Bibles into eastern Europe and worked with literature teams in India. His love of books grew during hundreds of hours on planes, trains, hovercrafts, boats, and trucks.

Eric got married in 1990, then graduated with a BA in Biblical Studies from Life Pacific College. In 2004, he published his first novel, *Dark to Mortal Eyes*. He has since published 5 supernatural thrillers, 6 mysteries, 5 film novelizations, and 4 nonfiction titles. His book,

Fireproof, spent 3 months on the NY Times bestseller list and helped pay for his daughters' braces.

Eric's heart is for those on the fringes of faith, those burned by religion and church upbringings, and those curious but nervous about a life of following Jesus. He believes no subject is off-limits. If Jesus is the Answer, why be afraid of the questions?

Info

BOOKING AND OTHER DETAILS

TO LEARN MORE OR
TO PURCHASE COPIES OF THIS BOOK
Please visit Chains2Change.com.
Additional copies of *From Chains to Change* can be purchased for donation to prisons, recovery programs, and our friends on the streets.

TO DONATE TO THE MINISTRY
Please give at HomeStreetHomeTN.org,
Facebook@HomeStreetHomeTN,
Instagram@HomeStreetHome_TN,
through Venmo@HomeStreetHome,
PayPal.me/HomeStreetHome, or
by texting: TheyMatter to 44321

TO BOOK SPEAKING ENGAGEMENTS
Please contact Steven at Steven.Chains2Change@gmail.com

ALL PROCEEDS FROM THIS BOOK GO DIRECTLY TO
HOME STREET HOME MINISTRIES.

Discussion Guide

FOR THOSE WANTING TO GO DEEPER

PART ONE

1. As Steven faced childhood abuse, how do you think his parents could have dealt with it better, or did you think their response was appropriate? Have you dealt with similar secrets in your life or family?

2. Were you happy or worried for Steven as you read about his first marriage? How did you react to his date at Chaffin's Barn Dinner Theater? Was his incident on the bridge understandable in light of his choices to that point?

3. Have you also reached points of life-threatening desperation? Are you there right now? Do you harbor anger toward God over any issues from your own past?

PART TWO

1. Did Steven con the system while in prison the first time, or did he rise above and use his educational options to better himself?

2. What did you think of Steven's fathering to his biological son and his various stepdaughters? How did he follow in his parents' steps and how did he make better decisions?

3. Steven's gambling became an addiction. What relationships and freedoms did he lose as a result? What has addictive behavior cost you in your own life?

PART THREE

1. In Tennessee prisons, Steven found ways to earn money despite a lack of support from home. Was this a good or bad thing? How did his survival skills help or hurt him in the future?

2. How did you feel about the Kentucky jailer's handling of Steven, especially in regards to Steven's father? In what ways has God shown you unexpected mercy?

3. Steven exposed the horrible conditions at Parchman Prison, in Mississippi. How would you handle the things he encountered in the penitentiary there? What effects, positive or negative, do you think the correctional system has on inmates?

PART FOUR

1. Alone and penniless, Steven ended up homeless on the streets. What were the real causes of his situation? What did you think about the ways he was treated?

2. When you see homeless people, what are your first thoughts about them? Do you see them any differently after reading Steven's story? Considering Mike's impact on Steven, what are some ways you too could be a positive influence in your own community?

3. Steven began ministering to the homeless while still essentially homeless himself. What is God calling you to do today? What excuses are holding you back?

PART FIVE

1. Steven's redemption came in fits and starts. It was not the overnight transformation we often hear described. How have you

changed over time? Have those changes come in big or small steps?

2. Even as Steven changed, he still smoked and occasionally cussed. Would you have preferred a PG-version of this book, or did you like the raw honesty? How do you think God feels about it?

3. Were you surprised by Steven's remarriage? How did you expect his ex-wife to respond to him? Together, they have grown in their walk with God. Much of this is through connection with church family. How are you growing spiritually? In what ways can you show more grace in your own friendships and romantic relationships?

Steven would love to hear your responses to these questions.
Feel free to email him at:
Steven.Chains2Change@gmail.com

ADVANCE PRAISE FOR
FROM CHAINS TO CHANGE

"*From Chains to Change* is incredibly raw, heartbreaking, and vulnerable. So many times the emotions I felt reading Steven's words first paralyzed me, then overwhelmed me to tears. Yet what was most moving to me was to see the heart of Jesus calling Steven back to Him from such a dark and broken world time and time again. He never gave up on Steven. A most beautiful and real picture of redemption. Steven's story really shows readers how each human heart is so alike. We don't need to be reminded of where we've fallen short, but instead, be assured of how truly loved and adored we are by our Creator no matter our mistakes or circumstances. And then just let Jesus take it from there."

> —**LAUREN AKINS**, *NY Times* bestselling author of *Live in Love*, Love One International, wife of country music star Thomas Rhett

"If you want to read a story of God's present-day miracles, this is the book for you. It tells the captivating story of a man named . . . Jesus. It's a story of hearts once given over to darkness that changed into hearts full of light. Steven's life story and ministry is a mind-blowing journey proving the power of Jesus. His obedience to what God has called him to do is remarkable. It gives hope to the hopeless and conviction for Christians around the world to to help the overlooked, hungry, and homeless."

> —**APRIL TOMLIN**, CEO, April Tomlin Interiors

"What a ride! *From Chains to Change* has it all. A true story of redemption. Refreshingly raw and absolutely beautiful!"

  —**CAROLYN ROSE**, Singer/Songwriter/Actor

"If you've ever doubted the integrity of humanity, questioned if there is any good in the world, or needed proof of the redemption and tenderness of our faithful God, Steven's story will replace your faith deficits with abounding hope. Through a random series of events, I was introduced to Steven and have been blessed by his friendship and ministry. Everyone needs a Steven in their lives and every city needs a Home Street Home. The homeless matter, and I know that because of how much Steven matters to me and the countless lives he has already impacted."

  —**CATHERINE NAIL**, Event Specialist & Coordinator

All proceeds from your purchase of this book go directly to our homeless friends through Home Street Ministries. Please consider buying a second copy to be donated to and read by those in prison and on the streets.

HomeStreetHomeTN.org